Smyrna's Ashes

Smyrna's Ashes

*Humanitarianism, Genocide,
and the Birth of the Middle East*

MICHELLE TUSAN

Global, Area, and International Archive
University of California Press
BERKELEY   LOS ANGELES   LONDON

The Global, Area, and International Archive (GAIA) is an initiative of the Institute of International Studies, University of California, Berkeley, in partnership with the University of California Press, the California Digital Library, and international research programs across the University of California system.

University of California Press, one of the most distinguished university presses in the United States, enriches lives around the world by advancing scholarship in the humanities, social sciences, and natural sciences. Its activities are supported by the UC Press Foundation and by philanthropic contributions from individuals and institutions. For more information, visit www.ucpress.edu.

University of California Press
Berkeley and Los Angeles, California

University of California Press, Ltd.
London, England

Library of Congress Cataloging-in-Publication Data
A catalog record for this book is available from the Library of Congress

21 20 19 18 17 16 15 14 13 12
10 9 8 7 6 5 4 3 2 1

).

Contents

Illustrations

TABLE

Acknowledgments

It is with much appreciation that I acknowledge the people and institutions that made this book possible. A sabbatical and Research Development Award from the University of Nevada, Las Vegas, provided support for the initial research and writing. Funding was also provided by a Curran Fellowship from the Research Society for Victorian Periodicals, University Faculty Travel Committee, and the UNLV History Department Travel Committee. A fellowship from the Black Mountain Institute provided support to revise the manuscript.

   The book started as a story of the maps that I found myself obsessively collecting on my research travels. Peter Mandler's invitation to Cambridge University to present at the Modern History Seminar gave me an early opportunity to talk about "Mapping the Middle East." Peter also kindly agreed to read the entire first draft of the manuscript and provided critique and encouragement. Tom Laqueur generously supported this research with invitations to present at the Berkeley/Stanford British History Seminar, where I had another opportunity to talk about my maps. Later, Tom invited me back to lecture on and discuss the project at the Berkeley Scholars Workshop. Peter Stansky encouraged me in my interest in Gladstonian liberalism and gifted me hard-to-find books that I needed for my research from his private library. I also appreciated the opportunity provided by Stephan Astourian and the Armenian Studies Program and the Institute of Slavic, East European, and Eurasian Studies at Berkeley to lecture on my research. Parts of the project have been presented at national and regional meetings of the North American Conference on British Studies and at the "Empire State of Mind" conference at Lingnan University in Hong Kong. The Black Mountain Institute

Seminar offered a venue to present an overview of the completed project and I thank the graduate students, colleagues, and fellow fellows, Uwem Akpan, Daniel Brook, and Mary-Ann Tirone Smith, who participated.

Thanks go to my colleagues, students, and friends who have supported my work over the past several years. Kelly Mays gave me the gift of her keen insight in our discussions of the manuscript and her friendship. At BMI, Carol Harter provided an intellectual home and Richard Wiley gave timely and thoughtful advice about writing. Erika Rappaport offered her support and provided an early opportunity to write about an old story, the Eastern Question, in a new way for *History Compass*. Deb Cohler, Jordanna Bailkan, Anne Stevens, and Elizabeth Fraterrigo offered wise counsel and many kindnesses at different points in the process. In London, Claire Sibthorpe, Murali Shanmugavelan, Miranda Wallace, and Corey Cook provided me with friendship and good company. Others who read parts of the project and offered me the benefit of their expertise include Peter Holquist, Dennis Dworkin, Lawrence Klein, Greg Hise, Colin Loader, Paul Werth, David Tanenhaus, and Andy Fry. Thanks to the graduate students in my Human Rights seminar for reading parts of the manuscript and offering me their perspective. Thank you to Nathan MacBrien, who helped foster me through the editing and publication process. My parents, Bill and Elizabeth Tusan, and in-laws, Donald and Martha Muelrath, offered encouragement each in their own way and it was my father-in-law who one day over dinner suggested the subtitle for the book. In Boulder City, Jan Bunch and Patty Kearns showed me a cool oasis in this funky desert town during the long, hot summers while I wrote. My sister, Christina Tusan, put me in contact with invaluable regional resources and her strength and support served as a constant reminder of why I took on this project in the first place.

Very special thanks to James Vernon for believing in the project and remaining a rigorous and honest editor during the revision process.

I am grateful for permission from the Armenian Film Foundation to reference the film version of *Auction of Souls*. Thanks to Walter Karabian, who put me in touch with Michael Hagopian before his passing and later Jerry Papazian at the foundation. A version of chapter 4 appeared in *Victorian Studies* as "The Business of Relief Work: A Victorian Quaker in Constantinople and Her Circle" (summer 2009); I thank Indiana University Press for permission to include a revised version here. I have made every effort to identify and seek permission from copyright holders of collections referenced in this book and regret any unintentional oversight. The Religious Society of Friends in Britain Library in London was full of unexpected discoveries and provided an excellent place to work thanks to the generosity of archivist Josef Keith. I also thank Friends House for allowing me to reproduce images used in chapter 4 and to quote from the collection. I acknowledge The Trustees of Lambeth Palace Library and the Keeper of Special Collections, the Bodleian Library, University of Oxford, the Bodleian Library of Commonwealth and African Studies, University of Oxford, for permission to cite manuscript collections in their care. At the Middle East Center Archive at St. Antony's College Oxford, archivist Debbie Usher provided generous assistance and very good tea. David Vereker both granted me permission to quote from the papers of his father, Commander S. L. Vereker, and provided me with an invaluable collection of photographs of the burning of Smyrna from his own private collection. My father helped me think about how to best use one of these images on the cover. I thank the executors of the Comdr. C. H. Drage papers and the copyright holder of the papers of Captain C .S. B. Swinley for allowing me to quote from the respective collections. At Lied Library, humanities librarian Priscilla Finley, Richard Zwiercam, the folks at interlibrary borrowing, and Dan Werra in the media lab went above and beyond in helping me to track down and make use of difficult-to-find source material.

This book is dedicated to my mother, Elizabeth Tusan, who made this work possible by flying in and taking over for me at home and caring for my precious little ones, Nicholas and Sophia, when I traveled for research and conferences. For her love and many kindnesses I am always grateful. My husband, Scott Muelrath, could not have been a better partner in the writing of this book. If, as my grandmother used to say, marriage is like a watermelon—you don't know if you have a good one until you get it home and have a taste—then ours has been truly sweet.

Boulder City, Nevada
May 2012

A Note on Maps

Many of the historical maps reproduced and discussed in this book were originally published in outsized format, with extraordinary detail and subtle coloring. It is impossible to reproduce these maps adequately in a book of this kind. Therefore, high-resolution digitized versions of all maps have been published in a gallery accompanying the online edition of this book. Interested readers may find them at http://escholarship.org/uc/item/5626s1fw.

"Smyrna's Wall of Humanity." George Grantham Bain Collection, Library of Congress, Prints and Photographs Division, LC-B2-5851–11 [P&P].

Introduction

As the last fires smoldered in Smyrna at the end of September 1922, the 300,000 refugees left homeless sat on the pier under the watchful eye of the Turkish military. Waiting for Allied humanitarian transport ships that would take them away from the city burned to the ground by Turkish nationalists, a shout went up: "Long live Mustafa Kemal Pasha, long live!" One refugee remembered thinking as he joined in the cry, "Yes, long live Mustafa Kemal Pasha. We will be forever grateful to him for what he has done: after butchering thousands of Christians, after robbing and ruining this rich city, he has subjected hundreds of thousands of people to an untold misery. Yes, long may he live."[1]

Out of the ashes of Smyrna came a new city, Izmir, and a new Turkish nation. One year after Smyrna burned the Allies and Turkey divided the spoils at Lausanne. In the 1923 treaty that marked the end of World War I a vision of a Muslim East—the product of state-sponsored genocide, nationalist ideals, and Western imaginings—came to fruition in an agreement that uprooted 400,000 Muslims and 1.2 million Orthodox Christians.[2] The Ottoman Empire's attempt to rid Anatolia of its Christian minorities, legitimized by the Allies in the population exchange mandated by the Lausanne Treaty that moved Ottoman Christians to Greece and Greek Muslims to Turkey, confirmed a vision of a Muslim East divided from a Christian West. "I recognize Mitilini which I had visited ten years earlier when the island was still under Turkish rule and when the governor was Faik Ali Bey, my poet friend who was Kurdish by origin and a great friend of the Armenians," Garabed Hatcherian recalled after disembarking in Greece as a penniless refugee. He understood that times had changed. "Involuntarily, we settle down in Mitilini even though we know it is not an appropriate place for us."[3] Here in a newly reconstructed East the lines between Muslims and Christians were starkly drawn in a way that seemingly only made sense to Lausanne's mapmakers.

Today the West tends to understand the Middle East primarily in terms of geopolitics: Islam, oil, and nuclear weapons. But during in the nineteenth century, this place was conceived of differently. The story of Smyrna suggests that the interplay of geography and politics found definition in a broader set of concerns that included humanitarian and religious questions. This book reevaluates these considerations as part of a series of debates that defined Western proprietary interests in the Eastern Question. The "shifting, intractable and interwoven tangle of conflicting interests, rival peoples and antagonistic faiths," as the British journalist and politician John Morley called it, made the Eastern Question one of the most pressing humanitarian problems of his generation.

This history of the Eastern Question explains how the Middle East emerged as a site of politics through a competing set of military and humanitarian interventions that pulled the region into the moral sphere of British imperial interests. News of atrocities committed against minority populations in the Ottoman Empire started to filter back to Britain in the late nineteenth century and helped construct a liberal democratic ethos that cast humanitarianism as part of its political mandate. Reformers, politicians, and missionaries cultivated a sustained interest in campaigns that raised awareness and funds intended to stop crimes against civilian populations including the 1876 atrocities against the Bulgarians, the Ottoman massacres of the mid-1890s, the 1915 Armenian Genocide, and the burning of Smyrna in 1922. The impulse to aid distressed minority populations remained a problematic legacy of these encounters as it came up against the seemingly insurmountable realities of Total War that culminated in the tragedy at Smyrna.

In this context, the Eastern Question offered new ways of seeing the East. Starting in the mid-nineteenth century, the East came to hold a central place in both the imperial and cultural imagination as a Christian borderland. Religion worked in tandem with geography and politics to draw the land of the Ottoman Empire and its Christian populations closer to Europe. The British were the first to use the term "Near East," a designation that suggested an intimacy that went beyond mere geographic association. The notion of a "Middle East" necessarily relied on first securing a conception of the East as divided into "Near" and "Far" regions. The latter, a product of the seventeenth century, found its complement in the invention during the 1850s of a Near East situated between the Balkans and Persia.

The idea of the Middle East came almost half a century later. The journalist and Foreign Office operative Valentine Chirol put the Middle East in an imperial context soon after the American Captain Alfred Thayer Mahan made use of the term in 1902. "The Middle Eastern Question," Chirol declared in the *London Times,* was merely "a continuation of the same question with which we have long been familiar in the Near East." This question of the East encompassed what he called the "moral, commercial and military" commitments of the British Empire.[4] Over the course of the nineteenth and early twentieth centuries the contest over the Eastern Question came to determine imperial claims and humanitarian commitments in a place Britons would first refer to as the Near and, later, Middle East.

To understand the birth of the Middle East in Western thinking this book focuses on the geographical idea that preceded it: the Near East. Britain certainly was not alone in this project of mapping the Ottoman Empire as adjacent to Europe. France and Germany also had their own ways of understanding the region. Although the German and French conceptions of the Ottoman Empire are beyond the scope of this study, it is important to note that Germany's *Naher Osten* and France's *Proche Orient* were inventions of the post–World War I period. Terms like the *Levant* in the French case and *Orient* in the German broadly encompassed the region the British had claimed as their Near East.[5] These broad conceptions divided the world in terms of Occident and Orient, with little distinction made between the Ottoman Empire, India, and China. The early organization of the East in terms of Near, Middle, and Far proved for the British a means of linguistically marking claims to the Ottoman Empire.

Such conceptual nearness had particular resonance due to imperial ambitions in the Far East. The hold on India made these lands particularly important as a gateway to its eastern empire. One of the things that reassured Britain in staking its claim in the Near East was an imagined kinship with Eastern Christians, who many believed shared a common origin with Anglican Protestantism. The opposition of Eastern Orthodoxy to Rome secured these connections by forging a sense of solidarity against a Catholic other. Pulling these regions closer to the British sphere of influence relied on ethnographic and religious associations with the land and particularly the people that made these connections tangible. Though little enthusiasm existed to formally incorporate the Balkans, Anatolia, and Persia into the British Empire, arguments for informal control over internal Ottoman affairs grew louder after the Crimean War ended in 1856. Attempts to strengthen the hold over this region after the 1850s included offering humanitarian aid, mapping the region, and increasing the presence of diplomatic officials.[6]

An obsession with the Ottoman Empire as both the cradle of civilization and Holy Land gave heightened meaning to these interventions.[7] During the second half of the nineteenth century Britain set out on an ambitious project to survey, map, and expand its diplomatic footprint in the Ottoman Empire. As James Scott has observed, acts of mapping presuppose particular modes of knowing.[8] In the case of the British, knowing the East entailed defining not only *where* it was but *who* lived there. The rise of the discipline of ethnography, a means of classifying groups based on ethnic and religious origins, provided a point of entry into this world. This science of society starting in the 1850s divided the Near East between Orthodox Christians and Muslims, a cosmography that remains an important legacy of the Victorian period. Missionaries also began to see the region as fertile ground to spread their message among the Christian minority populations, mainly Greek, Bulgarian, Assyrian, and Armenian.[9] By the late nineteenth century a mission had been launched to convert Muslims.[10] This conception of the Ottoman Empire in terms of religious ethnography helped revive interest in the Near East as the birthplace of Christianity. The embrace of the emerging field of biblical archeology further secured the Holy Land as a place of religious and scientific exploration.[11]

Casting the East solely in terms of geopolitics thus would have seemed strange to Victorians like Morley and Chirol. For them, the idea of the Middle East found expression in the shifting geography of the Eastern Question, which called into existence an East that was both territorially vague and conceptually specific. At stake was more than a contest over claiming space for the British Empire on a map. The Holy Land, considered the historic site of Christianity, animated contemporary thinking and led to the embrace of the plight of Eastern Orthodox Christians as an ancient peoples persecuted by a despotic state. The crises that preceded the 1878 Russo-Turkish War and culminated with Smyrna's destruction in 1922 cast geopolitical concerns in terms of a humanitarian responsibility to victims and served to articulate a vision of a moral and just British Empire. The new post–World War I map that unevenly divided the world between Christian and Muslim was in part a product of such cultural imaginings.

LIBERALISM'S HUMANITARIAN CONSCIENCE

The understanding of an East divided by ethnic and religious strife took root in a culture of diplomacy that made foreign policy a matter of conscience. Moral, humanitarian, and religious preoccupations with the Ottoman Empire played an important role in defining a liberal vision of Britain in the world. This notion came to prominence under the leadership of W. E. Gladstone in his highly publicized campaigns against Ottoman atrocities during the last third of the nineteenth century.[12] A radical moralizing diplomacy offered new focus to the Eastern Question as the problem of the declining Ottoman Empire's treatment of Christian minorities. Although most closely connected to Gladstonian Liberal Party politics this idea found its broadest expression in a valorization of a shared belief in British liberty that defended freedom against tyranny. A sense of national identity rooted in notions of liberation clearly belied the exploitive nature of Britain's own empire. Pledges to defend subject peoples against foreign despotism, particularly in the Near East, resulted in part from the rise of a free, popular press starting in the 1850s that offered the public access to information on international affairs. This, coupled with mid-nineteenth-century evangelical religious revivalism, helped construct humanitarianism as a shared Protestant value.

The humanitarian voice of liberalism cast the Eastern Question as a national moral crisis that required a political solution born out of British leadership. As the public embraced the notion that the British Empire had a special responsibility to aid persecuted minorities, others worried about the effect intervention into Ottoman domestic affairs would have on imperial prestige. This raised the larger question of whether or not foreign policy should be used to resolve humanitarian abuses abroad creating a potential disconnect between high politics and the larger body politic. The humanitarian ethos that animated interest in Christian minorities also found expression in other campaigns against slavery and the exploitation of laborers in Africa.[13] Atrocities committed against civilians in the Near East powerfully directed this impulse towards a place of strategic and commercial importance and among a people considered akin to Europe for the first time. At the heart of this story came first of the plight of the Bulgarian and later the Armenian, Greek and Assyrian peoples.

The Eastern Question posed in terms of intervention on behalf of these subject minorities unfolded in three phases. The first placed the Bulgarians at the center of the story. Popular interest in Christian minorities emerged soon after the Crimean War thanks in part to press coverage that focused attention on both the conflict itself and Ottoman minorities. Orthodox Christianity, the faith of the great majority of this population, had captured the imagination early on of High Churchmen like Gladstone, who cast humanitarianism as a moral and religious crusade.[14] The claim that Orthodox Christians represented an authentic Christianity from which all churches derived began to hold sway thanks in part to the campaign he waged on behalf of persecuted Bulgarians in the 1870s. The firestorm at home over the so-called Bulgarian Atrocities put diplomatic pressure on treaty negotiations after the Russo-Turkish War to support some protection for minority populations, for which Britain agreed to take responsibility to enforce. After the Treaty of Berlin that ended this war created a Bulgarian state in 1878, public interest in the Eastern Question shifted farther east to the Armenians, Assyrians, and Greeks living in Anatolia.[15] Armenians dominated the territory in Eastern Anatolia, today part of modern Turkey, making them the largest Christian minority in the empire after Bulgaria ceased to be an Ottoman territory at the end of the 1870s.

This second phase began with pledges to revive the culture of a people who shared a distant religious and cultural past with the British. Some, like Lord Curzon and the Church Missionary Society, placed Muslims (who they referred to as Aryan relatives) in this trajectory. However, it was the persecution of Christian minorities that continued to capture the public imagination. The events of the Armenian massacres of the mid-1890s and 1909 and the Genocide of 1915 put Armenians at the center of the story through World War I. Called "the oldest of the civilized races in Western Asia" by the historian Arnold Toynbee, Armenia viewed through this lens held special status as "the first state in the world to adopt Christianity as its national religion."[16] Renewed interest in the plight of Greeks and Assyrians that culminated with the burning of Smyrna after the Armenian Genocide and mass displacement of hundreds of thousands of Assyrians during the war, resulted in advocacy efforts that considered the plight of Armenians alongside these other groups. In this final phase of the Eastern Question Greeks and Assyrians joined the considerations of Armenians as oppressed minorities worthy of sympathy and material support.

After World War I, this humanitarian vision of the Near East lost its purchase. Historians have suggested that political pragmatism coupled with an exhausted and war-weary electorate spelled the end of a vision that had shaped Britain's encounter with the Near East for over seventy-five years. Yet this explains only part of the story of diminishing interest in victims of massacre and genocide in the Near East. The debate over the Eastern Question gave us a modern understanding of the state as a moral actor. At the same time, as the ground began to shift after World

War I, a region once considered near moved farther east in British collective imaginings, reducing the possibility of compassion for victims of wartime atrocities. The complete disappearance of a once widespread Christian community, the result of massacre, state-sponsored genocide, and Lausanne Treaty mandates, severed an important historical connection with the region. As this population scattered as a widening diaspora spanning from Persia to Europe to the United States, so too did the focus of a humanitarian ideal that once championed its cause. Such a reading calls into question the notion that a disinterested abstract universalism determined the shape of early humanitarian intervention.[17] Although the culture of humanitarianism remained, the possibility of empathy with human suffering diminished in a new Middle East where interest in oil and exploitable resources forged other ties.

The legacy of the Eastern Question gave shape to a humanitarian ethos informed by both the material and geopolitical, which later would influence human rights campaigns into the twenty-first century. Today, we accept humanitarian considerations as a companion to foreign policy concerns, from peacekeeping missions to rebuilding infrastructure for former enemies after military victory. The idea that a state or international body has an obligation to act on behalf of a universal set of humanitarian principles continues to animate contemporary foreign policy debates.[18] This story of the Eastern Question serves as a reminder that calls for a moral foreign policy did not always exist in their current form but rather as a set of contingent historical relationships. Such configurations have as much to do with material representations of the place and the people at the center of concern as they do with ideological commitments. How a humanitarian standard is applied to particular groups at particular moments then requires historical explanation.

THE MIDDLE EAST AS BRITISH HISTORY

The study of how the West represents and engages the Middle East has shaped recent work in British history. Drawing largely upon methods from cultural history, historians have interrogated the perceptions of missionaries, writers, and travelers in an attempt to explain the nature of Western hegemony in this region.[19] Diplomatic historians have taken a different approach rooted in an older tradition, analyzing the successes and failures of missions to the region by consuls, diplomats, and other high-ranking officials to understand the nature of military conflicts and treaty negotiations with the so-called Sick Man of Europe.[20]

This volume brings these literatures together by providing a cultural history of diplomacy and the Eastern Question. It explores what happened in the space between political expediency and the humanitarian ideal, how foreign policy handled the question of conscience. Debates within the press reveal a divided policy on the Near East, with one side supporting direct intervention on behalf of Christian minorities and the other taking a more pragmatic view when news of atrocities against civilians came to light. At the same time, the stories of missionaries, aid organizations, and military and diplomatic consuls told in this book offered very real points of contact, identification, and association with the region's people. These encounters shaped a discourse that understood the Near East as a site of political engagement from both a strategic and humanitarian perspective.

In the attempt to bring the east nearer, Victorians created a Muslim and Christian typology that belied easy categorization. Many of the ways the British characterized both Muslims and Christians during the nineteenth century fall into the worst orientalist stereotypes.[21] My intention in analyzing these racialized dichotomies is to offer another way of seeing how orientalism worked to ossify characterizations of religious difference. Metaphors of Orthodox and Aryan kinship worked discursively to render familiar peoples of the Ottoman Empire through narratives of kinship. At the same time, notions of a "barbarous" Muslim other distinguished Christian populations as a unique charge of Protestant Britain. How these notions were mobilized to understand and de-orientalize Ottoman Christian minorities remains a central part of this history of discursive invention.

"Smyrna's Ashes" also builds upon the recent work on humanitarianism in the United States and Europe particularly as it relates to Ottoman atrocities and genocide. Attempting to tell the stories of victims of humanitarian disasters can be problematic when viewed through the perspective of aid workers, missionaries, and public officials. However inadequately, I hope to have left space on the page to read these narratives as more than representations of someone else's suffering. This is a story I wanted to tell. My grandmother was born in the Ottoman Empire. As a member of the large minority Christian population massacred before and during the war she understood the Eastern Question personally. When I asked Grandma Vicky years ago where she got her Anglo-sounding name she replied, "During the turn of the last century, every Armenian family had a girl called Victoria." My memory of the Alberts, Richards,

Williams, and Marys of that generation who once called themselves Ottoman subjects serve as a reminder of the extent of Britain's reach into the villages devastated by war and genocide in the heart of eastern Anatolia. In this small way, the story of British intervention in the Near East is part of my own.

1. Humanitarianism and the Rise of the Eastern Question

"The ground on which we stand here is not British nor European, but it is human. Nothing narrower than humanity could pretend justly to represent it," declared W. E. Gladstone to a cheering crowd of 6,000 supporters at an overflow town meeting convened by the Lord Mayor in September 1896 in Hengler's Circus, Liverpool. The occasion of what would prove Gladstone's last great public speech was a rally to protest the massacre of Ottoman Armenians. Dubbed a "humanitarian crusade" by the *Times*, the former Prime Minister asked his listeners to act on behalf of a common set of values that had come to define popular discourse on the Eastern Question.[1] All across the country in late September public officials, relief groups, and religious organizations held dozens of meetings and passed resolutions in support of a "national movement" and "unified action" to force the government to do something to stop the two-year campaign of violence under Sultan Abdul Hamid II that would leave some 200,000 dead.[2]

When Gladstone came out of retirement to rally the Armenian cause in 1896 he drew upon a decades-long discourse that posited a moral obligation to minority Christians. Indeed, he was a key architect of the liberal humanitarian ideal that found voice during the "Bulgarian Atrocities" controversy of the mid-1870s. Gladstone strongly condemned war crimes committed by the Ottoman military against Bulgarian subjects on the eve of the 1878 Russo-Turkish War. This event had shocked the nation and solicited an outpouring of sympathy for Bulgarian victims while precipitating the ascent of the Liberal Party to power in 1880. By the time of the Armenian massacres, the public had grown accustomed to narratives of suffering among Ottoman Christian minorities in the press, in political debates, and from new organizations that lobbied for human rights. While some favored diplomacy, others argued for direct military action on behalf of victims. The Armenian controversy prompted a crisis of leadership in the Liberal Party when in early October 1896 then party leader, Lord Rosebery, resigned due to "some conflict of opinion with Mr. Gladstone" over the Eastern Question.[3]

The high political drama of the Eastern Question extended beyond determining the fortunes of the Liberal Party. As the timing and reception of Gladstone's speech suggests, over the course of the last third of the nineteenth century humanitarianism had found a populist voice under the leadership of the former Prime Minister. This chapter tells the story of how this liberal humanitarian ethos took hold in Victorian Britain through an engagement with the Eastern Question. Why would news of massacres that happened so many miles away prompt a populist humanitarian response and make foreign policy considerations a matter of public debate? Such a convergence did not happen everywhere or completely. In Germany, news of the persecution of minority Bulgarian, Armenian, Greek and Assyrian populations during this period solicited an entirely different response. German public opinion sided not with Christians but the Muslim elite.[4] In Britain, an important part of the story of the Eastern Question was humanitarian. This prompted its own counternarrative that such concerns amounted to unrealistic moralizing in foreign policy. Then Prime Minister Benjamin Disraeli's scornful dismissal of the Bulgarian Atrocities agitation as "coffee house babble" had its complement in his characterization of Gladstone's emotive leadership on the issue. "Humanitarian politicians," Disraeli asserted to a crowd of supporters, "do not always look before they leap."[5]

Though critics contested the championing of minority causes in the Ottoman Empire as sentimental politics, it was the very appeal to human sympathy for a group that many had come to see as representative of British moral and religious values that gave the narrative its purchase. Contributors to this narrative included radical and liberal politicians, journalists, secular and religious advocacy groups, and feminist activists. This diversity gave British humanitarianism its particular character, moving between a discourse of obligation to fellow Christians to a broader language of imperial and moral duty. That these early crusades favored Christian minorities over other needy subjects tells us something important about why this humanitarian ethos took such powerful hold around the Eastern Question. As different constituencies appropriated the cause as their own, the campaign came to define itself as much by what it was not as by what it was. "This is no crusade against Mahommedanism,"

Gladstone admonished the crowd in Liverpool. Rather, it favored intervention on behalf of a particular oppressed minority. Liberalism's humanitarian conscience needed a clear corollary in order to forge an intimacy that motivated action.[6] During the second half of the nineteenth century, the nearness of fellow Christians represented as sharing a common set of values and religious origin inspired this association. This connection formed gradually in the wake of the Crimean War as humanitarian and imperial interests converged in a place Victorians came to know as the Near East. By the turn of the century debates over the Eastern Question provided the region with its geographical and ideological boundaries by creating a portrait of a people living in a not too distant land with ties to an imagined British past.

THE BIRTH OF THE NEAR EAST

In November 1856, *Fraser's Magazine*, a progressively minded periodical of religion and politics, coined the term "Near East" by describing it as the land "for the integrity of which we went to war with Russia."[7] That year Britain had just finished fighting the Crimean War (1854–1856) alongside her European allies to check Russian ambition and establish a more formal influence over the Sublime Porte, the seat of Ottoman government in Constantinople. Called "the people's war" by the *Times*, it marked the first military conflict that had widespread coverage in the media.[8] The war captured the attention of the public as politicians and pundits began to ask how Britain would further secure its status as the reigning European power in the region. The first step would be to define the Near East itself.

The post-Crimea moment offered the Near East its early geography as a place close to Europe. Drawing the East "near" afforded an opportunity to make a clearer taxonomy of the notion of the Levant, a catchall category that generally described the "countries of the East."[9] *Fraser's* argued that the newly won influence over the sultan and his territories in the Near East should translate into improving British routes to India via the Ottoman Empire. Here the advantages of closer connections related to the proposal to build the Euphrates Valley Railroad joining the Mediterranean and Persian Gulf. The railway "carried through the heart of Asiatic Turkey, and touching close upon the confines of Persia, may at some future period exert a vast influence on the civilization of the Near East, and that it will recreate and become the channel of commerce renowned in antiquity, but of which at this day faint traces remain."[10] In other words, closer economic ties would advance civilization by reviving a lost relationship between East and West while facilitating better trade with the East. An unbroken rail line across the desert would secure this connection and map new efficiencies over less reliable caravan routes.

Fraser's choice of "Near East" to describe parts of the Ottoman Empire at this time is important. First, the term is defined in "contradistinction" to the Far East, a huge category that included China, Australia, Japan, and India and whose usage dated to the seventeenth century. Both regions relied on the existence of the other for their definitional and geographic integrity. Ultimately, the ability to engage in commerce united the "Near" and "Far" parts of the East in this worldview: "the whole of the Far East is, as it were, opening to us. The idea has been abandoned that the Eastern trade must be limited to gold, ivory, spices and dyeing stuffs, silk, tea, coffee, rice and tobacco. Cotton is expected from India, and Australian wool has wrought the almost utter confusion of the sheep of Germany and Spain."[11] These lines conjured up the image of an economy reliant on imperial trade networks and foreign products. Closer ties with the "Far" regions of the British Empire made the East seem closer through a geographical sleight of hand that rhetorically incorporated the Ottoman Empire into its imperial network. In this way, the Near East provided a literal and metaphoric gateway to Britain's Far East.

Second, this new nomenclature emerged as a means of defining the indefinable: a region with porous borders that resisted easy to decipher geographical boundaries. For the British, the Near East gradually superseded both more specific labels like "Turkey in Europe" and general ones like the "Levant" on maps and in prose descriptions of the region. This meant that the Near East could include the Balkans, Asia Minor, and parts of Arabia, depending on the preoccupations of writers and mapmakers. *Fraser's* neologism accommodated the inclusion of all of these regions from Crimea to Persia. By describing the Euphrates Railroad as a project that cut through the "heart of Asiatic Turkey, and touch[ed] close upon the confines of Persia," the Near East spanned both the Western and parts of the Eastern Ottoman Empire. Building a railroad through "Asiatic Turkey" was understood as a way to exercise both economic and cultural influence over an amorphous region conceptually bounded by its changing relationship to the British Empire. Simply put, the finance and control of such a route would indelibly mark it as British.

Questions over the future success and security of the Suez Canal provided another important context for the emergence of the Near East as a discursive category. Egypt existed on the margins of British understandings of the Near East. Although nominally under the control of the sultan, Egypt maintained a problematic semicolonial relationship with Britain. These concerns over Suez made the possibility of an overland route, even one considered more risky and expensive, a secure alternative especially if Britain could exercise greater control over the Sublime Porte after the Crimean War. In the end, even after the opening of the Canal in 1869 proved an effective trade route to India and Egypt fell more securely within the purview of the Empire after 1882, the British helped finance the building of the Anatolian Railway, which connected Eastern parts of Asia Minor with Europe.[12] Only after German plans to take over the financing and building of the southern route, the so-called Baghdad Railroad, sparked public outrage in Britain in 1903 did these plans for an overland route fade.[13]

Understandings of the Near East further drew upon notions of the region as the cradle of civilization and the birthplace of Christianity, or the "Holy Land." Critics maintained that the end of the Crimean War offered a new opportunity for the West to reconnect with its ancient past in the East. "Since the 17th century there has been but little direct intercourse between the Orthodox East and the Protestant West," wrote the *Edinburgh Review* in 1858, "but the great events of the last few years, which have opened for England such a career in the East, cannot fail to bring the subject very prominently before every one who pays real attention to such matters." Anglicanism could now rejoin Eastern Orthodox Christianity in its birthplace: "A noble opportunity now presents itself in the memorial church about to be erected at Constantinople. That monument to the brave men who died in the late war ought to become a centre, not of proselytism, but of friendly intercourse with the members of the ancient churches of the East. There they ought to behold a communion, united with them in opposition to Roman corruptions and usurpations." This new Anglican Church, "assigned a conspicuous site upon the hills with crown the Bosphorus," was built as a war memorial to the British efforts in Crimea to represent "a trophy of our heroism and our faith."[14] A monument to Christianity, the church promised to connect Orthodoxy with Anglicanism against the "Roman corruptions" of Catholicism in a prominent and unmistakable way. For Anglican missionaries, victory in Crimea opened up similar opportunities that included restarting a previously abandoned Church Missionary Society project in 1858 focused on reviving the Eastern Orthodox Church in the Ottoman Empire.

These symbols of Anglican and Eastern Orthodox unity reinforced a sense of common cause in the Holy Land. New technologies would hasten the reuniting of Eastern and Western Christendom in a more material way, according to one critic in an article on the Eastern Orthodox Church: "Civilizing agencies are now wielded by European nations . . . The press itself, long the great instrument of human advancement, is transcended in its effects and invested with wider and more immediate influences, by the railway, the telegraphic wire, and the photographic process. These marvelous powers are spreading themselves gradually over the whole earth, and marking out the lines of future conquest. There are yet vast spaces to be reclaimed to civilization and Christianity in every quarter of the globe."[15] The notion that development went hand in hand with Christian civilization strengthened proprietary claims. *Fraser's* had argued on the eve of the Crimean War that Britain had a responsibility to not let the region fall under the influence of Orthodox Russia, which considered itself the natural defender of Ottoman Christians: "the climate is mild, the soil wonderfully fertile, and under a good government and with years of peace, these provinces would probably be unsurpassed in Europe for wealth and prosperity. At present they bear only the marks of the hard lot to which their position between Europe and Asiatic invaders has for centuries past reduced them; ill cultivated, half peopled, half civilized with few towns and scarcely anything that can be called a road."[16] British-led reform and development schemes would revive a Christian East by solving the political and material causes of underdevelopment.

In this line of thinking, forging more intimate connection with Ottoman Christian minorities would bolster trade while effectively challenging "Asiatic invaders," which included the Russians. Britain's future ties with the Near East, as a debate in Parliament during the Crimean War concluded, rested not in its Muslim rulers or Jewish minorities but in supporting the Ottoman Empire's commercially minded Christian races: "the system of the Porte, bad and corrupt as it may be in many ways, has yet been found compatible with the rise of a rich and increasing commerce. That commerce is almost exclusively in the hands of its Christian subjects." Accordingly, "Their gradual improvement and amalgamation in the course of time" would offer both "the peaceful solution of a question, of which the very prospect has long perplexed the world" while securing British predominance. The British also cast the Jews as having a proclivity towards trade during this time.[17] However, the predominance of Christian minorities particularly along the rural trade routes that followed the proposed Anatolian Railway singled out this population for attention. As the debate concluded, support for Ottoman Christians would ensure that "No one Power will be allowed to steal or to force a march on the capital of the East."[18]

Conceptions of Orthodox Christians bound by geopolitical and cultural ties to the Empire continued to animate thinking after the war in this newly minted Near East. Some writers went as far as to push for greater recognition of religious connections between commercially minded Christian races and the British: "It is strange that a nation like England, in whose inner life religion plays so important a part should be slower than almost any of the Continental nations to recognize the all-important influence of the religion professed by a people upon its institutions and character." This line of argument aligned British interests with support of the civil emancipation of Christians: "No country ever thrives on the strength of natural resources without industry, knowledge, equal laws, respect for personal rights and security for property–things of which a genuine Mussulman would never so much as dream. Hence their commerce is carried on by foreigners; their land, once tilled by serfs, remains waste and passes into the hands of bitter internal enemies; the master's share of the produce is virtually not rent but tribute."[19] The answer: forcing the Ottoman Empire to reform its legal and tax system to favor those mainly Christian minority populations carrying on trade in the cradle of civilization.

THE BULGARIAN CRISIS

As the Near East settled in as a familiar Victorian geography the Eastern Question began to occupy a growing space in public discourse. Between 1856 and 1900, over one thousand articles explaining, debating, and arguing the Eastern Question appeared in Liberal, Conservative, and nonparty periodicals.[20] As table 1 indicates, the mid-1870s witnessed the beginning of a general and sustained increase in interest in the Eastern Question that lasted through to the twentieth century. This rise directly coincided with the Bulgarian crisis.

The events precipitated by the Russo-Turkish War heightened interest in the Near East. Historians have treated the controversy over the massacre of Bulgarian civilians in 1876 as an isolated event, which has disconnected it from a longer set of debates over the Eastern Question.[21] Public outrage over what became known as the Bulgarian Atrocities had roots in a foreign policy that posited Britain as a defender of minority Christians in the Ottoman Empire. Britain along with its European allies had previously supported the Tanzimat reforms that protected of the rights of minority Ottoman subjects in the wake of the Greek wars of independence in the 1830s. At the end of the Crimean War in 1856, Britain

TABLE 1. Coverage of the "Eastern Question" in the Mainstream Periodical Press

(articles and book reviews)

	1856–75	1876–85	1886–1914
Blackwood's Magazine	15	86	44
Contemporary Review	8	57	57
Cornhill Magazine	6	5	3
Edinburgh Review	16	31	40
Fortnightly Review	30	102	134
Fraser's Magazine	23	33	n.a.*
Macmillan's Magazine	11	24	6
National Review	2	9	84
Nineteenth Century	0	68	59
Quarterly Review	11	48	37
TOTALS	122	463	464

Information from Proquest British Periodicals database, accessed January 28, 2009, http://britishperiodicals.chadwyck.com/home.do.

*Fraser's ceased publication in 1882.

helped negotiate a set of reforms that would protect Christian minorities as part of the peace.[22] Most realized the ineffectiveness of these reforms even before the Bulgarian crisis began. However, news of the extent of the massacres in Bulgaria focused new light on these pledges, raising the specter of British culpability in the face of the humanitarian disaster unfolding in the Near East.

Then Foreign Secretary Lord Derby understood the tangled nature of a diplomacy that tied imperial interests to humanitarian commitments. "The eternal Eastern Question is before use again," he declared on the eve of the crisis at a meeting of Conservative Working Men in Edinburgh in December 1875, "and I for one have no idea that the year 1876 will see it finally settled."[23] The Conservative government's purchase of Suez shares the previous month coupled with word of a revolt by Bulgarian nationalists brought the Eastern Question into the spotlight. A little more than six months after his Edinburgh speech Derby received a series of deputations from concerned working men, city officials, and prominent citizens protesting the slaughter of tens of thousands of Bulgarians by Turkish soldiers in the wake of the revolt.[24] What, they asked, would the government do to stop the atrocities and protect British interests? Derby was called upon to soothe imperial worries and moral consciences in light of Disraeli's derisive dismissal of the atrocities as a matter of little importance. Derby told the crowd what it wanted hear: "Equal treatment to Mahommedan and Christian; better administration for both; security for life and property; effectual guarantees against a repetition of such outrages . . . these are practical objects and for these objects we shall labour." Britain, he repeated in response to the well over 400 petitions he received by December, would honor its historic pledges to protect the Bulgarians.[25]

Gladstone's leadership in denouncing the Bulgarian Atrocities ensured that the controversy stayed in the news. It also gave the cause its particular religious and moralizing character.[26] Gladstone began to draw connections between Anglicanism and the Eastern Orthodox Church starting in the 1850s. The belief that the Orthodox Church had a special connection with an authentic early Christianity drove this sympathy for Ottoman Christians and came out of the Anglican High Church tradition.[27] Victorian liberals who followed Gladstone's line of thinking led the charge particularly after news of the slaughter of Bulgarians reached Britain in May 1876 through reports published in the *Daily News*. An image of a meeting held by supporters of the Bulgarian cause at St. James's Hall in December 1876 published in the *Illustrated London News* in figure 1 depicted the mass appeal of liberal arguments on behalf of Ottoman Christians. "Attended by more than a thousand delegates from all parts of the United Kingdom to express public opinion" who came to discuss the "responsibilities of Europe and England in particular, in reference to the Eastern Question," the delegates list read as a who's who of liberal statesmen who vowed to uphold British interests by supporting a system that would insure the implementation of minority reform provisions in the Ottoman Empire.[28]

The Bulgarian Atrocities agitation offered a way of seeing the Eastern Question as the problem of a declining Ottoman Empire, particularly in regard to its treatment of Christian minorities. This understanding predominated throughout the last third of the nineteenth century and beyond thanks in part to sustained coverage in the popular and political press.[29] Writing in the 1930s, historian R. W. Seton-Watson credited Gladstone's moralizing foreign policy with ushering in a new way of thinking about the Ottoman Empire: "While then Disraeli clung to the very last to his illusions on Turkey and identified British interests with the artificial maintenance of a decadent state, Gladstone saw that the future lay with the nations whom Ottoman tyranny had so long submerged."[30] Gladstone had successfully marshaled public sentiment against fighting

Figure 1. Illustration of W. E. Gladstone speaking at St. James's Hall on the Eastern Question. *Illustrated London News*, December 16, 1876.

a war with Russia by publicizing Ottoman war crimes against Bulgarian civilians. His pamphlet "The Bulgarian Horrors" made a convincing case for a foreign policy that took into account humanitarian concerns, selling over 200,000 copies after its publication in September 1876. In it Gladstone "entreat[ed] my countrymen" to put pressure on the government "to put a stop to the anarchical misrule" in Bulgaria. The eventual demise of the Disraeli government in the wake of the controversy challenged over a generation of pro-Ottoman policy (see figure 2).[31]

Gladstone's crusade made moral and religious questions a populist form of engagement with foreign affairs. What Britain should do to alleviate the suffering of Ottoman Christians was elevated to one of the key questions of the Victorian period. This concern prompted the founding of humanitarian advocacy institutions that included most notably The Eastern Question Association. Formed in 1876 "for the purpose of watching events in the East, giving expression to public opinion and spreading useful information," the organization boasted a list of distinguished members led by the Duke of Westminster as president and the Earl of Shaftesbury as vice president. Clearly hoping to influence the outcome of what would later become the Treaty of Berlin, the association issued a

PUNCH, OR THE LONDON CHARIVARI.—May 26, 1877.

"WOODMAN, SPARE THAT TREE!"

Lord Beaconsfield sings—

"WOODMAN, SPARE THAT TREE!   *THE* ASIAN MYSTERIE,
I LOVE IT, EVERY BOUGH;   THAT IT HAS LIVED TILL NOW!"

Figure 2. Cartoon of Gladstone as a woodsman toppling the tree of Turkish rule in the wake of the Bulgarian Atrocities while Disraeli (Lord Beaconsfield) appeals to him to stop. *Punch*, May 26, 1877.

series of twelve pamphlets written by politicians, women's rights activists, and churchmen published together in one lengthy volume in 1877.

Instead of dwelling on the Bulgarian case the Eastern Question Association used these pamphlets to introduce readers to the "races, religions and institutions" of the Ottoman Empire through its Armenians, Assyrians, and Greek inhabitants. *Papers on the Eastern Question* included "Armenia and the Lebanon" by J. W. Probyn, "The Slavonic Provinces of the Ottoman Empire" by W. E. Gladstone, "Fallacies of the Eastern Question" by Rev. William Denton, and "The Martyrs of Turkish Misrule" by Millicent Fawcett. The association continued into the twentieth century much along these same lines as a "non-partisan and non-governmental" organization. As Frederic Harrison claimed in his presidential address at the annual meeting in 1910, the association saw as its mission to help the "various peoples of the East of Europe in resisting the oppression of a sanguinary tyrant."[32] The Eastern Question remained on the minds of Victorians due in part to the efforts of Liberals, Nonconformists, and journalists who argued for a radical Christian version of humanitarian diplomacy. For that story, we turn to two of the most vocal proponents of this vision.

HUMANITARIAN CRUSADERS:
E. A. FREEMAN AND W. T. STEAD

Both E. A. Freeman (1823–92) and W. T. Stead (1849–1912) came to the Eastern Question early in their careers. For Freeman it started with a fascination with the Eastern Orthodox Church in the 1850s. Stead came later to the Eastern Question through a critique of Conservative policy over the Suez Canal and brought a new intensity to the debate. To Freeman's professorial didacticism Stead brought a popular appeal. Together these two writers helped secure the ascendancy of a Gladstonian moral diplomacy and helped shape over a generation of thinking about the Eastern Question.

Converted to the liberal cause in his teens, Freeman considered Gladstone his "captain" in matters political and religious. He attended Oxford and later served, on the recommendation of Gladstone, in the Regius Professorship of Modern History. His spirited defense of the Greeks, Assyrians, and Armenians living in the Ottoman Empire came out of his Oxford-influenced belief in the intimate connections between the Eastern Orthodox Church and High Church Anglicanism. Calling the Eastern Church "one of the great phenomena in history," he asserted that its brand of Christianity proved an authentic source of connection between Englishmen and the Christians of the East.[33] He argued for the unity of Eastern and Western churches in dozens of articles, books, and pamphlets published starting in 1855, believing that improving relations between different Orthodox sects and Anglicanism would result in a successful challenge to Ottoman rule. Christianity, for Freeman, proved a defining cultural marker that unified British interests with the Eastern Question. As he most forcefully argued in *Ottoman Power in Europe* in 1877, religious kinship with Eastern Christians should operate as a moral compass for foreign policy.

Stead, as he would do with later campaigns like "white slavery" in England, took on the Eastern Question as a crusade, elevating the controversy to the level of a political movement.[34] As editor of the *Northern Echo* he built a career as a critic of the Conservative government. He first entered the debate over the Eastern Question in 1875 with a scathing critique of Disraeli's "secret" purchase of additional shares in the Suez Canal from the Egyptian Khedive, which gave England a majority stake and soon force Lord Derby on the defensive. "Startling News from the East," declared the headline of the *Northern Echo* on November 27, 1875, "Purchase by England of the Suez Canal." Not long after, the Bulgarian Atrocities agitation provided this Nonconformist radical with the opportunity to sharpen his critique of Conservative policy as imprudent and immoral. Although his politics mirrored Freeman's, his approach did not. The press was the starting point for Stead, who took his campaign from the pages of the *Northern Echo* to the public meeting hall. His ability as an organizer impressed Freeman, who admired how quickly the agitation took hold in the largely Nonconformist North where Stead counted forty-seven protest meeting during the months of August and September alone.[35] Gladstone so admired his work on behalf of the Eastern Question that he entrusted Stead with his papers in the hopes that he would write the history of the Bulgarian agitation.[36] His populist style of journalism, putting sensational reporting in the service of humanitarian crusades, carried over to his later work as editor of the *Pall Mall Gazette* and the *Review of Reviews*. As he characterized his career in 1894, "I am a revivalist preacher and not a journalist by nature."[37]

Freeman's and Stead's writing on the Eastern Question represented the clearest articulation of a liberal humanitarian critique of Conservative foreign policy. The so-called "philo-Turk" position of supporters of Disraeli came increasingly under fire by liberals including John Bright and organizations such as the League in Aid of the Christians of Turkey soon after news of the Bulgarian Atrocities reached Britain.[38] Freeman went as far as to accuse Disraeli of pro-Ottoman sympathies, using it as an excuse to attack his Jewish background and question his loyalty.[39] This critique went beyond a question of support for either cross or crescent. The threat from Russia supposed by a generation of politicians starting with Lord Palmerston found a counterpoint in a critique that understood Russia as an ally in the defense of Eastern Christendom.[40] Stead's *Northern Echo*, where he served as editor during the 1870s, and other liberal-minded periodicals such as the *Contemporary Review* further popularized the Eastern Question as a diplomatic problem with a moral solution. Conservative-minded critics dismissed this as naïve and sentimental politics, arguing that only military support of Turkey would keep Russia in check. By the 1870s this view had come increasingly under fire from liberals, who countered that Britain was backing the wrong ally. Freeman himself had broken ties with the *Saturday Review*, where he earned six hundred pounds a year for his writing, when the periodical expressed support for the Disraeli government's willingness to go to war against Russia in defense of Turkey.

None of these arguments would have taken hold without Gladstone's indomitable presence in the debate. In "The Paths of Honor and Shame," published in March 1878, Gladstone warned against going to war with Russia to save the Ottoman Empire: "A war undertaken without cause is a war of shame, and not of honour." Rather the British government should use diplomacy to promote reform in the Ottoman provinces: "The security of life, liberty, conscience, and female honor, is the one indispensible condition of reform in all these provinces."[41] Conservatives responded with the charge that this policy substituted one brand of prejudice for another. In "What is the Eastern Question?" one commentator rallied against Gladstone's "hypocritical mask of humanity, liberty and religion," which threatened to expel Muslims from Europe.[42] Others worried alongside Disraeli that government by "sentiment" would make a mockery of British power and prestige. To this, liberals responded with appeals to British justice: "It is not a question, be it remembered as is often imagined, of Mohammedan as against Christian; it is a question of the ruling Turk as against all his subjects alike, whether Christian or Mohammedan."[43] Another argued that England "must be on the side of humanity, freedom and progress, if it is to be in harmony with both her interests and her duty."[44] For Gladstone, the specificity of the Bulgarian case elevated humanitarianism to the status of a common cause: "Rich and strong we are; but no people is rich enough, or strong enough to disregard the priceless value of human sympathies."[45]

Freeman's and Stead's writings on the Eastern Question cast Bulgaria's revolution as a beginning meant to inspire other oppressed minorities. In 1875, Freeman drew attention to the Turkish response to the revolt in Montenegro, which he called "a genuine revolt of an oppressed Christian people against Mahometan masters." "The true Eastern Question," according to Freeman, hinged on "whether European powers shall go on condemning the nations of South-Eastern Europe to remain under barbarian bondage." As he concluded, "The so called Turkish government is then, I say, no government at all."[46]

By the 1890s both men had published numerous articles advocating civil and political reform in the Near East. Freeman's religious moralism and his "devotion to the cause of righteous government," according to his biographer, kept him writing.[47] Freeman kept the Eastern Question before the public in articles such as "Bulgaria and Servia" (1885), "Present

Aspects of the Eastern Question" (1887), "Ancient Church Endowments" (1891), "Dangers to the Peace of Europe" (1891), and "Progress in the Nineteenth Century" (1892). Stead's journalism carried on in the same vein. Articles published in the *Northern Echo* included "England and the Eastern Insurgents" (1876), "Our Policy in the East," and "The War," which gave him claim to the title of the people's representative in the Eastern Question. Up until his death aboard the *Titanic* in 1912 he continued to write about the plight of Eastern Christians. The *Review of Reviews* featured articles on the Armenian massacres of the 1890s, the Russian and Armenian churches, and Anglo-Ottoman relations. A set of articles profiling Gladstone in the *Review of Reviews* in the 1890s championed the liberal statesman as defender of Eastern Christians. In the wake of the Young Turk Revolution that brought on another wave of sectarian violence in 1908, Stead published articles arguing that Britain should put pressure on the new Ottoman government to reform its minority policy.

Stead used the Bulgarian Atrocities campaign to launch a brand of moral crusading that helped make his name as a journalist. After the controversy that he claimed in characteristic overstatement "was in a great measure my work," Stead reflected on the moral imperative that set him writing. "What is true of Bulgaria is true of larger things," he wrote in his journal in 1877. Religious piety combined with a moral sense of the public good led to his vow "to stimulate all religious men and women, to inspire children and neighbours with sense of supreme sovereignty of duty and right." England's leadership as an empire ("keep[ing] the peace of one-sixth the human race") and in protecting female virture ("The honour of Bulgarian virgins is in the custody of the English voter") were part of his set of core principles.[48] This world view drew upon Gladstone's assertion that England had a duty to defend "female honor." This call to defend rape victims cast Bulgaria itself as a wronged woman. The sexualizing of the Bulgarian Atrocities thus introduced another moralizing strand to British diplomacy. Stead later used this tactic to spectacular effect at home during his 1885 newspaper expose of child prostitution in London in the "Maiden Tribute of Modern Babylon," and in his condemnation of the Boer War as an "immoral" war that threatened the honor of the female Outlander in the Transvaal.[49] In the case of the Bulgarians, a compelling melodrama of religion and sexuality helped keep the issue before the public.

Secular and religious activists alike had something to take from the branding of the Bulgarian case as a humanitarian crusade. Gladstone's moral leadership, Stead's populism, and Freeman's fiery diatribes offered a powerful counter to conservative charges that cast this campaigning as wrong-headed sentimental politics. The founding of institutions that supported this ideal further enabled this liberal humanitarian vision of the Eastern Question to take root. The increasing professionalization of charity networks tapped into British ideas of benevolence and humanitarianism by giving individuals a stake in ameliorating human suffering by donating money to causes like "Bulgarian Relief" and later "Armenian Relief." The indefatigable Adeline Paulina Irby and her army of female helpers oversaw aid funds and institutions in the Near East. Philanthropists like Lady Strangford continued in this vein well beyond the end of the Bulgarian agitation at home. By the summer of 1877, English-based relief funds had contributed over 250,000 pounds to relief work in the Balkans.[50]

Offering aid through donations was one thing, making Britons feel a moral obligation to Eastern Christians was still another. The story of the decision of Nonconformists to support Gladstone's campaign offers a well-studied example of how this idea took root during the Bulgarian agitation. Nonconformists, as Richard Shannon has argued, represented "the temper of moral seriousness in the public life of nineteenth-century England" and played a central role in transforming the argument to assist Christians in need into a crusade. Although the agitation spread across England, Wales, Scotland, and Ireland, Nonconformists in the north and southwest played a disproportionate role in the agitation.[51] These mainly Methodists, Unitarians, and Quakers saw their own second-class status as parallel to that of Eastern Christians. At the same time, the nineteenth-century fascination with the Holy Land as a birthplace of Christianity gave Nonconformists reason to understand Eastern Christians as authentic representatives of early Christianity. Gladstone recognized early on the importance of Nonconformity in forging connections between Britons and Eastern Questions, praising the "exertions made by the Nonconformists in the cause of humanity and justice" during the Bulgarian crisis.[52]

At the heart of the Nonconformist response rested the belief posited so strongly by Gladstone himself that Eastern Christians shared a kinship with Anglican Protestantism. Stead and Freeman made this connection by attempting to strengthen British claims over the Holy Land. Freeman's anti-Semitic attacks on Disraeli aimed to widen the perceived gulf between Judaism and British Protestantism with respect to the Near East. Freeman also represented Eastern Christianity as anti-Catholic, which he claimed afforded it a natural affinity with Anglican

Protestantism: "The High Church section of the English Church take a natural interest in a communion which like their own, protests against the usurpations of Rome, while it sympathizes with their special views of ritual and discipline, of sacramental efficacy and Episcopal government."[53] These Protestant values, according to Freeman, should also appeal to "Broad Church" believers who understood Christianity as a crucial link between East and West. In this line of argument, the connection between the Eastern Church and the "Reformed Churches of the West" that began during the Reformation could find needed revival through projects such as the Crimea Memorial Church built by Britain in Constantinople to commemorate the Crimean War.[54] A union of faiths had emerged out of the crucible of war to create a sense of common faith and purpose among Christians in the East and West.

For secular-minded skeptics, Freeman offered a kinship model based on an evolutionary and racialized view of history. "One special feature of what is called the Eastern Question is the direct and immediate connexion into which it brings the earliest and the latest times of history," Freeman argued in "The Geographical Aspect of the Eastern Question" in 1877. "The lands between the Hadriatic [sic] and the Euphrates" offered Britons a glimpse of their own past. In the Near East, "the past and the present are in being side by side" and distinctions of race and religion become more pronounced from West to East.[55] The "political geography" of the Eastern Question, according to Freeman, was that of a slow march forward where religious distinctions would give way to national identities as they had done in Western Europe. Until that time, Freeman suggested a type of imperial federal structure that would allow for a more peaceful and democratic coexistence and bring the western Ottoman Empire closer to Europe.

Stead and Freeman both held up the "desire for liberty" as a defining characteristic of Eastern Christians. Even with "all their shortcomings" according to Stead, "they represent the cause of progress, of humanity, of civilization." Disraeli's support of Turkey in its conflict with Serbia and Montenegro led Stead to declare that the premier would "tarnish England's glory and disgrace the English name by assisting to defeat the heroic men who have gone forth against the Turk under the banners of Independence, with the war-cry of 'Liberty or Death.'"[56] Freeman considered the Ottoman's "an army of occupation" and maintained that the desire for self-government set Eastern Christians apart from their Muslim rulers.[57] The responsibility of England to those seeking freedom from Ottoman rule rested in the "English political belief" that "freedom and just government were indeed righteous and holy thing to be striven after by all men."[58] This support for the aspirations of minority Christians thus reflected a deeper English value that had its roots in a culture of justice and liberty. As Stead asserted, "the day when Englishmen cease to sympathise with those who are struggling for freedom will date the downfall of their own liberties."[59]

By 1880, the liberal argument that favored intervention on behalf of minority Christians deeply informed considerations of the Eastern Question. That year witnessed the landslide victory for the Liberal Party under Gladstone's leadership. Historians credit Gladstone's role in the Bulgarian Atrocities agitation with securing his victory against the pro-Ottoman Disraeli government.[60] Freeman likened the event to a "deliverance" from conservative tyranny that revealed that the people of Britain "have a conscience." This moral diplomacy informed future Liberal administrations and the response of Lord Salisbury's Conservative government to the Eastern Question during the mid-1890s. This had not little to do with the discourse of humanitarian reform that took hold in the wake of the diplomatic resolution of the Russo-Turkish War.

A MORAL FOREIGN POLICY

The Treaties of San Stefano (March 1878) and Berlin (July 1878) cast the Eastern Christian "desire for liberty" as a problem to be solved by Great Power diplomacy. At stake was the question of how to adjust the territories of the western Ottoman Empire to offer greater autonomy to the Bulgarian, Romanian, and Serbian populations while protecting the Assyrian, Greek, and Armenian populations still living under Ottoman rule in Anatolia. Treaty negotiations, widely reported in the British press, proved of only limited success in resolving the minority question (see figure 3). While the westernmost provinces of the Ottoman Empire were granted a measure of national autonomy, other reform provisions fell flat. Conservatives had played a central role in negotiating the terms of peace and helped to soften the harsh terms of the Treaty of San Stefano that favored greater autonomy for subject minorities. When the Treaty was rewritten as the Treaty of Berlin four months later, British negotiators had removed the clause that would have forced reforms on the Ottoman government. Article 61 of the Berlin Treaty formalized British responsibility for the treatment of Christian subjects but offered little by way of enforcement.

The diplomatic maneuverings that seemingly resolved the Bulgarian

Figure 3. Sketched portraits of diplomats attending the Eastern Question Conference. *Graphic,* January 6, 1877.

issue through the creation of a semiautonomous Bulgaria had done little to quell calls for more liberty for other minorities. The lack of an enforceable minority protection clause for in the Berlin Treaty kept the plight of Ottoman Christians in the news. In the wake of Berlin, the watchword of "reform" of the Turkish administration provided a point of departure for both liberal and conservative public opinion. Failed attempts to enforce the reforms of the Tanzimat period shaped ideas regarding how and by whom these changes would be carried out. Liberals favored removing territories from Ottoman rule while conservatives largely favored influencing the sultan through diplomatic pressure. "Are Reforms Possible Under Mussulman Rule?" asked Malcolm MacColl in an article by the same name in the *Contemporary Review* in August of 1881. Concerned primarily with placing "the Christian subjects of the Sultan on a footing of equal rights with the Musselmans," MacColl argued that "The only possible hope is in the withdrawal of Armenia from the direct rule of the Sultan ... Appoint a Christian or at least a non–Mussulman Governor and make him practically independent of the caprice of the Sultan and the intrigues of the Palace and the Porte. There will then be no difficulty in introducing reforms in all branches of the administration."[61]

The unresolved issue of minority rights cast a long shadow over the postwar settlement. Bulgarians occupied the role of the victim in the negotiations at San Stefano and Berlin. The creation of the nominally independent territory of Bulgaria came as a response to the controversy over Ottoman war crimes. To "protect" them from misrule by the Ottomans the negotiators separated Bulgarians from the Ottoman Empire. Negotiators believed they had solved the minority problem through a national solution. Instead of promises of British protection, the treaty gave Bulgarians their own semiautonomous territories. The so-called Big Bulgaria proposed in San Stefano quickly gave way at Berlin to a group of smaller, weak states drawn along ethnic and religious lines. With the stroke of a pen the newly invented Bulgaria, Servia, and Roumania promised to solve the Eastern Question by eliminating the causes of sectarian strife and thus foreign entanglements with Ottoman internal policy. At the same time, this agreement offered a more indirect form of protection by drawing these religio-ethnic states closer to Western Europe while pushing the Ottoman Empire farther east.

Reports that the Treaty of Berlin had failed to introduce reforms to protect minorities in remaining Ottoman provinces offered a powerful platform for humanitarian advocates. Invoking notions of kinship among "Christian nations" during his 1879 Midlothian campaigns, Gladstone launched his re-assent to the Liberal Party leadership by heralding a moral foreign policy that "should always be inspired by love of freedom."[62] After winning the election the liberal press served as the mouthpiece for this program. This included mainstream and advocacy publications such as the Anglo-French newspaper *Armenia* edited by a former delegate of the Berlin Conference. By 1889, a ninety-eight-page parliamentary report on the "Condition of Populations in Asiatic Turkey" found its way into an article in the *Contemporary Review* and argued for immediate action on behalf of oppressed Assyrian and Armenian Christians.[63] That next year James Bryce, a man who would prove to be a pivotal figure in wartime debates over the Eastern Question, started the Anglo-Armenian Association with the explicit purpose of enforcing Article 61. The article outlined Britain's commitment to the Ottoman Empire: "Under the 61st clause of the Treaty of Berlin we are bound in certain eventualities to defend Turkish territory; but the obligation rests on the preliminary condition such reforms as England shall approve are carried out. The responsibility for the delay of such reforms is therefore at our door . . . From the time of Milton's appeal for the Waldenses down to the Bulgarian troubles of our time the English people have always rejoiced to show their sympathy with populations of their own faith in time of persecution."[64]

A more urgent call for reform came from those who represented Christian minorities as allies under threat. In "Shall the Frontier of Christendom be Maintained?" J. W. Howe asked, "Is this world nation willing that unarmed and unoffending communities shall be swept out of existence? . . . The Turk is now the ally of Russia. See to it England that these despotisms, united, do not for all time deprive you of your natural allies the Christians of the East!"[65] This call to honor a "natural" alliance with minority Christian communities, others argued, had at its core a set of cultural values that came out of a common faith. "Christianity is a religion of humanity," claimed one commentator on the eve of the San Stefano Conference. "Its social idea is industrial, not predatory or military."[66] Such views followed the Gladstonian line that had animated his northern Nonconformist supporters. For Gladstone, the loyalty of Eastern Christians was a prize worth fighting for: "I am selfish enough to hope, in the interest of my country that in the approaching Conference or Congress we may have and may use an opportunity to acquire the goodwill of somebody. By somebody I mean some nation, and not merely some government. We have repelled and I fear estranged twenty millions of Christians in the Turkish Empire."[67] Here moral obligations dovetailed with strategic interests. Supporting minority reform, according to this argument, would produce loyal allies to Britain and protect its imperial interests in what one commentator called "the whole Oriental world."[68]

The eroding of the Ottoman Empire's hold on Christian minority populations in the Balkans represented in the new Bulgaria and treaties of San Stefano and Berlin failed to quell calls for reform. Rather, a new crisis in the Ottoman Empire shifted focus from Bulgarians to other Christian minority groups, namely the Greeks, Assyrians, and Armenians. The resolution of the Bulgarian issue in the Treaty of Berlin focused attention on the Armenians in particular due to their status as a large, historically persecuted Ottoman minority who adhered to the Eastern Orthodox faith. By the time the Armenian massacres started in the mid-1890s this other persecuted minority had captured the imagination of liberal humanitarianism.

THE ARMENIAN MASSACRES

The Armenian cause gained momentum as a corollary to the Bulgarian Atrocities agitation early on. Humphrey Sandwith introduced the issue of "How the Turks Rule Armenia" in the midst of the Russo-Turkish war treaty negotiations. In 1878, he argued that Britain's pro-Ottoman policy made it complicit in the slaughter of innocent Christians and went as far as to advocate the annexation of Armenia. As David Feldman has argued about the Jews, Christian minorities' connection with Britain rested on their "industrious" nature and embrace of liberal values.[69] Religious affinities further strengthened this bond. Sandwith cited case after case of Christians subject to unfair tax burdens and thwarted and sometimes killed in their attempts to accumulate wealth through trade and industry.[70] Others argued for greater British intervention by presenting a more problematic view of Britain's long-standing interest in Eastern Christians. Isabella Bird understood British interest in Armenians in this vein: "while the Nestorians, Chaldeans or Assyrians (as they are variously called) from their comparatively small numbers, general poverty and total lack of mouth pieces, excite no interest at all, the interest felt in the Armenians is seldom a cordial or friendly one. . . . The Armenian is too self-interested to be lovable, too politic to be trusted and too proud to be patronized, and too capable and often too rich to be despised." "Armenians," however, she concluded "cannot be ignored."[71]

The "Armenian Question," as some began to call the Eastern Question in the mid-1880s, took on an air of urgency after the massacre of Armenian civilians began in Anatolia in 1894.[72] Interest in the Armenians of the Ottoman Empire grew steadily in the years preceding and following the massacres. Coverage in the *Times* increased from 14 mentions in 1886 to 61 the following year. By 1890, articles on the Armenian Question numbered 122.[73] Between 1890 and 1897 dozens of articles appeared in the *Nineteenth Century*, *Spectator*, *Contemporary Review*, *Blackwoods*, and *Fortnightly Review*.[74] The call to aid Armenians during the massacres themselves reverberated throughout the press much as it had in favor of Bulgarians twenty years earlier.[75] "It is a simple unvarnished fact that unless Russia does occupy Armenia the Christian population will be exterminated," one commentator claimed in the wake of the first wave of massacres in the Anatolian villages of Sasun and Mush. "No other Power can save them; and when England understands the alternative she will applaud rather than resist the advance of Russia as she did after the massacres in Bulgaria."[76] *Punch*, in one of its dozens of depictions of the Armenian Question illustrated this connection in 1895, depicting Gladstone and the Duke of Argyll, another long-time supporter of minority rights in the Ottoman Empire, as "Brothers in Arms Again: Bulgaria, 1876 and Armenia, 1895" (see figure 4).

Frustration with the lack of response by the government during the

Figure 4. Cartoon of Gladstone and
the Duke of Argyll campaigning on
behalf of Armenians in 1895, as they
had done almost twenty years earlier
for Bulgarians. *Punch*, May 18, 1895.

Bulgarian Atrocities shadowed considerations of the Armenian crisis.
"The time has come for every reasoning inhabitant of these islands deliberately to accept or repudiate his share of the joint indirect responsibility
of the British nation for the series of the hugest and foulest crimes that
have ever stained the pages of human history," wrote E. J. Dillion in the
Contemporary Review in 1896.[77] Dillon's "vehement protest against these
hell-born crimes" attempted to force the Liberal Rosebery and successor Conservative Salisbury governments into action. Memories of the
unwillingness of the British government to respond to the Bulgarian
massacres led commentators to ask for concrete reforms. Citing the failure of minority protections provisions in the treaties of Paris and Berlin,
one writer in the *Fortnightly Review* asserted that Britain was being
misled again by the sultan: "The whole of Europe has been outwitted,
defied, humiliated, and held at bay by a Prince whose throne is tottering
under him. . . . Christendom with all the might and all the right on its
side, is powerless."[78] Under Gladstone's urging Rosebery came up with a
sympathetic though largely ineffectual policy that did little to help either
Ottoman Christians or Liberal fortunes in the next election. "In spite of
the circumstance that the late Liberal government was in possession of
these an analogous facts," argued one commentator regarding the mas-

Figure 5. Sketch of members of the British Government Cabinet Council deciding the future of the Eastern Question. *Illustrated London News,* November 30, 1895.

sacres, the government "found it impossible to have them remedied and unadvisable to have them published." Hope for resolution would rest with the newly returned Conservative government: "There is fortunately good reason to believe that Lord Salisbury . . . will find efficacious means of putting a sudden and a speedy end to the Armenian Pandemonium."[79]

The spirit of reform that animated debates over the status of Ottoman Christians gained momentum after the Treaty of Berlin in both Conservative and Liberal Party circles. Salisbury, during his time as one of Disraeli's ministers in 1878, had argued forcefully in favor of a pro-Ottoman policy against Russia. When Salisbury led the Conservative Party to power in 1895 public opinion guided his own plan for self-government for Ottoman Armenians that met with widespread approval. As Lord Sanderson put it, in the wake of the Armenian massacres, "Lord Salisbury declined to pledge the British Government to any material action in support of the Sultan or of the Rule of the Straits, on the ground of the alteration of circumstances and the change in British public opinion."[80] In November 1895 the *Illustrated London News* published a two-page rendition of a meeting of the "Cabinet Council" on the Eastern Question that depicted the main players engaged in serious debate. On the reverse was printed an article critical of the reign of Sultan Abdul

Hamid (see figure 5). Salisbury's overtures, designed in part to keep his critics on the defensive, did not amount to any more than Rosebery's earlier ineffectual pledges.[81] "Public opinion in England has spoken loudly and decisively on the Armenian question," asserted H. F. B. Lynch in the concluding article of his series on Armenia in the *Contemporary Review;* "two ministries have taken energetic action, yet, from some reason which has not yet been sufficiently explained, their intervention remains without result."[82]

Frustration with ineffective government action spawned an extra-parliamentary response. William Watson's 1896 *The Purple East: A Series of Sonnets on England's Desertion of Armenia* implored the administration in a collection of verse "to smite the wronger with thy destined rod" or risk "The gathering blackness of the frown of God!"[83] The reformer George Russell took a more pragmatic approach, founding a new advocacy organization: "The Forward Movement in relation to Armenia is an attempt to do by the moral force of the Liberal Party that which the 'non-party' movement so grandly auspicated a year and half ago, has signally failed to do." The "Forward Movement" was inspired in part after hearing the Armenian Church Liturgy performed "under the shadow of our august Abbey." During this church service "the binding pressure of a common Christianity" drove listeners to form a movement based on "an inexorable command of conscience which bids us to GO FORWARD."[84] P. W. K. Stride offered a yet more practical course of action. In "The Immediate Future of Armenia" he offered a plan that placed Armenia in the hands of an international body: "To be strong enough, such an organization must be military; to be imposing enough, it must be non-national, or rather open to, and supported by the Great Powers; to be above suspicion it must work without thought of gain and whatever surplus there may be of income over expenditure must be devoted to the further development of agriculture and industry. An institution—call it a Brotherhood, a Society, a Company, or what you will—conducted on these lines would have at any rate the chance of great usefulness."[85]

As during the Bulgarian Atrocities agitation, critics cast the response to the Armenian massacres as imprudent sentimentalism. Ghulam-us-Saqlain in "The Musselmans of India and the Armenian Question," wrote of the "alleged Armenian atrocities" in the *Nineteenth Century,* raising the specter of Muslim subjects in India rebelling against the British Empire as a result of its Ottoman policy.[86] Similarly, in "A Moslem View of Abdul Hamid and the Powers," R. Ahmad blamed "British Christian opinion" for stirring up trouble in the Ottoman Empire. Although Ahmad could not understand why "England alone of all the Powers has whipped herself to fever-heat" over Armenia, he, too, made the case for reforms to the Ottoman system based on rule of law. As he concluded, "The misgovernment in Turkey is injurious alike to the Christians and to the Turks and all reforms must benefit the two races equally."[87] The critique that humanitarianism served as a cover for anti-Muslim sentiment first voiced during the Bulgarian Atrocities now made a broader pitch for humanitarian diplomacy rather than rejecting it out of hand.

News of the massacres led to a series of nationally coordinated advocacy efforts. The "National Protest against the Torture and Massacre of Christians in Armenia Public Meeting" held at St. James's Hall London in May 7, 1895, with the Duke of Argyll in the chair, offered publicity to the cause. The number of relief organizations eventually grew so large that in May 1897 the National Conference of British Societies engaged in working for the Relief of Armenians in Distress was formed under the leadership of James Bryce to coordinate relief efforts. Prominent relief organizations included the Friends of Armenia, which raised tens of thousands of pounds for relief efforts, the International Association of the Friends of Armenia, Quaker relief organizations, and the Women's Relief Fund.[88] The National Conference met first in London and later in Cardiff under the auspices of the "Friends of Armenia Branch" there with the goal of securing "permanent" relief by coordinating efforts of societies operating throughout England, Scotland, and Wales.[89] This national organization did not seek to consolidate societies but rather benefit both small and large organizations by publicizing and pulling together resources. Large organizations like the Friends of Armenia—with headquarters in London and branches throughout the British Isles, including those in Manchester, Edinburgh, Paisley and Liverpool, for example—worked with smaller funds like the Irish Armenian Relief Fund run by the Lord Mayor of Dublin that had a more localized constituency. Such institutions alongside others that would come out of causes that included the feminist movement made the Eastern Question part of the fabric of Victorian humanitarian discourse.

GENDERING THE EASTERN QUESTION

A Nation's History! How shall it be writ?
With tears of blood—in a sealed book of shame.
For when the weak and persecuted call her name
The mighty heart of England—slept![90]

A. Bradshaw's poem "Deserted Armenia" appeared in the feminist periodical *Our Sisters* in 1897. Starting in the early 1890s a discourse of "sisterhood" encouraged feminist activists to take up the Armenian cause as their own. The *Women's Penny Paper* announced the founding of the Women's Vigilance Association in London in November 1890 "for the purpose of calling attention to the condition of the women in Armenia." Through a "series of addresses and meetings" the association intended to draw attention to the kidnapping of Armenian women to "sell as slaves."[91] Feminist perspectives on the Eastern Question appeared in feature articles, book reviews, and biographical sketches of women activists in all of the major women's papers including the *Woman's Herald, Woman's Signal, Women's Penny Paper, Our Sisters* and *Shafts.*[92]

Feminist human rights campaigning added weight to the argument in favor of intervention on behalf of Christian minorities. Assuming the role of Britain's moral conscience, liberal feminists found in the Armenians a just cause for reform. In 1895, *Shafts* published a letter addressed to Lady Henry Somerset, a key voice in this campaign, from the Armenian women of Constantinople that described the massacres in that city in 1895. Somerset's response to the letter, signed "Your Suffering Sisters," concluded with a specific call to English womanhood: "Will English women be deaf to the voices that call to them in the hour of their supreme agony? Will they not rise to demand that such steps be taken at all hazards as will secure the rescue of this tortured people?"[93] Others echoed Somerset's gendered notions of British justice. "We should be callous indeed, if our sympathy remained unmoved by the fearful crimes in the Turkish dominions," wrote one correspondent in *Shafts.*[94] *Our Sisters* published reports of the massacres in Diarbekir, describing events like the mass murder of "the defenseless crowd of men, women and children" gathered in a church set fire to by Kurds who lived in the hills surrounding the village.

Such coverage suggests that by the time of the Armenian massacres in the mid-1890s readers of feminist papers had come to understand the Eastern Question as a women's issue. Somerset, a well-known women's rights activist, used her newly renamed paper, the *Woman's Signal,* to sound the alarm on behalf of victims. In an address at the annual meeting of the British Women's Temperance Association she argued: "The Turkish Empire has been kept alive by treaties which have been broken again and again and yet in a great crisis when our fellow Christians cry to us in their death agony, we as a country are powerless to move and are obliged to acknowledge that we are impotent to save the people we agreed to defend."[95] Coverage of the Women's National Liberal Association included a similar line of argument, claiming that "[t]he sufferings of the Armenians appealed to the sympathies of all" present at the meeting.[96] Lead articles contained references to "the persecuted Armenian" and appealed to readers to heed "the bitter cry of Armenia." News briefs referred to the "attacks on Armenians in the very heart of the Turkish government's rule" while describing the actions of Sultan Hamid.[97]

Somerset, a liberal committed to the Gladstonian line on the Eastern Question, understood England's affinities with Armenians in terms of both religion and gender. "The situation in Armenia does not seem to improve," Somerset lamented, "As our readers know, Russia and France have withdrawn from the Conference of the Great Powers, and have left England to work out Armenia's salvation alone, or else to leave the unspeakable Turk to exterminate a people who have been Christian since Christianity was."[98] Gladstone's eighty-fifth birthday celebration provided Somerset with the opportunity to make the case for "A Call to Action" in her columns. On this occasion, London Armenians presented a chalice to Hawarden church in honor of what Gladstone "had done for their nation."

The story of Mrs. Bedros, who escaped the massacres in Sasun and sat next to the Somerset at the birthday celebration, was told by a missionary after dinner. Somerset related to readers in graphic detail the murder of Mrs. Bedros' three-month-old baby and her two aunts by Turkish soldiers. The young woman was saved by remarkable circumstance, according to Somerset: "'Don't kill this woman,' said one of the brutal Turks. 'She is young and pretty; I will take her along with me.' But she struggles with her brutal captors with all her strength. 'If you are such a fool,' said the Turk, 'as not to go with me quietly, we shall kill you at once.' She still struggled. They tore her clothes off her back. Her fate was near, the worst of outrages and death at the hands of the men who had just killed her baby before her eyes."[99] When coins that her husband had fastened to her belt fell along the ground, she escaped to the woods while the soldiers picked up the gold and quarreled over the money.

Somerset's dramatic retelling of the story in the press echoed W. T. Stead's Bulgarian Atrocities narrative twenty years earlier. Outrages of rape, violence, and greed figured prominently in the story as retold by Somerset, who spoke for Mrs. Bedros through her missionary patron interpreter. This narrative provided Somerset with a call to action. "The Christian womanhood of England as presented by the *Woman's Signal* can be depended on to demand that the extermination of these people shall be stopped."[100] Moral responsibility for Armenia, in this representation of the massacres, rested on the protection of womanly virtue. Somerset's outrage was strengthened by her status as a woman. Unlike Stead and his depictions of outrages against Bulgarian virgins, Somerset held a unique position of ownership over such narratives of injustice. She represented to her audience an authentic voice of sympathy and thus added moral weight to her call for action.

The call to forge a sisterhood with rape victims resonated with liberal feminists who came to see the Armenian Question as a corollary to the Woman Question. One correspondent suggested in a letter entitled "Our Sisters in Armenia" the franchise for women in England would result in real change for Armenian women.[101] Somerset's growing disillusionment with the Liberal Party due to its lack of commitment to either votes for women or the Armenian cause most likely influenced her decision to turn to an extra-parliamentary approach. The occasion of the "national protest against the Armenian atrocities" held at St. James's Hall in the spring of 1895 gave Somerset the opportunity to make her case in a public forum. Like the national meetings held to protest the Bulgarian Atrocities, a list of distinguished speakers spoke to a massive crowd on the need for intervention.

Somerset's authority in a group otherwise made up entirely of distinguished male speakers relied on the claim that she represented the voice of the womanhood of England and Armenia. Her speech "touched a new note," according to one report, "pointed as it was by the presence of 'the child-mother' to whom she alluded with a touching pathos." The retelling of the story of Mrs. Bedros who stood on the stage next to her husband moved the crowd to cheer Somerset's call to intervene on behalf of the martyred Christians of Sasun, who, she claimed, "Died that the untrammeled beneficent, consecrated life of England's purest womanhood might slowly come to women in their own beautiful and pleasant land."[102] This language of mutual sacrifice contained within it the seeds of redemption. For Somerset, helping Armenian women would elevate English womanhood.

In 1896, Somerset launched the idea for the Armenian Rescue Fund. The *Signal* was now under the editorship of Florence Fenwick Miller, who helped create the "Woman's Signal Armenian Refugee Fund" distributed through Lady Somerset. Donations ranged from 100 pounds to 1 shilling and totaled for one week in October 1896 over 240 pounds. Prayer meetings, British Women's Temperance Union branches, Congregational church members, individuals, and anonymous donors including "An

English Sister" contributed to the fund, whose purpose was "not only to cover and feed these suffering ones, but to see that they have homes and work." Potential donors were assured of the worthiness of the 600 refugees helped by the fund: "Let it be remembered that they do not drink, that they are devout and earnest, exceedingly docile and kind and remarkably quick-minded."[103] Despite these industrious credentials refugees would be resettled in Marseilles, not London. The fund eventually came to serve the destitute Armenians still living in eastern Anatolia. Somerset claimed in March 1897 that she had raised enough money to support a three year program to educate and care for orphans in Van. To Fenwick-Miller and the readers of the *Signal* she offered her thanks. The money collected from readers served as "eloquent proof of the worth of your paper which has gathered round it the best hearts of the womanhood of England."[104]

Narratives of kinship between Britons and Ottoman Christians living in the cradle of civilization played a powerful role in the mid-century conception of the Near East. By the turn of the century, a discourse of culpability, responsibility, and proprietorship refined how this relationship came to be represented. Politicians, journalists, diplomats, travelers, and missionaries all participated in this process, telling stories about the Near East that connected the land, its people, and their customs to a distant Christian past that created bonds of kinship from discourses of suffering and subjugation. In many ways, the casting of the Eastern Question as a humanitarian issue had as much to do with its status as one of the great religious questions of the day as it did as a problem of European diplomacy. Nowhere was this more apparent than in the geographical representation of the Near East on the map. Over the course of the late nineteenth century, a project of ethnographically mapping the Ottoman Empire represented British imperial interests as intimately connected with Eastern Christians. The next chapter describes the material and discursive processes that conceptually drew the Near East closer to Britain as a Protestant borderland.

2.   Mapping the Near East

By the end of Victoria's reign, a common awareness of the Eastern Question meant that few would have failed to recognize the idea of the Near East, though most understandably might have been hard-pressed to trace its physical borders on a map. As Larry Wolff has argued, marking Europe in terms of East and West was part of a larger Enlightenment project that shifted the way Western Europe understood its place in the world.[1] This reorientation of the map from a division based on Northern and Southern Europe to one divided by East and West held particular resonance for Britain, as it shifted an imperial gaze from North America to India.[2] During the mid-nineteenth century, the "Near East," the land separating Britain from India, the Empire's geographical anchor, took on new significance. By the late nineteenth century, Britain drew the Near East closer to its empire through reconstructing the region considered just beyond Europe as a Protestant borderland.

The project of orienting the Near East in relationship to the British Empire relied on Victorian religious and ethnographic preoccupations. Geographical imaginings of the region in prose descriptions and drawings of surveyors, diplomats, travelers, and missionaries made this world legible. The rise of geography as an academic discipline, bolstered by high-profile expeditions funded by the Royal Geographical Society and the Palestine Exploration Fund, contributed to representations of the Holy Land as adjacent to Europe.[3] Improvements in communication and travel through transportation schemes like the Baghdad Railway shrunk the cultural and temporal distance between the Balkans, Anatolia, Mesopotamia, and Western Europe while trade, once tied to the monopoly Levant Company, encouraged business ventures that made the Eastern lands of the Ottoman Empire seem near.

Significantly, Ottoman Christians, spread across the Balkans and Anatolia, resided at the geographical epicenter of this capacious vision of the Near East. This chapter considers the importance of ethnographic mapping to this process of invention and incorporation. If the Enlightenment divided the world in terms of East and West, then Victorians reoriented it again in terms of religion and ethnicity. Put another way, the East/West divide was refined in terms of a Muslim/Christian distinction, which organized difference and defined geographical space on the map in a new way. The Near East in this cosmography had a number of different priorities mapped onto it: commercial, imperial, and religious. It was this last category that most distinctively animated this reorientation producing a cultural geography based on ethnographic markers.

The term "Near East" sounds quaint to modern ears. It has largely lost its usefulness in political geography and instead evokes the distant religious and cultural world of ancient Mediterranean peoples living along the Adriatic, Aegean, and Black Seas. Travelers, missionaries, and civil servants certainly shared this romantic sense of the cradle of civilization populated by a mix of Orthodox Christians and Muslims living in and around the Holy Land. Victorians, however, also understood the ethnographic boundaries of the term lending it a deeply political meaning that rendered significant the Christian populations of the Ottoman Empire. To understand why, it is important to retrace the contexts in which the Near East first emerged as the geographic marker of the Eastern Question.

A NEW MAP

The earliest maps of the Near East necessarily relied on the Victorian imagination. The difficulty of compiling an accurate topographical survey of the Ottoman Empire coupled with a growing preoccupation with the religious ethnography of the Holy Land gave nineteenth-century maps of the region their particular character. Actual survey work undertaken by the British government only began after the 1878 Russo-Turkish War and continued in fits and starts up through World War I.[4] Reliance on "a pot-pourri of sketch maps, travelers' itineraries and anecdotal material," rather than "systematic survey," insured the protracted nature of this process.[5] Even after the Intelligence Department of the War Office began systematizing its output of maps, plans and drawings in 1881 the ad hoc nature of information gathering in Ottoman lands continued to hinder mapmakers. Worries on the part of the sultan with the "sinister intentions" of surveyors, along with "foreign competition and jealousy," put roadblocks in the way of meaningful survey work. As late as 1907 one surveyor complained that "our maps" of the Ottoman Empire "are very bad or inaccurate."[6]

The unevenness of military surveys opened up a space for an ethnographic ordering of the Near East to take root. Here the pen and ink renderings of the Victorian mapmaker came to rely on literary representations. Ethnographers began to focus attention on the peoples of the Ottoman Empire immediately after the Crimean War. Robert Latham's *The Varieties of the Human Species* (1856) explicitly linked the study of ethnography to geography. For Latham, considered the father of ethnographic science, understanding the "nations of the world" relied first on charting the "varieties of the human species." His 1856 "Ethnographic Map of the World" depicted a Europe connected to the East by a small swath of "Indo European Caucasians" that included Armenian and Assyrians (see figure 6).[7] For Latham the Turanians, or "Turks," occupied a space between, fully part of neither Europe nor Asia.[8] The liminal status of the ethnographers' "Turanian" peoples reoriented the map according to ethnic considerations that drew the Near East, via its "Indo European Caucasian" populations, geographically closer to Europe.

Military and academic preoccupations with the mapping of the Ottoman Empire found their complement in a growing popular interest in maps in general and Near East geography in particular. Maps themselves began to take on a new cultural significance during the second half of the nineteenth century. Improved lithography techniques and marketing by commercial mapmaking firms made the mapmaker's renderings more widely available through cheap reproductions found in books, newspapers, and other periodicals. The invention of the thematic map during this period captured the Victorian imagination by offering a new way of orienting oneself to the world by depicting religious distribution, climate, and social status, the most noteworthy in the latter category being "Booth's Poverty Map of London." Thematic world maps offered Britons another way of seeing the globe beyond national and imperial borders.

Maps of the Near East became a regular feature in periodicals, travel books, and literature starting soon after the Crimean War. Depictions increased substantially after the Russo-Turkish War. The rising popularity of the atlas in particular helped shape British geographical understandings of the Near East. The renowned Edinburgh mapmaker A. K. Johnston's *Worldwide Atlas of Modern Geography*, published in 1892, for example, contained two maps of the Near East: "Turkey in Asia" and

"Turkey in Europe and Bulgaria." Complete with blank maps for students to practice geography lessons this atlas made no mention of the "Ottoman Empire" by name and instead reoriented the Near East in relation to Europe and Asia.[9] Johnston also marketed individual maps to consumers including a large portrait-sized map of the "Near East" that sold for one shilling.

The first widely produced British maps of the Near East came out in the 1870s during the publicity surrounding the Bulgarian Atrocities. Edward Stanford's 1876 *Ethnological Map of European Turkey and Greece* sold for one shilling sixpence and included a long introductory essay with accompanying statistics on population distribution by ethnicity and religion. Sir George Campbell, a former lieutenant governor of Bengal who spoke at the St. James's Conference on the Eastern Question, worried that "as a nation we seem to have been content not at all to trouble ourselves about the fate of the Christians."[10] His 1876 book, *A Handy Book on the Eastern Question,* went into multiple editions and argued that Britons needed to see the Christian-dominated regions of the Ottoman Empire as connected to Europe.[11] His "Map Showing the Distribution of the Christian Races in European Turkey" (figure 7) offered, with accompanying statistics, a thematic portrayal of Europe mapped along religious and ethnic lines. This map erased Muslim presence even in places like Albania where by his own estimates this group made up half the population.[12] Campbell advocated a physical remapping of the region in the wake of the Bulgarian Atrocities that followed this division: "the Bulgaria written across our maps, as applied to the long strip of territory north of the Balkans is a use of the term known neither to Turks nor to the Christians of Turkey. . . . It is clear that the Bulgaria to be dealt with must be the ethnological Bulgaria and not the Bulgaria of mapmakers."[13]

Others supported this vision of a map oriented along religious and ethnic lines. Rev. William Denton argued in 1876 in his book *The Christians of Turkey* that Britons had both a moral and economic reason for supporting Ottoman Christians in both "European" and "Asiatic" Turkey. Christian races, in contrast with Muslims, were natural allies due to their "superior industry and morality." Frequent massacres, heavy taxation, and threats from nomadic peoples had historically stood in the way of Christian minority populations getting ahead.[14] Denton used this argument to counter claims by Turkophiles who shared Disraeli's view of the Ottoman Turk as Britain's true partner. According to Denton, "the Turks are neither consumers of foreign goods nor producers of articles of commerce to any appreciable amount; and that when the whole race has

(continued on page 48)

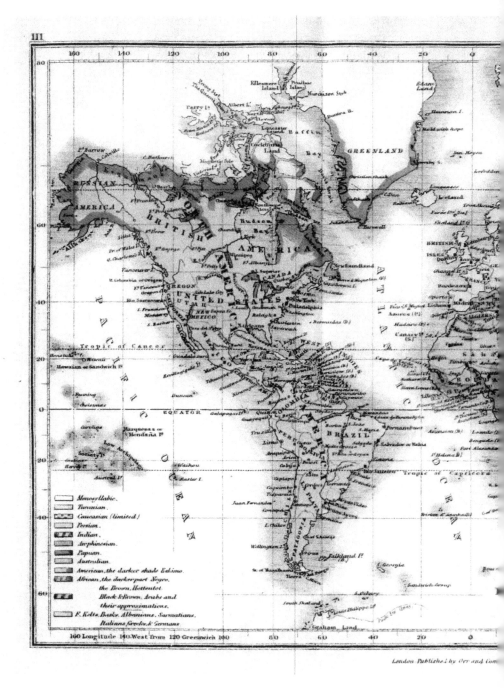

Figure 6. Ethnographic map of the world showing the similarities between peoples of Europe and the Near East. From Robert Latham, *The Varieties of Human Species* (London, 1856).

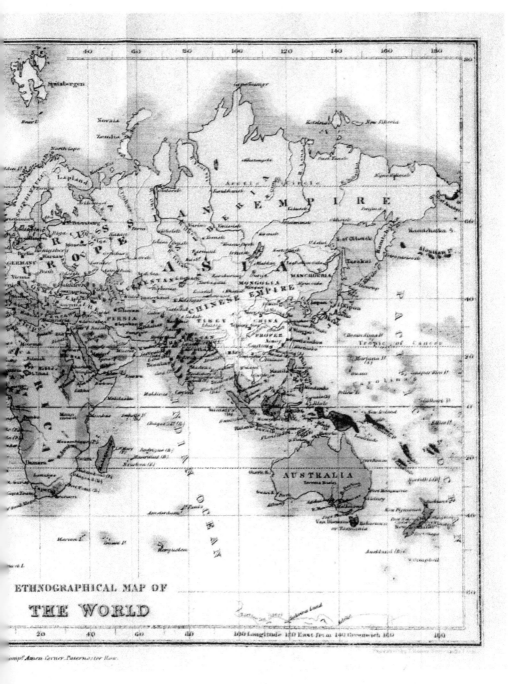

Figure 7 *(overleaf)*. Religious and ethnographic map of Europe and
the Near East. From Sir George Campbell, *A Handy Book on the
Eastern Question* (London: Houlston and Stoneman, 1876).

MAP SHOWING THE DISTRIBUTION OF THE

London: John Murray.

Greeks

Roumans

Albanians

South-Slaves

Bulgars

disappeared from the countries which it occupies . . . then, not merely will the peace of the rest of the world be less frequently menaced, but its commerce will be largely augmented."[15] As evidence of the advantages of Christian rule in the Near East, Denton cited Greece as an example of a country that successfully entered the European system after Ottoman rule ended in the 1830s.[16] Ottoman Christians, in this reading, shared a common kinship with their Anglican Protestant brothers due to business acumen and similar cultural sensibilities. These were the "polite and commercial people," to borrow a phrase from Paul Langford, of the Near East.

The resolution of the Russo-Turkish War in the Treaties of San Stefano and Berlin in 1878 called for a physical remapping of the westernmost regions of the Ottoman Empire. As discussed in chapter 1, minority protection clauses proposed in the Treaty of San Stefano made a nominally independent Bulgaria and the reform of Ottoman laws that disadvantaged Christians a priority. Negotiators abandoned strong minority protection provisions when they superseded San Stefano with the Treaty of Berlin four months later. The spirit of San Stefano's defense of minority Christian populations, however, lived on in attempts to remap the Near East along ethnic and religious lines, which advocates argued, in the end, would best protect minorities and promote British interests.

Sir John Ardagh, the man who led the team that drew the new border, embodied this belief. Born in 1840 in Waterford, Ireland, Ardagh started his career as part of the Royal Engineers, which eventually led to a post in 1876 with the Intelligence Department. In 1878 he attended the Congress of Berlin as a "technical military delegate attached to the special embassy," where he produced a first draft of the new boundary.[17] Ardagh met the other members of the Bulgarian Boundary Commission after the Conference in Constantinople, setting out on horseback to survey the country to be divided. Infighting among the German, French, and Russian surveyors opened up a space for Ardagh's team of English surveyors to contribute twenty of the thirty-four sketches of the new border. Three different surveys undertaken over the course of two-and-a-half years ("the task of fitting all these together was no easy one," Ardagh recalled) produced a largely British drawn twelve-foot map.[18]

The disproportionate role played by British topographers in the survey work was reflected in the final map. Ardagh's inability to decipher the world of political, religious, and ethnic rivalries on the ground made his hope of an "impartial" adjustment impossible. As he soon discovered, "By the Treaty of Berlin 'the ancient frontier' is to be maintained and according to the inhabitants, both Turk and Bulgarian, its actual position differs widely." Continued conflict between Turks and Bulgarians made accurate survey work difficult at best. The new map, Ardagh continued, "would have been finished long ago but for the delay in furnishing the topographers with the safe-conducts necessitated by the disturbed condition of the country."[19] His letters complained of constant "interference" by residents who considered the boundary commission a "Mixed Army of Occupation."[20]

Ardagh himself, having worked closely with the Turkish army as a British intelligence officer, showed little sympathy for the Bulgarians, whose attempts to influence the location of the new border he considered "a disgrace to the new Principality." Nevertheless, Ardagh's new map "pressed on the Turkish Government" in 1880 at a reconvening of the conference at Berlin shifted the imperial orientation of this former part of the Ottoman Empire to an ethnographic one that approximated the Christian/Muslim divide that animated popular and academic thinking about the region after the Crimean War.[21]

At least four different British cartographers rendered thematic maps of the boundary map over the next thirty years. Significantly, the borders of San Stefano, which had favored an ethnological "big Bulgaria" that encompassed the majority of the region's Christians, lived on in popular maps even though it had been superseded by Berlin, which provided for a series of small Christian states organized more sharply along ethnic lines. Edward Stanford's map of the failed Treaty of San Stefano (figure 8) continued to be reproduced well into the twentieth century. The "Map to Illustrate the Treaty of Berlin" issued after the ratification of this second treaty (figure 9) showed the changes to the war settlement and included, in pink, the territorial shifts of the nullified San Stefano settlement.

These two maps offered a glimpse into the process by which the European powers attempted to balance Turkish and Russian power by bringing the Near East into the fold of Europe. In San Stefano we see the independent states of Campbell's Christian Europe come into view. Berlin's revision of San Stefano took the blanket division based on religion (that is, putting all of the Christians together) and refined it along ethnic lines, fragmenting "big Bulgaria" into three different principalities. S. Augustus Mitchell's 1880 "Map of the Berlin Congress Treaty" (figure 10) offered a similar view but included in its title "Map of Turkey in Europe." In the end, these maps secured in the mind of a generation of Victorians the ethnographic boundaries first introduced by Latham after

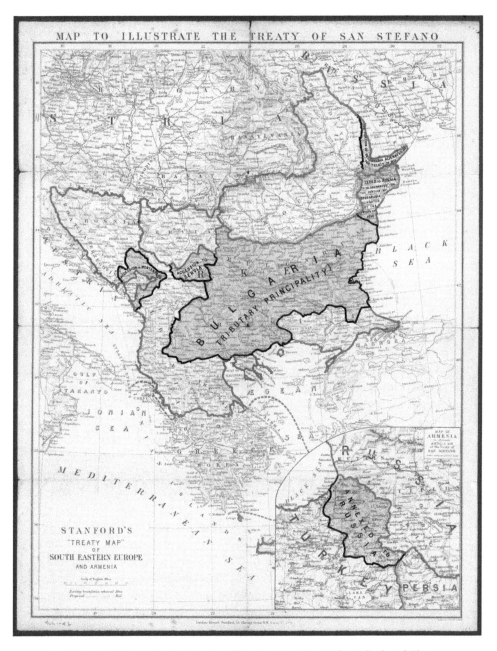

Figure 8. Edward Stanford, "Map to Illustrate the Treaty of San Stefano." This widely reproduced map illustrates territorial boundaries as negotiated but never enacted under the Treaty of San Stefano. Courtesy of the National Library of Australia.

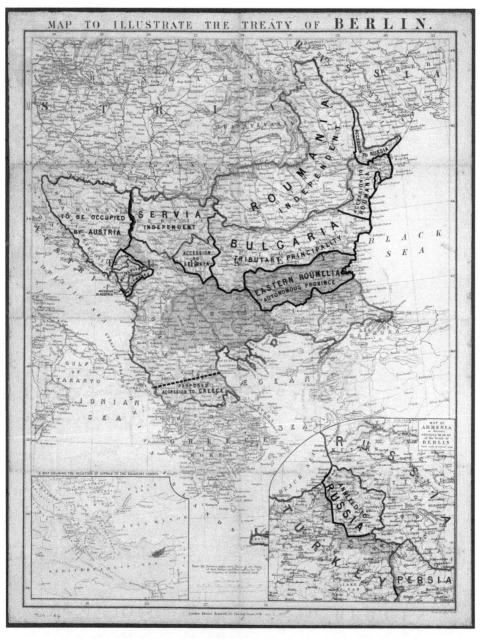

Figure 9. Edward Stanford, "Map to Illustrate Treaty of Berlin," illustrating
territorial boundaries as renegotiated under the Treaty of Berlin to limit
Ottoman influence in the Near East. Courtesy of the National Library of
Australia.

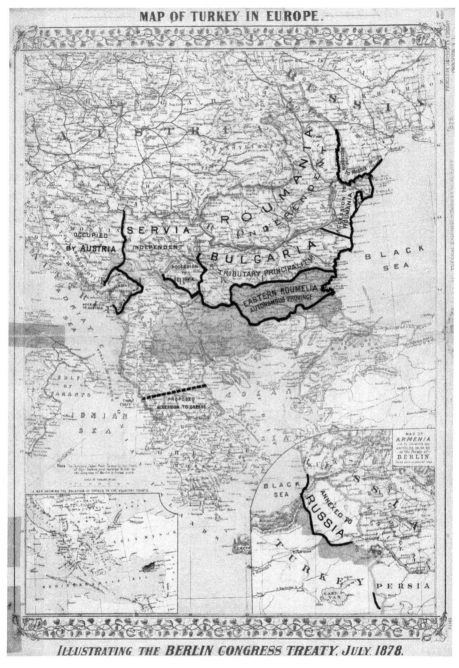

Figure 10. S. Augustus Mitchell, map illustrating the Treaty of Berlin settlement (London, 1880).

the Crimean War, applied by Campbell and Denton during the Bulgarian Atrocities agitation of the mid 1870s and later codified by Ardagh.

Significant sections of all three thematic maps included insets of Armenia and its Christian minority population. Stanford's Treaty Maps included in former British Ambassador to Constantinople Stratford de Redcliffe's 1881 account of the Eastern Question offered an even wider view (figure 11). Here eastern Anatolia finds itself connected to the Balkans by a single line that bypasses the majority Muslim region of western Anatolia. This reorientation of the map along religious and ethnic lines after the Treaties of San Stefano and Berlin relied on assumptions that joined imperial and humanitarian impulses. As Campbell and Denton argued in the wake of the Bulgarian Atrocities and on the eve of the Russo-Turkish War, the Near East by virtue of its Christian populations belonged in Europe. Commercial prosperity, humanitarian concerns, and political stability for Europe and the Ottoman Empire in this narrative relied on strengthening this connection.

In 1908, the mapmaker and publisher A. K. Johnston issued another thematic map of the two treaties. Sold for one shilling, the map (figure 12) put the by-now thirty-year-old crisis again at the center of Western European concerns. The insets of Europe in 1815 and 1875 demonstrate how the changing of the map below fits into the larger narrative of European politics of the previous century. This version remains virtually identical to similar maps published in the 1870s with the important exception of the title: "Map to Illustrate the Near Eastern Question." With war between the Triple Alliance and Triple Entente only narrowly avoided over Bosnia in 1908, interest in the Near East and the treaties that helped invent it would have justified this rechristening.

THE NEAR EAST MOVES EASTWARD

So far the maps and descriptions discussed in this chapter have considered the Near East as beginning and ending, with the important addition of lands occupied by Armenian and Assyrian Christians in eastern Anatolia, in what is today Eastern Europe. Indeed, as late as the 1890s many still considered this the important physical and psychological borderland of the Near East. As the traveler William Miller put it: "When the inhabitants of the Balkan Peninsula are meditating a journey to any of the countries which lie to the west of them, they speak of 'going to Europe,' thereby avowedly considering themselves as quite apart from the European system. So far as 'Europe' is concerned this geographical

(continued on page 58)

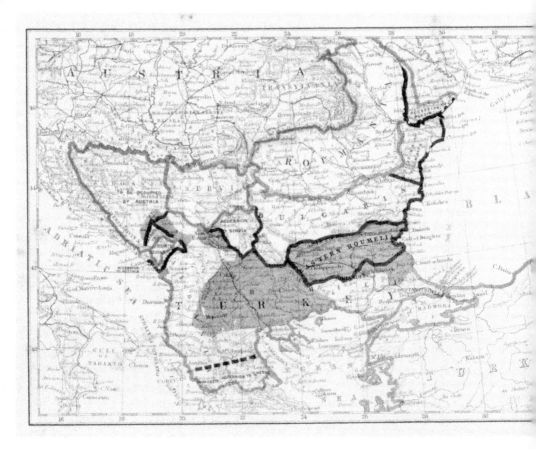

Figure 11. Treaty map that includes both the San Stefano and Berlin territorial agreements that geographically connect Eastern Christians in the Near East. From Stratford de Redcliffe, *The Eastern Question* (London: John Murray, 1881).

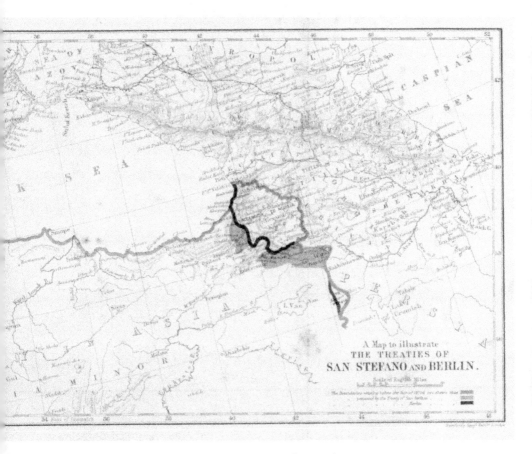

Figure 12 *(overleaf)*. A. K. Johnston, turn-of-
the-century geopolitical map of the Near East
(Edinburgh: W. and A. K. Johnston, 1908).

EUROPE
IN 1815
English Miles

EUROPE
IN 1875
English Miles

OCCUPIED AND ADMINISTERED
BY AUSTRIA UNDER TREATY OF BERLIN

THE BOSPORUS
& CONSTANTINOPLE

CEDED TO BULGARIA BY IMPERIAL FIRMAN.
ISSUED 6TH APRIL, 1886.

REFERENCE

Boundaries in 1861
Boundaries proposed by Treaty of San Stefano 3rd March 1878
Boundaries as fixed by Treaty of Berlin 13th July 1878
Boundaries as at present
Turkey in 1861
Turkey as at present
Austria-Hungary in 1861
Austria-Hungary as at present

inaccuracy possesses considerable justification. For of all parts of our continent none is so little known to the average traveler as the Near East."[22]

Writing in 1898 Miller recognized the Near East as beginning where Europe ended. At the same time he emphasized the Near East as a lesser known part of "our continent." Miller's inside/outside conceptualization of the Near East reflected a growing preoccupation by British geographers and travelers alike to mark this territory as European. Miller, not satisfied with the thematically-oriented maps commercially available in Britain declared that "No good English map of the Peninsula" existed and decided "to use the best German map" to illustrate his book, which "necessitated leaving the bulk of the names in the map in their German dress."[23] During the late nineteenth century, diplomats, politicians, and travelers embarked on a project of mapping that included the Balkans as well as Anatolia and Persia, as Miller put it, "in English." Significantly, the War Office launched its first official mapping surveys of Eastern Anatolia, the area considered the center of historic Armenia, starting in 1893.[24]

This cosmography offered an enlarged European-oriented Near East (figure 13). Miller's oversized three-foot-wide map of the Balkan Peninsula included as a large foldout insert at the back of his book reached into Anatolia, including all of Constantinople, regions around the Black Sea, the Mediterranean, and the Aegean Seas. A small legend at the bottom of the map translated Serbian, Bulgarian, Greek, and Turkish geographical terms into English. Large swaths of land covered by ethnic groups rather than national borders covered the map. It ignored all national boundaries including those drawn at Berlin in 1878 that had laid down the borders of Roumania, Bulgaria, Servia, and Eastern Roumelia for the first time.

This seemingly gross oversight made sense since Miller most likely used the German geographer Heinrich Kiepert's ethnographical map produced before the Russo-Turkish War settlement.[25] However, Miller's readers would not have known this, since he neglected to give any credit to Kiepert. Laziness or concerns over plagiarism might have explained Miller's choice to translate Kiepert's map into English rather than offer a more accurate map that showed new national boundaries. More likely, his decision to include this particular map reflected the trajectory of his narrative organized around a host of ethnographic observations on what he called "barbarism and civilization" during his travels. This explanation suggests that ethnographic conceptions of the Near East continued to exist alongside national considerations long after the European powers divided the region into a chain of small nation-states.

Although Britain, Germany, Austria, Russia and France all compiled their own ethnographic maps during this period, the British made this cosmography their own by tying ethnography to commerce and empire.[26] In Britain, the science of "human geography" grew out of the theoretical framework laid out by Robert Latham at mid-century and tried to explain social progress through ethnographic markers.[27] Geographers such as Marion Newbigin popularized the use of topography, location, and climate to explain why some societies prospered while others languished. In her widely read *Modern Geography,* Newbigin rejected notions that national boundaries could take the place of geographically bound racial and ethnic divisions that had determined the evolutionary development of societies both in and outside of Europe.[28] The Holy Land offered Newbigin a useful case study in ethnographic determinism. Concluding the book with a chapter entitled "The Coming of the Turks," she remarked that after the Ottoman invasion "civilized man had outgrown his cradle," leaving "the Midland Sea for the greater world beyond."[29] This portrait of a conquered Mediterranean stuck in its infancy under Ottoman rule made it a place ripe for a modern revival.

The geographer D. G. Hogarth offered an ethnographic portrait of a Near East tied to Britain by both religion and commerce. His book *The Nearer East* was published in 1902 as a volume in the series Regions of the World, which targeted a popular audience. Hogarth, an archeologist, traveler, and fellow at Magdalen College Oxford, expanded the borders of the Near East beyond Eastern Europe using human geography: "The aim of this volume is to present the causative influence of geographical conditions upon Man in a certain region." Here his ethnological map of the Nearer East mirrored Miller's by showing Albanians, Montenegrins, Armenians, Turks, and Arabs, with specific attention paid to Islamic designations spread across what is today Eastern Europe, Turkey, the Arabian Peninsula, Greece, Egypt, and most of Iran (figure 14).

The logic of the designation "the Nearer East" relied on its relationality to the West. First, the "cradle of civilization" represented the birthplace of Christian Europe and the Holy Land. Second, Hogarth's Near East was the present source of "luxury products" such as spices, food stuffs, silks, and carpets that Europeans valued. Echoing the characterization of the Near East by *Fraser's* magazine in 1856 discussed in chapter 1, Hogarth described a world where these two elements, Christian and commercial,

Figure 13 *(overleaf)*. Turn-of-the-century travel map of the Near East. From William Miller, *Travels and Politics in the Near East* (London: Unwin, 1898).

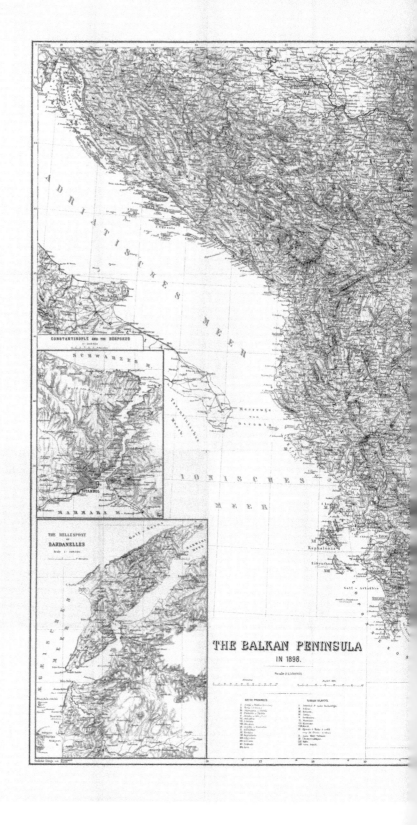

THE BALKAN PENINSULA
IN 1898.

Figure 14. "The Nearer East" defined by region according to religion and ethnicity. From D. G. Hogarth, *The Nearer East* (London: W. Heinemann, 1902).

constituted what he referred to as the region's contribution to the "corporate human body."

As with earlier maps, Hogarth's ethnographical divisions relied on a distinction between Christian and Muslim populations. However, he offered a more unified vision of place than others, like Campbell, presented twenty-five years previous. Here an expanded geography divided Christians and Muslims in a patchwork of ethnic affiliations, from the eastern edge of the Balkans to Persia, that brought these populations together in an entity called the Near East. Hogarth remained conscious of the tenuous nature of this designation, however, claiming that the Near East existed as a series of "Debatable Lands" loosely joined together by their relationship to Europe. Hogarth hoped to use his work to encourage the accurate mapping of the Holy Land. Better maps, he maintained, would lead to a clearer understanding of human social origins and consumer relationships that gave the Nearer East its geographical integrity. The final section in his introduction included a list of the most up-to-date maps of each region covered in the book along with their deficiencies. Pointing out the inaccuracies of these maps arguably made his own conceptual renderings of the region that much more influential.

The journalist and traveler David Fraser found Hogarth's ethnographic map particularly useful when he wrote *The Short Cut to India* in 1909. Fraser argued that Britain should fund the completion of the Baghdad Railway across Anatolia to Persia. Improvements in rail travel, the Orient Express's service to Constantinople began in 1883, and better communication technology already had begun to connect these regions more concretely to Britain.[30] To make his case for strengthening these links he cited Hogarth, claiming that "it is essential to take into consideration the idiosyncrasies of the people, and the character of the country and climate." Traveling along the route of the proposed railway route in 1908 in the midst of the Young Turk Revolution in the Ottoman Empire, Fraser understood the risks of investing British capital in such a venture. He used Hogarth's categories to counter claims that an inland route through a sparsely populated region would not be cost effective. For although it might be difficult to find Arab laborers to build the railway, he argued, Near Eastern Christians were a particularly industrious race who eventually would make good use of the route and bring further development to the region. According to Fraser, "They are nearly all Arabs (along proposed route) to whom manual labour is as repulsive as it is to the unemployed in Trafalgar Square." By contrast, he maintained that "Armenians are really the most useful element of the population, for they are diligent farmers, expert craftsmen, capable shopkeepers and when education avails, they become skilled in the professions." "Hearsay" evidence from doctors Fraser had met in the region reassured him that the Christian population was reproducing much more rapidly than the Muslim, which he concluded would bode well for the venture.[31]

Ethnography influenced military mapping as well. The decision to map "Eastern Anatolia" came in anticipation of a conflict on the border between Russia and the Ottoman Empire. The Intelligence Branch completed the Russo-Turkish Frontier in Asia map as mandated by the Treaty of Berlin in 1880. Attention then turned to a very detailed survey of the towns, topography, and people of the eastern Ottoman Empire. Significantly, each section surveyed began with a detailed description of the majority populations. In the case of eastern Anatolia, the site of historic Armenia and the first region to be mapped in this survey, these included the "Turks, Armenians and Greeks."

Led by Captain F. R. Maunsell, the government project relied on surveys by British consuls serving in the region, Royal Geographical Society (RGS) expeditions, and the observations of travelers.[32] Maunsell, himself a fellow at the RGS, was educated at Cheltenham College and the Royal Military Academy and entered the Royal Artillery in 1881. During the course of his more than fifty-year career, he wrote extensively on the Eastern Question and served as vice-consul in various posts in eastern Anatolia.[33] The government handed over the final map to the RGS, which made this information available to the public, publishing the final version of Maunsell's map in its journal in 1906.

The military was not done with Maunsell's map, however. The RGS took what they called the "Map of Eastern Turkey in Asia, Syria and Western Persia" and put it through multiple revisions, adding territory and railroads as information became available. In 1917, the War Office bought the original plates of the Maunsell map, as it became known, from the RGS. Retitling it "Map of Eastern Turkey in Asia, Syria and Western Persia: Ethnographical," the military gave Maunsell's map a color-coded overlay that separated the people of the region according to ethnicity and religion.[34] The Germans published their own version of Maunsell's map one year later.

The persistence of this ethnographical frame, which grew to accommodate the Balkans, Asia Minor, and parts of Persia, speaks to its usefulness as a way of organizing the East. Between 1897 and 1939 the Near East appeared in the titles of over fifty advocacy, travel, and historical monographs. The RGS magazine during this period also began indexing the "Near East" for the first time. The increasing number of index entries in this category charted the growing interest in maps of the region. Hundreds more references occurred in the press and within scores of other texts. Some titles, like *The Situation in the Near East: A Brief Account of the Recent Massacres* (1904), made a case for humanitarian involvement, while others, like *British Policy in the Near East* (1897) and *Our Allies and Enemies in the Near East* (1918), advocated a stronger British military presence.

The Near East, though generally referring to the lands dominated by the "European and Asiatic" parts of the Ottoman Empire, still remained a place where its actual physical boundaries remained in flux. In part, this was because the easternmost regions remained only partially mapped by British geographers up through World War I despite efforts by the War Office to make the mapping of the Near East a priority in the 1890s.[35] The problem, however, went beyond more accurate survey work. The multiethnic and religious character of the region had always resisted easy classification. No map could make sense to Western eyes of the maze of overlapping societies that had existed side by side for centuries, sometimes at peace and sometimes at war. In the British imagination the Near East represented an amalgam of cultural markers that linked imperial interests in part with the fate of the region's Orthodox Christians living in the cradle of civilization.

A PROTESTANT HOLY LAND

For missionaries, this conceptual mapping of the Near East had particular resonance. The rise of a vibrant missionary press during the second half of the nineteenth century offered Victorians a religion-oriented geography through coverage of foreign mission projects.[36] As the Ottoman Empire emerged as a focus of evangelical work during the second half of the nineteenth century, the religious press began to offer prose and iconographical descriptions of the Near East. This interest in the Ottoman Empire as a site of mission work contributed to ethnographic representations of the Holy Land.

Some of the most compelling of these depictions came from the flagship journal of the Church Missionary Society (CMS), the *Gleaner*. Representations of the CMS's Mediterranean and Persian missions described a land made familiar by the attempt to revive a lost kinship between Britons and Eastern Orthodox Christians. "From the earliest days of the infant Society, the Committee's eyes had been upon 'the East,'" claimed one CMS historian writing in 1899, "that is, those Oriental lands where ancient Christian Churches were living a barely tolerated life under the oppressive rule of the Turk." This afforded new opportunities for mission work. As he continued: "'If those Churches,' they said, 'could be brought back to the knowledge and love of the sacred Scripture' might they not become 'efficient instruments of rescuing the Mohammedans from delusion and death?'"[37] The CMS set out to "revive" these ancient Christians that had languished under Ottoman rule.[38] A renewed Christian Orthodox church in the Holy Land advocates believed would also "have an effect on the Mohammedan and Heathen World."[39]

This project began in earnest as British influence in the region grew in the period surrounding the Russo-Turkish War.[40] Stories in the *Gleaner* defined the Near East as an obvious place of interest to the CMS in historical and geographical terms: "It was natural that the eyes of the early Committee of the Church Missionary Society, surveying the vast fields of labour open before them, should rest with peculiar interest on the lands of the Bible." These "lands of the Bible" initially included Greece, Turkey, Asia Minor, Syria, Egypt, "and even Abyssinia," though the CMS soon abandoned its failed efforts in Egypt and Abyssinia. These regions were seen as united as a birthplace of Christianity now under both Muslim rule and the influence of ancient Eastern Churches "steeped in ignorance and superstition."[41] This framing of mission work as an effort aimed at bringing back a "corrupted" Christian church to its origins required forging connections between Anglican Protestants and Eastern Orthodox Christians.

Coverage of the society's "New Mission to Persia" in May 1876 reinforced these connections. Rev. Robert Bruce, the founder of the Persian mission, provided an intimate portrait of the Holy Land.[42] In the pages of the *Gleaner*, Bruce invited the CMS community to travel with him to "see" the mission for themselves: "Dear readers, will you accompany me on a journey to Persia? You will never understand our Mission till you pay it a visit." On this "visit" he offers an ethno-religious reimagining of the region: "I must tell you first there is no such kingdom of Persia. Persia is a misnomer: the Shah calls himself not the Shah of Persia but of Iran. Persia is only a province of Iran and Iran is the same word as Aryan, which reminds us that the Iranians are our near of kin, and like all true Aryans, have great capabilities, so that if they could only be made Christians they would be as noble a race as their cousins the Anglo-Saxons."[43] Bruce's travel tale connected Persia with Britain's own story of origin. Even the geography of Persia was drawn closer to British shores through the promise of bringing "Aryan" people back into the fold as Anglo-Saxon kin who had the potential to adopt Christianity. This reading drew upon Victorian understandings of the category of "Aryan" that could include both Muslims and Christians.[44]

Missionary stories of travel in the Near East mapped the region as both a familiar and a welcoming land. "A Holiday among the Mountains of Persia" represented the region as the perfect place for a missionary to take a much needed rest with his companions. The travels of Bruce's successor, Rev. C. H. Stileman, through the mountains outside Julfa reminded him of home: "We could now almost imagine ourselves in Devonshire, as we were in a well-watered, fertile valley everything green around us, with narrow lanes passing between orchards full of ripening apples and plums and other fruit."[45] Another story, "By-Ways of the Pleasant Land" by "A Lady Missionary," told of a picturesque journey taken by a female missionary and her entourage of "native helpers" on the "Sultan's Highway." Lacking geographic specificity, the tale offers a similarly idealized portrait of a not-unfamiliar rugged land: "Imagine a brilliant June morning," she began. "The night dews only too quickly rolling away from the hills, but still hanging here and there in faint white vapour; vineyards in fragrant blossom, green with the bright, fresh verdure of early summer, a western breeze tempering the scorching rays of the sun."[46]

Even tales of failed missionary efforts could serve to broaden the connections between the Christian community in Britain and the one the CMS hoped to revive in the Near East. The Constantinople Mission had been plagued by difficulties from the beginning. Started in 1818, it was closed three years later "owing to an outbreak of popular fanaticism" and then restarted in 1858 in the wake of the Crimean War only to end again in 1877.[47] The end of the Russo-Turkish War afforded new opportunities. In 1879, the *Gleaner* reported that "several friends urged upon the CMS the importance of resuming its work in Turkey and Asia Minor, in view of the increased opening of those countries which will probably result from recent political changes."[48] The CMS focused its work on existing mission stations where it ministered to both Eastern Orthodox Christians and nomadic and settler Arab populations in Palestine, despite prohibitions against Muslim conversions.[49] The New Mission Church at Jerusalem, in place of the failed Mission at Constantinople, emerged as the center of this work in the heart of the Holy Land.[50]

Narratives of the challenge of conversion were accompanied by stories that offered small encouragements from the field. "Islam and Christian Missions" cast Muslims as intractable: "The Gospel in the Mission Field has no more powerful or bitter foe than Islam."[51] Converts were brutally punished and missionaries who entered Muslim homes often quickly were kicked out. Stories of proselytizing efforts, however, demonstrated an eagerness to draw in Muslims despite strict restrictions on conversion. "Although we are nearly always well received," wrote Miss J. Ellis from Cairo, "perhaps I ought to tell also that we have been literally turned out of four houses by the husbands of the women, one of them (a teacher in one of the Government schools) being exceedingly rude, and telling us 'never to come there again' but it is a marvel to me, visiting entirely among Moslems as we do, that we are not oftener subject to this kind of treatment."[52]

This conceptualization of the Near East populated by a revived Christian church and potential Muslim converts was accompanied by a more concrete form of mapping in the pages of the *Gleaner*. "A journey to Iran is not so formidable an undertaking as some think it to be," opined the Rev. Bruce in 1894. Much as his wife had done in her travel log published twenty years earlier, Bruce wrote a piece that took the reader on a journey from London to Iran that ended in familiar territory. In this case, "the Northern Liverpool of Iran": "Twenty-four hours will take you from London to Berlin and fifty more thence to Odessa. In from three to five days you will cross the Black Sea to Batoum and in thirty-six hours you will get across the Caucasus by train to Baku. . . . A sail of thirty-six hours, in a good Russian steamer on the Caspian ought to complete the journey and land you at Enzelli, the Northern Liverpool of Iran."[53] A journey that had taken forty-five days, thanks to improvements in railway communication funded in part by British capital, now could be completed in fewer than ten days. Bruce's accompanying map entitled "Mohammedan Lands" situated the region that much closer to Britain by showing Persia's proximity to both Europe and India.

A little more than ten years later, the "Moslem Fund Campaign" project mapped this geography. "Our needs are so great and urgent that we must seek to enlist the help of all classes," implored a writer in the "From the Home Field" column. A square collection box, the "Moslem Box," was decorated with a map that split the world between Christian Europe and the Muslim East (figure 15). At the center lay the Near East mission projects of the CMS, with arms extending to all Muslim-ruled territory: "The 'octopus' map which demonstrates very vividly the Moslem Menace, is in itself a powerful plea."[54] With Europe pictured above and India to the far right of the picture, a pie chart on the opposite side characterized the number of people living under Christian rule, a number augmented by the British Empire's hold over India and East Africa.

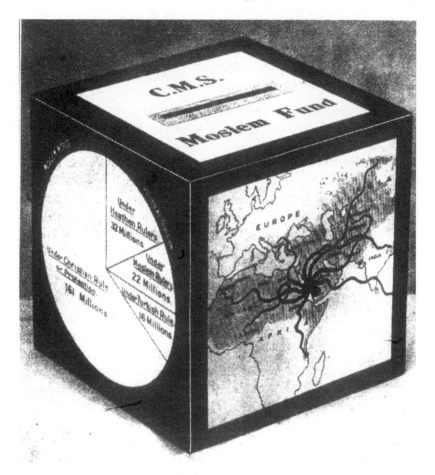

Figure 15. CMS charity "Moslem Box" to promote Christian missions in the Near East. *Gleaner,* February 1910

By the eve of World War I these stories and visual representations added up to a portrait of the Near East that spanned from Eastern Europe to the borders of India and encompassed Christian minorities and Muslims alike. Campaigns like the "Moslem Box" provided a material representation of this world view to those who held, studied, passed, and then contributed to the cause of bringing those areas of the map "under Christian rule." The extending of the geographical scope of Britain's Near East thus relied in part on an ethnographic understanding of the peoples of this region as distant kin in need of revival in the case of Christians or conversion in the case of Muslims. This religious and ethnographic reading contributed to other narratives that envisioned a Near East that spanned from the Balkans to the Indian border.

CURZON'S BIG NEAR EAST

Political pragmatists also found something compelling in ethnographic and religious understandings of the Near East. A look at George Nathaniel Curzon's writing reveals a view of empire deeply informed by such conceptualizations when it came to the Eastern Question. In the years just preceding his taking up of the post of viceroy of India, Curzon wrote three books that defined the importance of the empire in the East: *Russia in Central Asia* (1889), *Persia and the Persian Question* (1892), and *Problems of the Far East* (1894). In the final volume of his series on what he called "Asiatic Problems," Curzon with typical hubris mapped the Near East at the center of the British Empire: "What I have already endeavoured to do for Russia and Central Asia and for Persia or the countries on this side of India, i.e. the Near East—what I hope to be able to do hereafter for two other little-known Asiatic regions, directly bordering upon India, i.e. the Central East—I attempt to do in this volume, and in that which will follow it, for the countries lying beyond India, i.e. the Far East."[55] Here in the middle of Curzon's map sat India. The Near East, defined as regions to the west of India remained distinct from those to its East, the Far East. The concept of the Middle East, or Central East as Curzon called it, was still in its infancy and included only those regions, namely Afghanistan, on India's western border.

This capacious definition of the Near East proved of use to Curzon in making his argument that the British must increase investment in railways, trade, and infrastructure to thwart European and Russian competition in the region. The Near East here included Persia and Arabia as a corridor for Britain to access India. As Curzon continued in his introduction, "As I proceed with this undertaking the true fulcrum of Asiatic domination seems to me increasingly to lie in the Empire of Hindustan. The secret of the mastery of the world, is, if they only knew it, in the possession of the British people."[56] This idea of the lands of the Ottoman Empire as a gateway to India certainly did not originate with Curzon, who believed "without India the British Empire could not exist."[57] However, his travels in the region and political influence over policy, survey work, and mapmaking, (as a gold medalist and president of the RGS)[58] popularized the notion that of a big Near East.

Significantly, Curzon's geopolitical vision of the Near East relied on ethnographic imaginings. His work included an extensive discussion of *who* inhabited his Near East, contributing to discourse on the nature of the Muslim/Christian divide. Curzon did not seek to erase Muslims from his expanding Near East as Campbell had done earlier in his map of the Balkans, a task that even for someone like Curzon by this time would have proved difficult. A great believer in the salutary effects of the British Empire on populations under its influence, Curzon instead embraced the notion that Muslims as a monotheistic people shared the potential for kinship with the British that could be cultivated through the spread of English education and values. This secular conversion narrative adapted Rev. Bruce's religious ideal of kinship with the Aryan peoples of Iran. Curzon thus populated his vision of the Near East with Aryan kin who shared a common ancestry with the British: "it ought not be difficult to interest Englishmen in the Persian people. They have the same lineage as ourselves. Three thousand years ago their forefathers left the uplands of that mysterious Asian home from which our ancestral stock had already gone forth . . . They were the first of the Indo-European family to embrace a purely monotheistic faith."[59] Curzon of course understood the peoples of the Near East, Christian and Muslim alike, only as distant kin. Page after page of his two volumes on the region are filled with descriptions of habits he finds appalling and customs he cannot understand, leading his biographer to wonder why he wrote so long about people he did not like very much.[60] Idealizing ethnic and religious connections with both Christians and Muslims in the Near East was central to Curzon's cosmography, however. Mapping the Near East in this way made it possible to cast the problem of geopolitical power in the region as an imperial civilizing mission.

Curzon's vision of the Near East as stretching from the Balkan frontier and into Asia and beyond tapped into a growing common sentiment. Guide books such as *Practical Hints for Travelers in the Near East*, published in 1902, began to include North Africa, the Balkans, Turkey, Syria, and Palestine as part of the region. Missionaries also found opportunity in expanding the geography of the Near East.[61] The Near East, according to the *Gleaner*, encompassed "'Moslum' and Oriental lands" "which lie between the Mediterranean and the frontier states of India."[62] What would incorporate these regions for missionaries like Bruce was the potential for conversion, which would make them "as noble a race as their cousins

Figure 16 (*overleaf*). British map of the Near East. From the *Harmsworth Atlas and Gazetteer* (London: Carmelite House, 1909).

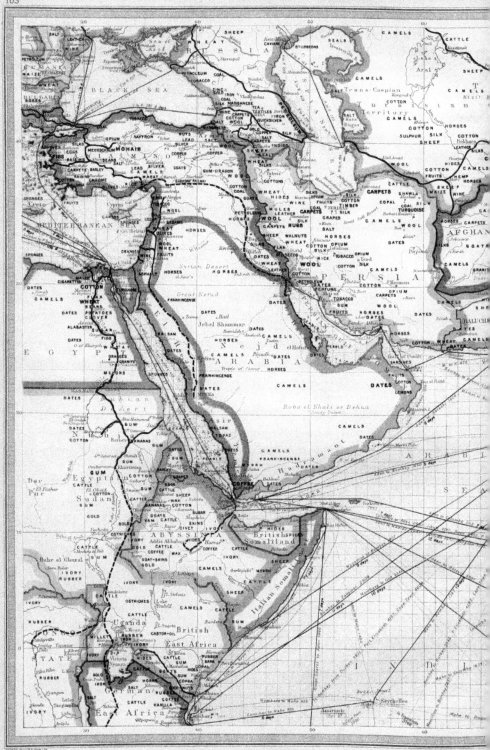

GEORGE PHILIP & SON L^TD

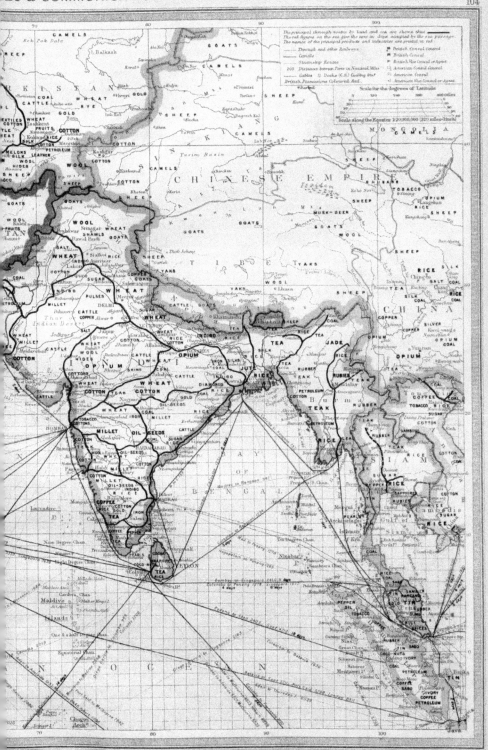

the Anglo-Saxons."[63] Like Curzon, Bruce's view of the Near East relied on notions of distant kinship. Others like Valentine Chirol understood the Eastern Question in terms of Curzon's expanded geography: "Thus in the brief course of some forty years—say between 1860 and 1900—the area of that Eastern question, which only a generation ago appeared confined mainly to the southern and eastern shores of the Mediterranean and the Black Sea, has been extended, not only across the Caspian and the plains of Central Asia, but to the far-away coast of the Pacific."[64]

This expanded geography joined geopolitical and ethnographic conceptions of the Near East in a familiar revival narrative. Writing in 1907 the traveler and journalist William LeQueux argued that "[t]he countries denominated by the general name of the Near East are, by their geographical position and fertility, of immense importance. They have been the cradle of the ancient civilization and of rich and powerful empires. The reason of their gloomy present does not lie either in the exhaustion of the soil or in the loss of their geographical importance, but only in the administration which the Turk has established for centuries over them. A change in the administration will bring resurrection." Britain had the ultimate responsibility to bring these changes to the Ottoman peoples by "call[ing] forth in them an immense economical development" in a region that rival Germany had already "thrown covetous eyes."[65]

The big Near East of the early twentieth century, firmly rooted in Victorian ethnographic understandings, offered a canvas on which to map geopolitical priorities. By the early twentieth century the Near East emerged as an important feature of conceptualizations of the British Empire. In 1909, the *Times*'s proprietor, Alfred Harmsworth (later Lord Northcliffe), published the *Harmsworth Atlas of the World*. In it he presented a vision of the Near East as a land connected to Britain by modern lines of communication populated by endless natural resources (figure 16). This thematic map created by the London Geographical Institute included the supposed location of products that had already captured the British imagination. Silver, saffron, and lead from Asia Minor; wool, salt, opium, and tobacco from Persia; wheat, coffee, and camels from Arabia all lay within easy reach of British Possessions ("colored in red").

The future Lord Northcliffe's geographical hubris matched and even exceeded that of Curzon. From the Balkans to the horn of Africa to Persia to India to the Malay Peninsula, the map entitled "The Near East: Industries and Communications" depicted the Near East at the center of a British Empire that knew no bounds. In the west, the national designations of Bulgaria, Turkey, and Armenia, the latter still part of the

Ottoman Empire, joined Asia Minor, Persia, and Afghanistan to the British Empire in the East. This rendering of the Near East effectively erased the Ottoman Empire as a designation from the map. Small black flags punctuated the landscape, designating the expanse of British consular outposts established in the immediate wake of the Russo-Turkish War. These outposts lined the trade route where an abundance of railways, canals, steamship routes, and cables connected the Near East in a vast imperial web.

This Near East spanning from the Balkans to India and beyond projected a new authority over the people and resources of the Ottoman Empire during a moment when British imperial power in the "Far East" was at its height. The 1878 Treaty of Berlin had set the stage for the conceptual dismantling of the Ottoman Empire. By the turn of the century maps more frequently used designations such as "Turkey in Europe" and "Turkey in Asia" over the term "Ottoman Empire" or, as in the case of Harmsworth, erased it altogether, decades before World War I brought the Empire itself to its actual end. Such commercial and imperial representations were not invented in a vacuum. Rather, they came out of and contributed to ethnographic understandings of the Near East drawn along religious lines.

Geographical renderings of the Near East reflected Victorian understandings of the Eastern Question that shifted both the humanitarian and imperial gaze farther eastward. Extending the boundaries of the Christian Near East through the Balkans, Anatolia, and around the Mediterranean expanded the geography of British responsibility particularly during the Bulgarian Atrocities agitation and later during the Armenian massacres of the 1890s and massacres of Orthodox Christian populations during World War I. The next two chapters trace the institutionalization of a worldview that coupled proprietary interest with humanitarian responsibility.

3. Humanitarian Diplomacy

Consular work is the public face of British diplomacy.

FOREIGN OFFICE REPORT, 2000

The Consuls in the Levant have duties of a higher description to discharge than those in any other part of the world.

LORD PALMERSTON, May 7, 1855

In May 1876 Lord Stratford de Redcliffe (formerly Sir Stratford Canning) presented a plan to transform the way British foreign policy worked in the Near East in a lengthy letter to the *Times*. Considered the elder statesman on the Eastern Question, the former ambassador outlined an ambitious program to establish "equality of all classes before civil law" as reports of unrest in Bulgaria began to reach Britain.[1] He suggested a new kind of hands-on diplomacy where British consular representatives would oversee the implementation of changes to Ottoman civil and legal administration. Doubts raised about the "practicability" of such a plan led Lord Redcliffe to "draw up a fuller statement" six months later as the Bulgarian Atrocities agitation raged at home. His memorandum on "Suggestions for the Settlement of the Eastern Difficulty" promised to transform the consular service in the Near East into a network of political, military, and juridical posts scattered largely throughout the Christian provinces of the Ottoman Empire.[2]

For men like Redcliffe, the answer to the Eastern Question rested in part with a more activist foreign policy when it came to Ottoman internal affairs. Transforming consular work from a loose network of commercial agents to the wider duties envisioned by Redcliffe would do just that. Britain had pushed the project of reforming the Ottoman legal and civil code with then Ambassador Canning's attempt to reinforce the Tanzimat reforms in the 1856 Crimean War settlement.[3] The failure of this effort took on a sense of urgency in the wake of the Bulgarian Atrocities with calls to better enforce reforms outlined in the 1878 Treaty of Berlin. This chapter traces the rise of new diplomatic beliefs and practices through the experiences of some of the agents charged with this task. Diplomats, civil servants, and their families served in both official and unofficial capacities in the Near East while engaging in humanitarian advocacy work and philanthropic activities. More than mere representatives of government policy, their work narrated diplomatic interests in terms of a growing belief in humanitarian responsibility for subject populations.

The civil service began expanding in the Near East after the Crimean War and drew diplomats and consuls more intimately into Ottoman internal affairs. In addition to the ambassador's residence in Constantinople, a network of 62 consular outposts in the Ottoman Empire employed in the 1860s around 350 consuls, vice consuls and consuls general. By 1900, a well-established network of official consular posts extended from Belgrade to Basra.[4] These agents, initially charged with protecting the interests of the nearly one million British subjects living in the region, took on another directive. Beirut Consul Elridge, for example, reported in 1870 that he would periodically put aside his commercial and juridical duties to intervene in religious and political conflicts among the local population.[5] As one government report put it in 1871, "No body of men are more usefully employed in securing the extension of commercial enterprise, the welfare of the people among whom they live and the maintenance of peace."[6]

A major restructuring of the consul system in the Ottoman Empire occurred under the title of the "Levant Consular Service" in 1877. The name, borrowed from the defunct crown-chartered Levant Company, intended to connect local administrative and peacekeeping functions of the consuls with their traditional role as commercial agents that dated back to the sixteenth century. In practice, when it came to the westernmost lands of the Ottoman Empire and Anatolia, places with the largest concentration of Christian minorities, commerce took a back seat to political administration. The introduction of the category of "military consul" after the Russo-Turkish War made mediation a central duty of the consul. These men watched the border while they supervised the implementation of treaty agreements that protected minorities living in towns along the Russo-Turkish frontier.[7] The presence of this group of paid agents of the crown in politically volatile areas necessarily involved them in work that often blurred the boundaries between civil and military functions. The fallout from the Bulgarian Atrocities in the late 1870s and the Armenian massacres of the mid-1890s brought diplomats and consuls more deeply into local matters that included arbitration for subject populations, relief work, and legal defense. Out of this configuration came a diplomacy that made humanitarian advocacy a legitimate part of foreign policy.

REFASHIONING DIPLOMACY IN THE NEAR EAST

Changes in the way diplomacy operated in the Near East came out of debates during the Crimean War. In 1855, Lord Palmerston argued that the structure of diplomacy should reflect the special nature of British interests in the Ottoman Empire: "in the East the consul, besides his strictly consular duties, had certain judicial and even diplomatic, duties to discharge. He was the channel of communication in all matters of complaints within his cognizance with the centre of the Government." These "higher duties," as he called them, allowed Palmerston to argue on behalf of expanding both the number of consuls and their function.[8] In 1825, Ambassador Canning had set the stage for this shift by dissolving the Levant Company and transferring the administration of the consular system to the government. This opened up the possibility of making consuls more than commercial agents employed by a chartered company with a mandate to protect and promote mercantile interests. The outbreak of the Crimean War necessitated better defining what this meant. The growth of the government-run consul service to five times its previous size by 1856 resulted primarily from appointing representatives with "judicial and political functions" to areas of little commercial value to trade.[9] "Every consul in the East," one former consul observed in an interview in 1903, "bears a more or less political character and is daily engaged in the conduct of negotiations with the native authorities which require all the tact and intimate knowledge of men that are supposed to be the essential qualifications of the trained diplomatist."[10]

Percy Ellen Algernon Frederick William Sydney Smythe, later the eighth Viscount Strangford (1825–69), was an early proponent of the new diplomacy. "There are other sick things in Turkey besides the sick man," he wrote of the diplomatic service in 1863, "though they are not half such good subjects for declamation."[11] Described by one contemporary as having a "keen Oriental-looking face and beard" with an extreme "shortness of sight," Lord Strangford attended Oxford and later served as one of two student attachés to Constantinople in 1845, a position made official in 1849. Later, he served as Oriental secretary during the Crimean War.[12] His expressed love of geography and knowledge of numerous languages including Turkish, Sanskrit, Persian, Arabic, and Greek led to the characterization of him as the "the most varied linguist this country has ever produced." As president of the Royal Asiatic Society Strangford promoted what he called the "open race for the knowledge of this part of the world" between Russia and Britain.[13] After assuming his title on his brother's death in 1857, he split time between London and Constantinople, where he joined a Muslim fraternity and lived for a time the austere life of a dervish.

A committed ethnologist interested in the history of nations based on linguistic commonalities, Lord Strangford's intellectual interests deeply informed his politics. His ideas about the Near East found audience in numerous articles published in the *Pall Mall Gazette, Saturday Review,* and *Quarterly Review.* He adhered to the Palmerstonian line that both admired the Ottomans while seeing the end of the Empire as inevitable and maintained that the future rested with its Christian minorities. Though many of his generation thought Greeks would serve this role, Lord Strangford held that the Bulgarians would modernize the Empire. At the same time he had a deep respect for the Ottoman elite, whom he viewed as akin to Britain's aristocracy. This put him in line with many liberals of the time who believed that Christian rule would not come out of a revolutionary moment but as the result of a slow natural progression. The "Christians of European Turkey will be the ultimate masters of the country" by slow growth, not "convulsive" change.[14] The British would encourage this process not through military action but rather by making sure that Christian minorities could govern themselves, eventually freeing themselves from Ottoman rule. Writing in the 1860s, he argued that the Bulgarians, a "virtuous" and not revolutionary people, best demonstrated this capability for self-government.

Lord Strangford hated the notion of the Eastern Question. "The term Eastern Question is in itself a convenient way of expressing the whole aggregate of Turkish foreign politics in two words and it cannot well be dispensed with. But to predicate the 'solution' of it is simply to miss the point, which is that it is insoluble by any action from without, short of downright brute conquest. It is high time to get rid of so misleading a formula."[15] Rather, he understood what others called the Eastern Question as a process that would result in the eventual resolution of conflicts over the minority problem in the Ottoman Empire. No naïve idealist, Strangford exercised caution when it came to forcing reforms on the Ottomans that advantaged minorities. The British had an obligation to assist by introducing and enforcing the principles of good government among populations that demonstrated a readiness for democratic reform. As an ethnologist he argued against treating nationality "as a fixed and defined principle," believing that the Bulgarians would free themselves from Turkish rule because of their numbers and desire for independence.[16]

This worldview posited proprietary knowledge as the key to effective diplomacy. A. Vambery, a writer who fell under Strangford's influence, summed up this belief: "England's Perplexity in the East, her disquietude whenever the Eastern Question comes practically to the front, is mainly due to her want of true, sound knowledge of the Moslem Asiatic countries and peoples." Lord Strangford through his writing and patronage of men like Vambery attempted to correct this imbalance through a knowledge-based diplomacy that promoted English interests against Russia. As Vambery concluded, "It is from this cause and not on account of a superior number of troops that she is overreached by the Colossus in the North. What some few had done in Eastern Asia, some English diplomatists succeeded also in accomplishing in Western Asia, where they made the name 'Ingiliz' shine with a brilliancy which even the blunders of their successors have been unable altogether to obscure."[17]

"Knowing" the Ottoman Empire entailed both ethnographic and geographic understanding. "The geography of the country is very little known as regards European Turkey," Strangford argued, much in line with ethnographers and mapmakers of this time.[18] Britain stood to take advantage of its rivalry with Russia through a more thorough survey of the ethnographic complexity of the region's politics. "Past blindness" to national and religious considerations of the Eastern Question, particularly when it came to the "Christians in Turkey," had impeded British diplomacy.[19] Although skeptical of claims of nationality as a primary marker of the forms of nationhood, he maintained that Britain had to take this idea seriously since recognizing claims of "nationality" by minority groups had become a "treaty obligation" after the Crimean War. Strangford believed that only careful attention to ethnographic differences would allow Britain to fulfill these obligations. "Perhaps we shall end by having to appoint ethnological attaches and secretaries to Vienna and Constantinople," he mused, "and to send colporteurs with bundles of Dr. Latham's books for distribution among all our political consulates."[20]

Strangford made the case for the cultivation of knowledgeable and experienced civil servants in an 1863 essay entitled "Chaos." The appointed diplomat, he argued, "resides entirely at the capital," leaving him out of touch.[21] For the ambassador the "provinces are a mere abstraction," as his concern rested with mollifying the Ottoman elite at the Porte and countering anti-Turkish feeling at home. The consuls, on the other hand, who resided "wholly" in Turkey's "illgoverned provinces" "are politicians one day, merchants, advocates and judges the next" and often engaged in the protection and defense of minority interests.[22] While cautioning against using Christian morality as a rallying cry in diplomatic dealings,

Strangford maintained that paying clearer attention to reforming the status of minorities would strengthen Britain's proprietary claims over the region.

A new kind of civil servant was needed to foster administrative change on the ground while not alienating the Ottoman governing elite. "We want our nation served in Turkey . . . by the most perfect and highest type of English manhood," Strangford maintained, "we want it there more than anywhere due to the special nature of the work." This meant stationing "the best ambassadors, best attaches, best interpreters, the best consuls, the best railway and telegraph men" in areas "untrodden by European foot since Ovid."[23] Convinced that the consul system did not have enough good men, Strangford pushed to make the service more "English." This replaced the value of regional knowledge gleaned from the experience of local inhabitants, or "Levantines," who had long worked in the consular service with clearer ideological consistency.[24] "We must have Englishmen in our public service," Strangford maintained, "if we do not send out Englishmen then we must Anglicize our Levantines."[25] Anglicizing the foreign service through education to make it more "English" would give the government more direct control over consuls and better focus the message that they hoped to convey to local populations: "Freedom, broadening slowly down from precedent to precedent."[26] The *Times* echoed this sentiment soon after in a series of articles calling for reforms that put English-educated civil servants in Near Eastern posts.[27]

By the time the Bulgarian crisis forced the debate over diplomatic reform forward, Lord Strangford had died of a brain hemorrhage at age forty-three in 1869. His ideas, however, continued to have currency thanks in part to his wife, Lady Strangford (née Emily Anne Beaufort), who threw her energies into bolstering his legacy by publishing his writings in a series of well-received books during the subsequent decade.[28] Reforms announced by Lord Derby in July 1877 professionalized the service through competitive exams and linguistic education for English-trained consuls and interpreters. The newly minted Levant Consular Service would govern the civil service from the Balkans to the Chinese border. In the Ottoman Empire, agents took further advantage of the capitulations, a set of historical agreements that granted extraterritorial privileges. This coupled with the growth, professionalization, and increasingly national character of the service helped make British presence more widely felt.[29] Such changes would affect the practice of diplomacy from the ambassador's residence to the provinces beyond the end of the century.

AUSTEN HENRY LAYARD AND
HUMANITARIAN DIPLOMACY

When Austen Henry Layard (1817–94) arrived to take up his post as ambassador in Constantinople in spring 1877 he immediately had his hands full. The first cohort of six English-trained linguists of the Levant Consular Service arrived that November anxious to begin their work. With the new system barely on its feet and the anticipated extension of its mandate by Whitehall the Ottoman Empire's top-ranking diplomat also faced a volatile political landscape. Layard's five-year tenure at Constantinople witnessed the fallout from the Bulgarian Atrocities agitation, the beginning of the Russo-Turkish War, and its resolution in the Treaty of Berlin. How Layard executed the role of the diplomat had as much to do with his response to these crises as it did with the changing experience and structure of diplomatic practice in the Ottoman Empire.

From Huguenot stock, Layard was educated in Italy, England, France, and Switzerland mainly as a result of his father's search for a cure for his asthma away from the damp English climate. He finished his formal education in England and entered his uncle's solicitor's office in London in 1834. Having read *Arabian Nights* as a child and motivated by a desire to escape the drudgery of work as a clerk, he took an overland journey to Ceylon with an acquaintance to join an uncle who thought life as a barrister in the colonies might suit him better. Layard claimed in his autobiography that the real reason for his journey was to get away from "bigoted Tories," as he had formed "from my boyhood very liberal and independent opinions upon politics. These opinions extended to religious questions."[30]

The promise of adventure more than politics, however, seemed to have inspired his early interest in the Near East. As he described his first glimpse of Scutari, which for him marked the dividing line between East and West: "This was my first glimpse of Eastern life, and the scene as we passed through the bazaars crowded with men and women—Turks, Albanians, and Greeks of various tribes and races in their varied and gay costumes—was to me singularly novel and interesting. . . . The change since passing the borders of Christian Europe was now complete, and I felt myself, as it were, in a new world—in a world of which I had dreamt from my earliest childhood. I was not, on the whole disappointed."[31] This "new world" also afforded new opportunities. He adapted quickly to the demands of travel in the Ottoman Empire, taking advantage of the assumption by locals that "all European strangers are supposed to be consuls."[32] This allowed him to move through "unexplored" parts of Asia Minor with relative ease, where he decided to "follow a new route through Asia Minor and to visit parts of it which had hitherto not been explored by previous travelers." Connections with the Royal Geographical Society facilitated this course: "At that time the maps of the interior of Asia Minor, which we were about the traverse were almost a blanked, and we had nothing to guide us except our compass and such information as we could pick up in going from village to village and from the inhabitants of the country."

Layard embraced the role of amateur geographer, compiling information on the western lands of the Ottoman Empire whenever he could: "We passed through several flourishing villages, of which I obtained the names, carefully mapping our route as we went along, and keeping a road book, which I had marked off so as to enable me to keep a complete record of our progress. . . . Without the observations recorded in it being scientifically accurate they were sufficiently full and careful to enable me subsequently to lay down a fairly trustworthy map of the country through which we journeyed and which I afterwards sent, with a memoir to the Royal Geographical Society."[33] These efforts, along with his work "correcting" the map of Montenegro, earned him the gold medal from the society in 1849.

This work culminated in excavations near Mosul where he uncovered the Assyrian treasures that earned him fame at home and which reside today in the British Museum. It also initiated an enduring interest in the Assyrian people. He dedicated an entire section of his book *Nineveh and Its Remains* to the customs and religious beliefs of the modern-day Assyrians, claiming that to understand the artifacts one must understand the people and the "geography" of their position. "To Protestants, the doctrine and rites of a primitive sect of Christians, who have ever remained untainted by the superstitions of Rome must be of high importance," he asserted. In particular, Layard wanted to bring an understanding of the Assyrians through "the purity of their faith" and the plight of their "suffering" to the attention of the wider public. For Layard, his discoveries at Nineveh also unearthed a common cause: "our sympathies cannot but be excited in favor of a long persecuted people who have merited the title of the 'Protestants of Asia.'"[34]

The launch of his political career soon followed. Knowledge of Persian and Arabic that he picked up living among the local Arab population, along with the patronage of Ambassador Canning, who funded his earliest expedition, earned Layard recognition as "the discoverer of Nineveh."

This connection with Canning coupled with the popular success of his series of books on Nineveh led to Palmerston's appointing him as a paid attaché at 250 pounds a year in late 1840s. He then launched a brief career in Parliament marked by a crusade to end venal promotions in the civil service and an ultimately unsuccessful campaign against what he viewed as the maladministration of the Crimean War.[35]

Conscious of his status as a man on the make with a prickly personality that often alienated even his friends, he left to seek a career away from England. As might be expected, a position in the diplomatic service did not come easily for this stocky, untitled man who waited for years under Canning's encouragement for an official appointment. Aristocrats like Strangford had refused to take Layard seriously, poking fun at his political ambitions as little more than an extension of his role as an adventurer.[36] Eventually, his support of then Prime Minister Disraeli led to his appointment as ambassador at Constantinople in 1877. Dubbed the "first Liberal Imperialist" by his biographer, Layard believed Britain should "maintain the Turkish Empire in its present state until the Christian population may be ready to succeed the Mussulman."[37] "My conviction," Layard declared, "is that it is possible to do so, and that this policy is the only hope of a favorable solution to the Eastern Question."[38] Layard was encouraged by the growth of Protestantism among the peoples of Turkey, notably the Armenians and Greeks, and he hoped "that ere long this religious movement will bring about a political one and that we shall [see] the Protestant Christians of this country hold a very high and honorable position."[39] At the same time, like others of his generation including Lord Strangford, Layard held the sultan in high esteem and refused to support any efforts to destabilize the current regime.

He believed instead that Britain should lead by example. A visit to India in the wake of the 1857 Mutiny offered Layard an object lesson in bad administration. British oppression in India sent the wrong message to the Ottoman elite: "Are we to hold the Bible in one hand and the sword in the other? If so what can we say to the Turks and other nations who would oppress Christians?"[40] At the same time, Layard was disdainful of the popular agitation against the Bulgarian atrocities: "The English have these periodic lunacies particularly when religion is involved."[41] After reading Gladstone's pamphlet that sparked the Bulgarian Atrocities agitation at home, he wrote to a friend, "you cannot drive 3 millions of Turks out of Europe into starvation and hopeless misery. The wild humanitarian cry about Turkey will lead to serious mischief. It is grievous to see a man like Gladstone turned into a mere vulgar pamphleteer."[42] Layard, never one to keep his political opinions to himself, responded to Gladstone's campaign in an article in *Quarterly Review*, where he argued that Turkey should expire of its own accord, not pushed by military pressure or public opinion.

Layard embraced a hands-on approach to diplomacy that involved him in local and national Ottoman affairs. In 1856 he helped establish the European-modeled Ottoman Bank in order to develop the "material resources" of the Ottoman Empire.[43] He also began supporting humanitarian aid projects that promoted equality among Ottoman subjects: "I was anxious to promote the establishment of schools amongst the indigent Christian and Jewish populations of the Turkish capital—a matter with which Lady Canning took a very lively interest. We were able to open some schools in the poorest quarters of the city, and eventually one was founded for the education of children of the better classes without distinction of faith, it being meant for Christians and Mohammedans alike." Such projects, he believed would curry favor with the sultan, who himself later supported this institution.

The Bulgarian crisis necessitated a clearer joining of humanitarian and diplomatic concerns. In a September 1876 letter to Lord Derby, Layard chronicled a long list of interventions by British officials on behalf of both Muslim and Christian subjects. "They prove," Layard concluded, "that the case of humanity without reference to race of creed or any political interest has ever been upheld by England in Turkey." In another letter dated two days earlier to his mentor Lord Redcliffe he called for punishment for those who perpetrated the atrocities. At the same time he urged the government to "approach the Turkish question in a wise, moderate and statesmanlike spirit and not with passion and exaggerated sentiment." "A false step on the part of England at the crisis," he forebodingly concluded, "might be irretrievable and might be even fateful to the future of this country."[44]

As the top ranking diplomat in the Ottoman Empire, Layard intervened directly in humanitarian aid campaigns. The Stafford House Project, the National Aid Society, the Red Crescent Society, and the Turkish Compassionate Fund, along with a handful of American-run missionary projects, all relied on the support of the ambassador at one point or another. The ambassador's example inspired others, including most notably the widow of Lord Strangford. While editing her husband's writings, Lady Strangford had enrolled in a four year nurses' training course in England. In 1874 she published "Hospital Training for Ladies" and waited for a call to use her skills and capital. The Bulgarian Atrocities

Figure 17.   Charity hospital run by Lady Strangford and supported with donations from Britain. Inset: Sketch portrait of Lady Strangford. *Graphic,* May 26, 1877.

proved the perfect opportunity to use her husband's diplomatic network to launch her own campaign. Work with the order of St. John's Eastern Sick and Wounded Fund led to the opening of her own fund to help destitute Bulgarians. In August 1876, when atrocity reports began to filter back to England, she started the Bulgarian Peasants Relief fund pledging to raise 10,000 pounds to assist the homeless and went to Bulgaria to administer the aid personally (figure 17).

Such an aid scheme would not have survived without the cooperation of diplomats and consuls spread throughout the Ottoman Empire. Lady Strangford understood that the ambassador's assistance was the key to successful aid work. She worked on relief efforts with Layard, using his position to provide emotional and material support for her efforts. "I must say it is a great comfort in this terrible time to have you at Constantinople," wrote Lady Strangford to Layard in 1877 upon setting up her relief hospital in Adrianople.[45] Over the next three years she used Layard to secure funds from other aid organizations, ease her passage through hostile territory, and intervene on behalf of those under her patronage. Layard also served as a go-between in the management of the large amounts of cash that her funds brought in thanks to his connections with the Ottoman Bank and relationship with British consuls operating in the region.

Lady Strangford needed Layard both to help facilitate and offer diplomatic legitimacy for her projects. "I always give my ambassador as little trouble as possible," she declared after numerous requests that included the purchase of supplies and an escort for her and her large party out of Sofia on the eve of the outbreak of the Russo-Turkish War. In 1880, she wrote from her home to Layard regarding a new project in eastern Anatolia: "I was very unwilling indeed to take up the miserable state of Kurdistan and Armenia and for a long time would not consent to work with it. But I found that no one else would work and that not a penny would be subscribed if I did not come forward." Funds went through Layard's account at the Ottoman Bank and he then distributed them to the consuls at Van, Aleppo, and Erzeroom. Lady Strangford advised, "You will not . . . raise the hopes among the Consuls of any large fortune being at hand but yesterday I had the pleasure of telegraphing 400 pounds to you for the half of the northern districts and 300 pounds for the southern. The 400 was paid yesterday into the Imperial Ottoman Bank . . . the 300 pounds will be probably arranged today." The fund eventually raised over £13,500 from subscribers in Britain which Strangford gave to Layard to distribute, knowing that he shared her sensibility: "it is best for you to decide really to whom it goes . . . provided it is sent to the Kurdistan or Armenian country, and provided its bestowed without any distinction or preference to creed or race."[46] Strangford believed that Layard's authority as a representative of the British government would help legitimate humanitarian aid work as part of the larger mission: "we thought we might send the money through your hands, partly as a convenience to ourselves partly in order to give it an official flavor in the eyes of the receivers."[47]

Layard similarly used Strangford to further his own agenda. During the Russo-Turkish War, he asked her to investigate alleged atrocities committed by Bulgarians against the Turkish population that he hoped to use to counter Gladstone's anti-atrocity campaigns. In June and July of 1878 Strangford attempted to find evidence of atrocities committed by Bulgarians against Muslims. "I have not a single word of any 'terrible crimes'; much less 'revolting cruelties' such as you allude to." At Layard's urging she sent out Dr. Stephenson, the head of her hospitals, "to go up country for me" to "enquire into the reports of the Bulgarian atrocities both towards Muslemans and Protestants." Frustrated with the results of her search, she requested that Layard give her "a few memoranda of the places where such things have happened as reported."[48] Layard received no satisfaction from this investigation, which seemed to have strained relations between the two. A few months later before closing her hospitals and leaving the country for good, she admonished Layard for not taking a more active interest in her recent work: "I am sorry you did not think it worthwhile to visit my hospital as it would have pleased the Turks very much."[49]

By the early 1880s Layard's fashioning of himself as defender of both the Ottoman administration and its dispossessed citizens was untenable. The mood back in Britain had changed with the landslide election that returned Gladstone and the Liberal Party to power. "Mr. Gladstone is warm glowing cordial and appreciative to everybody," wrote Strangford to Layard on the eve of the election. Hoping that Gladstone would infuse new life into her relief projects, Strangford worried that her connection with Layard would not bode well for her projects: "I am in despair about our meeting on the 6th of May as Gladstone has given up coming, though that sacred cause is nearest to his heart, so he writes to the committee."[50] Layard fared much worse. Gladstone had not forgotten Layard's public rebuke and promptly dismissed him as ambassador. "My case is one of extraordinary hardship and cruel injustice," he declared soon after his dismissal.[51] It would be Layard's last official diplomatic position.

Ironically, at the very moment of his termination Layard found himself involved with a campaign that even Gladstone could have loved. One of the last acts that he performed at Constantinople was advocating on behalf of a "Protestant Constitution." This document, pushed by Great Britain and Germany would grant Protestants "those rights and privileges which were accorded to every other religious sect in his empire," according to Layard, who tried unsuccessfully over several months to use his personal influence to persuade the sultan to sign on. Fear that Ottoman Christian minorities would appeal to Russia for protection along with Layard's belief in religious toleration drove these negotiations. Layard argued that Christians should be appointed to higher government positions and after his own machinations failed went as far as to call on the National Assembly to pressure the sultan to accept these conditions.[52] Looking back on his career, Layard claimed, "Although it was not possible to obtain for the Armenians all that Lord Beaconsfield's Government desired to obtain for them, and which I was most anxious to secure, yet some progress was made towards granting to Armenia a better administration, in which the Armenians themselves might share."[53]

In the end, Layard's humanitarian diplomacy produced few results.

"The Constitution to be conceded to the Protestants of Turkey, promised to me over and over again by the Sultan and his Ministers, is still unsettled," Layard disappointedly wrote to Granville on the eve of the signing of the Berlin Treaty. "The conduct of the Porte in this matter has been without excuse. . . . The question has been in discussion with the Porte during the three years that I have been here."[54] His tenure, however, did have a lasting legacy. Layard embodied the idea promoted by the reforms to the consular service that diplomacy in the Ottoman Empire went beyond signing treaties and ceremonial meetings with the sultan. This new diplomacy posited that civil servants and diplomats had a legitimate mandate to gather knowledge and intervene in Ottoman minority policy even if that involvement rarely produced the intended effect. The following story of William Everett's tenure as a provincial military consul offers an on the ground perspective of humanitarian diplomacy.

HUMANITARIAN DIPLOMACY
ALONG THE RUSSO-TURKISH BORDER

> I never have been so struck with any place in Turkey as with
> this. . . . Not the East that we know up at Erzeroom but the . . .
> East that one reads of. The East where everything is bright . . .
> where grapes, figs, pomegranates and watermelons grow. . . . It is
> quite another country that we have got into and it is curious and
> most interesting. . . . How I wish you were here darling. I have
> never tasted in my life better grapes.
> WILLIAM EVERETT TO HIS WIFE,
> during a tour of his district, October 15, 1884

Consuls like William Everett (1844–1908) who found themselves in newly created posts in the Anatolian interior after the Russo-Turkish War encountered a different world than that of the ambassador at Constantinople. The area then known as Armenia and Kurdistan located several hundred miles east of the seat of Ottoman administration had the feel of the Mediterranean, containing fertile lands, a moderate climate, and the Empire's highest concentration of minority Christians.[55] These Armenian and to a lesser extent Assyrian and Greek minorities lived under the millet system that governed non-Muslim populations in villages that dotted the landscape of Anatolia. Despite the relative ineffectiveness of past attempts at administrative reform many in these villages welcomed the British consul as a potential liberator from oppressive taxes and unequal treatment.[56]

Consular service reforms in the Near East most directly influenced the practice of diplomacy in eastern Anatolia. Everett as part of the new cohort of "military consul" was responsible for a large district which separated him from other officials by high desert passes, long distances, and bad roads. This gave him wide discretion in day-to-day functions and dealings with local populations. Everett, like other consuls who lived on the border with Russia, operated as a modern-day explorer, mapping, administering, and keeping a close watch on other European and especially Russian activity. In addition, the Cyprus Convention that helped shape the Treaty of Berlin gave Britain the special responsibility to oversee reforms. This role as protector of minorities in these distant outposts superseded the traditional role of the consul as a guardian of distressed British citizens.[57] Civil servants assigned to these posts in the interior served as administrators, information gatherers, aid workers, and mediators in local political conflicts.

In 1878, Everett was appointed vice consul at Erzeroom, a mountainous town of about 40,000 people with a large Armenian population on the Russo-Turkish border. He lived with his wife, Maria Georgina Calogeras, formerly of Corfu, and two daughters until he resigned from the consular service in 1888. A skilled draftsman with extensive military experience, Everett attended Sandhurst after a term at Marlborough College and later joined the Cameronians regiment in 1864. Life as a consul entailed frequent travel and interaction with the local population, American and British missionaries, and occasional European travelers and administrators. The creation of Erzeroom as a "political" rather than "commercial" post defined Everett's duties in the broadest of terms. Information gathering, securing ties with local officials, and cultivating the loyalty of the minority Christian community rather than protecting mercantile interests necessarily involved him in the day-to-day activities of village life.

Information gathering largely involved mapping terrain and passing on knowledge of local populations. As the eyes and ears of the state, consuls traveled for two main reasons: district tours and survey work. Month-long tours over rugged territory with an entourage of local guides and assistants took Everett to the half-dozen Armenian millets that made up the core of his district. He stayed with local inhabitants along the way, hearing their grievances and meeting with Ottoman officials in his district. Although he held consul status, Everett and others like him did not have an official document from the Ottoman government, or *firman*, leaving him reliant on the acceptance of the local population to legitimate his role. On his way to the town of Bitlis he wrote to his wife: "The authorities have been excessively civil so far as we've got. As I daresay you remember I have no Firman for this villayet [sic] and was therefore a little [worried] as to whether they would acknowledge me as Consul, but there have been no difficulties."[58]

Everett brought the keen eye of the surveyor to his post. Mapping was something that military men did starting at the end of the Napoleonic wars in both official and unofficial capacities.[59] After the Russo-Turkish War this pursuit had heightened importance, particularly along the border between Turkey and Russia. Everett proved himself a skilled surveyor. He traveled to Rumelia as part of the Turco-Bulgarian boundary commission to map the Russian frontier and in 1880 helped set the eastern boundaries of the Ottoman Empire as a member of the Turco-Persian frontier commission.[60] As consul for Kurdistan between 1882 and 1888 he performed survey work around Erzeroom to document a region previously unmapped by the British. Using German maps, he participated in the ongoing project of chronicling the geographical, ethnological, and physical makeup of the Russo-Turkish border.

Cultivating ties with the local Christian population came primarily from worries over Russia. An obsessive concern with potential Russian intrigue colored Everett's dispatches to his superiors. Convinced that Russia was always about to invade, he kept a special watch over the Armenian population for any indication that they might be looking to Russia rather than England for protection. Armenians, he claimed were not "patiently awaiting the decision of Her Majesty's Government . . . as to their future fate" and believed that they could prosper as "Russian subjects" and even "become rich under Russian rule."[61] This threat was used to argue that Britain should increase its influence over Christian populations in order to thwart a potential Russian advance. "I have reason to believe," Vice Consul Eyres in Van wrote to Everett, "the Russian Vice-Consul for Van was sent by his Government expressly to foster the sentiment of friendship manifested by the Nestorians [Assyrians] towards Russia, to encourage them to look to that country for protection, and to cement, as it were, an informal alliance." Evidence of this intrigue rested on the Russian consul distributing "decorations to the Patriarch and other Nestorians [Assyrians]."[62]

Reports of the maladministration of minority communities under the millet system worried the Foreign Office. Granville implored his top diplomats to "communicate the substance of Consular Reports to the Sultan" and "point out to His Majesty the neglect to remedy the grievances of the Armenians is driving them into the arms of Russia."[63] Evidence suggests that authorities did just that. In a letter to Everett his superior reported, "I was very much struck both by your reports and Eyres and I had parts of them translated into Turkish in the hopes that if he read them in his native language the Grand Vizier might pay more attention to them."[64] Although such pressure did little to ameliorate conditions for minorities, it reinforced the idea that to outmaneuver Russian intrigues Britain had to beat them at their own game. Everett's report of Russian movements in his district solicited the following response from the Foreign Office: "Thanks to you for the interesting information contained therein relative to Russian proceedings in Armenia and the danger of Rumanian intervention in the event of no steps being taken to ameliorate the condition of the population."[65]

Everett responded by lobbying the British Government for a sizable aid package for his district. Layard meanwhile admonished Everett to be patient on the topic of reforms: "I am constantly pressing the question . . . and have of an accord assurances that justice shall be done to the Christians. . . . I am afraid that you have little reason to be satisfied with the manner in which affairs are going on in your district . . . the Armenians must have patience but cannot expect the institution of a country to be reformed in a day and they ought to feel that England is doing all she can for them."[66] The ambassador's wait-and-see attitude complicated diplomatic dealings with the Ottoman government on the one hand and minorities on the other. When mass violence did occur in the provinces dispatches from British consular representatives, in comparison with those of other eyewitnesses including missionaries and American consuls, often downplayed their effect.[67] This approach echoed that of consuls serving in Bulgaria at the time of the massacres there when newspaper reporters and advocates for the Bulgarian cause accused consuls of telling the Disraeli government what they wanted to hear.[68] Despite a political climate at home that could predispose consuls against the plight of minority populations in the communities where they were stationed, aid work continued as an important part of diplomatic dealings in the Near East.

On the local level, consuls, like other agents in the civil and imperial service, enjoyed a great deal of informal power. During his tenure Everett helped get rid of unpopular local officials, argued successfully on behalf of Armenian prisoners, mediated disputes, and administered humanitarian relief. In 1882, he employed the assistance of the French, Persian, and Russian consuls to replace officials who he believed obstructed his work.[69] Everett also asked his superiors for help. "I have induced them to get rid of the Vali of Van," Dufferin wrote to Everett in 1884, hoping he had done "it in time" to help him to resolve some administrative problems in the village.[70] Everett's campaign to free Armenian prisoners accused of schemes against local administrators drew in the Earls Dufferin and Granville at the Foreign Office. They chose to appeal directly to the sultan rather than exert pressure through the embassy to secure the release of a limited number of prisoners. "Had we engaged in an ostentatious and open advocacy of these poor people's interests," wrote Dufferin to Granville, "I have little doubt but that the Sultan would have refused to pardon any of them."[71] This kind of behind the scenes pressure characterized the diplomacy on behalf of minority rights and often alienated as many people as it pleased.

Overt humanitarian aid work provided a more direct route to securing a foothold among local populations. As Layard put it to Everett when famine hit his district in 1880, "if assistance came in this district from the English people it would greatly raise our prestige here which is waning fast. It is not pleasant either to be appealed to save life and to be unable to do anything."[72] In the background, as ever, loomed the threat of the Russians providing aid to those "under their protection." Everett recruited American missionaries to serve on the relief committee, as Layard had assured him that "the Americans will help us" with the project. One missionary complained that American missionaries "had not been sufficiently recognized in the Bluebooks" for their work. He also accused Everett of misappropriating funds, reportedly calling him a "conscience-less scoundrel," which made him furious.[73]

Fear of competition and mutual distrust with aid workers led Everett to take more direct responsibility for humanitarian work. In 1881, famine relief and the distribution of aid consumed Everett's official duties. His decision to throw himself into famine relief certainly had much to do with this semi-official policy that saw aid as the way to win the hearts and minds of the local population. It also had a good deal to do with how he understood this community. The notion that some of the people he served "have a strong bearing to our church" must have helped Everett sustain the task he had before him.[74] This aid was increasingly managed by British consuls. When Lady Strangford set up a new appeal in 1881, she put collected donations and supplies in the hands of consuls in affected areas. Everett investigated claims of starvation in his district in late January and received immediate approval to draw money from the fund administered by Layard for relief. By early February, Everett started investigating the prices of goods himself after receiving letters from his district that "report a bad state of things." His diary from this period records his constant worry that local officials would cheat him. He insisted always on seeing the grain before purchasing it himself. Everett also kept a regular record of expenditures made in each district while listing the price of grain, livestock and household goods, and the items he handed out. "Gave distribution of flour to 4 poor families," he recorded on March 9, 1882.[75]

Balancing consular duties with humanitarian commitments eventually took their toll on his family life: "How I wish you would come back soon," his daughters implored in their letters whenever he went out on tour.[76] In 1885, Everett was badly wounded in a home invasion. Upon learning the Armenian Catholic identity of his assailant he came to believe that he had fallen victim to a murder attempt by a disgruntled constituent during the execution of his duties.[77]After the attack, Everett had little desire to continue on in his post. The now Colonel Everett returned to London, where he accepted a position as professor of military topography at the Staff College.[78] He also continued his work for the Foreign Office and eventually joined his old friend from the Russo-Turkish boundary commission, Sir John Ardagh, as his assistant when he became director of Military Intelligence in 1896. Everett must have felt at home employed "in the semi-diplomatic work" of the Intelligence Division. Here he used his "special skill in unraveling the complicated tangle of frontier questions."[79]

This "complicated tangle" along the frontier got worse in the coming years. After the Armenian massacres of the mid-1890s, popular outcry in Britain resulted in another expansion of the consul service along the border. The role of the military consul to "supervise the reforms" meant that he had a preventative as well as activist function. The extent of the massacres resulted in establishing vice consuls at Van, Sivas, Adana, Khurput, Mush, and Diarbekir, where the threat of more violence continued. This further bolstered the notion that consuls had a diplomatic function both to administer justice and to provide relief. So important had this role become that some consuls came to see their main function as intervening on behalf of minority communities in their districts.[80] This new wave of expansion in the Christian provinces broadened the humanitarian face of the diplomatic mission.

The "higher duties" imagined by Palmerston at mid-century would eventually translate into a diplomacy that encompassed more than treaty negotiations, commerce, and securing the rights of British citizens. As part of the "wider world" of politics "diplomatic culture" during the nineteenth century "had to be constantly renegotiated" in the midst of changing priorities.[81] In the case of Britain, these changes drew upon ethnographic understandings of imperial responsibility that made diplomacy compatible with humanitarian advocacy. This did not happen necessarily by design but rather in response to activism at home and to geopolitical crises that brought structural changes to the practice of diplomacy in the Ottoman Empire. Diplomacy in this case became both a matter of conscience and the protecting of imperial interests.

Refashioning the mission and structure of diplomacy in the Near East did not necessarily serve its larger military purpose. Little evidence exists that attempts to win the hearts and minds of the local population secured the border and staved off Russian influence in the region. The integration of humanitarianism into diplomatic practice, however, did change the way many understood foreign policy as a disinterested affair of state. The institutionalization of this hands-on, knowledge-based diplomacy came from the growth, professionalization, and increasingly national character of the service and made British presence more widely felt. As the next chapter shows, missionary philanthropists came to rely on this consular network and an expanded official presence to see their projects through while they drew on a set of beliefs that cast Ottoman Christians as deserving recipients of sympathy and material support.

4. Missionary Philanthropy

When Ann Mary Burgess found herself on a ship to Constantinople in 1888 she did not anticipate the role she would play in shaping humanitarian aid work in the Near East. Swept up in the evangelical fervor of late Victorian life, this Quaker missionary from Yorkshire found her calling among Eastern Christians. After learning Turkish and Armenian she set up a program that promoted religious education and industrial employment for the needy. Her mission at Constantinople lasted for over fifty years and proved emblematic of Victorian thinking about humanitarian service and moral responsibility abroad.

While officials tied humanitarianism to diplomacy, others like Burgess viewed obligations to Ottoman Christians through the lens of Gladstone's liberal-radical Nonconformity. This vision found its clearest articulation in missionary and philanthropic projects that aid workers started to ameliorate the suffering of Armenians and Assyrians. Missionary philanthropy had roots in the Victorian evangelical movement.[1] Interest in the Holy Land prompted the Church of England to initiate contact with Eastern Christians as early as the 1830s. The Archbishop of Canterbury, citing common historical and religious ground between the Anglican and Assyrian churches, started a mission in the late 1860s on the border between Turkey and Persia to serve the approximately 100,000 Assyrian Christians living there.[2] Nonconformists found an even wider audience in their ministry to Armenians, among whom they set up the most successful and widely known of these missions. An estimated two million Armenians lived mostly in the eastern parts of Asia Minor before their massacre and deportation during World War I, making them the largest Christian minority population in the Ottoman Empire.[3]

Systematic massacres among these populations during the late nineteenth century created the impetus for a network of secular and religious humanitarian aid projects. Britain's role in enforcing minority treaty obligations found a corollary in the work of aid organizations that attempted to mitigate the effects of increasing sectarian violence that targeted these communities. Although greater diplomatic presence throughout the Ottoman Empire eased the establishment of missionary-run aid institutions, the ambitions of policymakers held little interest for most philanthropists and missionaries, who drew up relief schemes based on Victorian notions of charity and the deserving poor.[4] Women missionaries in particular played an important role in charity and industrial work schemes that supported the work of these missions.[5] In the midst of growing geopolitical uncertainty, missionary philanthropy guided charity projects among a population that Britons already had come to know as not just Christian but an industrious and commercially minded people.

MISSIONARY PHILANTHROPY AND THE ARMENIANS

Missionary philanthropy captured the imagination of religious organizations and the public by casting mission work in a broader humanitarian role. The goal of the Church of England Assyrian Mission, in the words of one early missionary, was not "to interfere" but to "afford them such assistance as it may be able to do, consistently with its own principles, in order that they themselves may be able to improve their own condition."[6] Interest in aid programs targeted specifically at persecuted Christian minorities grew in the wake of the Bulgarian Atrocities agitation. This was particularly true in the case of women, whose plight captured the attention of feminists like Lady Henry Somerset during this same time. While Somerset engaged largely in fundraising at home to provide food, clothing, and shelter for the destitute, evangelicals took a more hands-on approach that fit in with Victorian gender norms. In 1890, the order of the Sisters of Bethany established a medical mission and a school for girls among Assyrians dedicated to the "training and education of the women to be the fit wives and mothers of the Assyrian race."[7] It also set up a school of embroidery and employed its charges in sewing and packing fruit to sustain the work of the mission.

Burgess's contemporaneous Friends' Mission stood out as the most successful of these projects. The Constantinople mission institutionalized relief work as an integral part of the missionary enterprise. Although not usually associated with evangelicalism, Quakers and Quaker women more specifically had a significant presence in these social reform schemes.[8] The rise of the evangelical movement within English Protestantism at mid-century offered new opportunities for a people best known for their religious introspection and Quietist philosophy.[9] Foreign relief work globalized the reach of the Friends' Mission. Their deserved reputation as business leaders lent an entrepreneurial character to the business of relief work.[10]

Providence, Burgess believed, ultimately led her to her post in Constantinople. She initially thought she might do *zenana* work among secluded women in India but her then employer, Priscilla Peckover, told her she must "wait for a more definite call."[11] This call came when she spotted an advertisement in the Quaker magazine, *The Friend*, by an Armenian Quaker doctor who had married an English woman advertising for a nurse to assist him with his Constantinople mission. After a brief training course in nursing at Banbury, Burgess began her work with Dr. Gabriel Dobrashian at the Friend's Medical Mission.[12]

As a Quaker woman growing up in Victorian England, work among Ottoman Armenians would have appealed to Burgess on a number of levels. First, debates surrounding the Eastern Question and its relation to the status of Christian minorities in the Near East had shaped her generation's perception of the Ottoman Empire. For High Churchman such as Gladstone the Armenians' Orthodox faith linked them to an authentic Christian past.[13] Their early adoption of Christianity as a national religion and highly developed ancient culture furthered this connection.[14] As Gladstone posited, "To serve Armenia is to serve civilization."[15] Second, evangelical service had begun to play an important part in Quakerism's attempt to increase declining membership.[16] Finally, Quakers, like other religious denominations, had started to recruit single women as teachers in foreign missions with links to Britain and the Empire.[17]

Two events shaped the of direction Burgess's work after she arrived in Constantinople: the earthquake of 1894 and the massacres of the mid-1890s. Requests for aid by those widowed and orphaned after the earthquake prompted the mission to open twelve beds for this purpose. Two years later, the prolonged persecution of the minority Armenian population in Anatolia left hundreds of thousands dead.[18] W. C. Braithwaite, then secretary of the Medical Mission, appealed to Friends to provide the £700 a year needed to keep the medical mission going and "continue this body and soul saving work."[19] The massacres targeted the male population and forced the leader of the medical mission, Dr. Dobrashian, to flee to England with his family. Burgess along with two other English women "stayed at the mission and undertook relief work among the suffering women and children, as bread-winners had become very scarce."[20]

The combination of a lack of qualified doctors and Burgess's own limited medical training eventually forced her to close the hospital. Medical missionary work often provided a first point of entry into the profession but a lack of training and institutional support for female doctors led many to abandon medicine in favor of other humanitarian enterprises.[21] Burgess developed organizational, business, and fundraising skills to connect the mission with other aid workers in the region. This network of philanthropic and religious relief work spanned from Constantinople to the villages of eastern Anatolia to Cambridge, where the mission was headquartered. Here a team of Quakers that included W. C. Braithwaite, J. Hingston Fox, and William Henry Crook coordinated efforts in England for Burgess's work in the Ottoman Empire. Funding the orphanage and building the program of the mission became a top priority, though securing the necessary funding proved difficult at best.

The search for resources led Burgess to cultivate ties with secular philanthropic organizations and government institutions. The London-based branch of the International Organization of the Friends of Armenia set up operations in eastern Anatolia in 1897. Initially started to assist victims of the massacres, it soon developed its own network of patrons that Burgess would use to support her work in Constantinople. Women made up twelve of the fifteen members of the executive committee; they also held the majority of the forty-five positions on the general committee. The organization represented a who's who of nineteenth-century philanthropists and was run by Lady Frederick Cavendish with contributions and organizational support coming from women including the Cadbury sisters, Lady Henry Somerset, and a host of titled ladies. Twenty-seven branches of the British Women's Temperance Association also donated to the general fund.[22]

These women recognized Burgess as an important resource for their own work. Similarly, Burgess used the nascent organization's fundraising networks to lend publicity and raise much-needed capital for Armenian widows and orphans.[23] Burgess also employed her connections with the British consular staff at Constantinople, including Andrew Ryan and Robert Graves, to further her cause, attending embassy dinners in dresses made with material sent to her by supporters in England who recognized the value of cultivating political connections.[24]

By the late nineteenth century, Burgess emerged at the center of a network that joined missionary and philanthropic work. This shift from relying on religious institutional support to forging connections with secular humanitarian organizations and government institutions emphasized what Andrew Porter has called the "humanitarian character of Christian service."[25] Focus on humanitarian relief work over religious conversions shaped the evolution of the two related goals of the mission. As one supporter observed, Burgess wanted to "strengthen and revivify the spiritual life of the Armenian Church" rather than convert her subjects to the Quaker faith.[26] She also supported education to promote minority demands for civil and administrative reform.

The crisis years of the mid-1890s necessitated what amounted to a mixing of religion and politics. In the aftermath of the 1896 massacres, W. C. Braithwaite described how the mission bridged the roles of political advocate and spiritual guide, helping "prisoners in obtaining their release, in visiting and caring for the sick, in clothing the naked and in feeding the starving ones around us." As Braithwaite concluded, "It has been our blessed privilege, also as of old, to see that the poor have the gospel preached unto them."[27] Evangelicalism in this way served a larger humanitarian purpose. This also worked in the reverse. Secular organizations like the Friends of Armenia had little trouble supporting the attempt to revivify the Eastern Orthodox Church, recognizing the important role that religious organizations, both Protestant and Orthodox, played in providing aid to massacre victims and maintaining community ties.[28] Rather than understanding conversion itself as the goal, Burgess put evangelical activism in the service of humanitarian relief and political advocacy.

PHILANTHROPIC NETWORKS

The Armenian massacres made Burgess anxious to find a way to protect and offer long term financial support for the survivors, primarily women and children. As she recalled, "In the first weeks that followed this political out-burst of hate and fury, we could do little else besides giving out bread to women and children and listening to tales of woe. But seeing the distress would be of long duration, and that in a day not far distant relief funds would cease, and our power to relieve distress would end too, we opened our Industrial work in the way of Needlework, Knitting and Oriental Embroideries. We soon discovered that work for the people was the best healer, as well as a means of [earning a] living."[29] "Industrial work" generated funds through the production and sale of artisan crafts made by the needy. After the massacres Burgess completely transformed the buildings of the medical mission into a multifunction campus. She retained a resident English builder at a cost of £1,940 to create a "Meeting Hall, two Schoolrooms, Workrooms for the Industrial Department, Dining and Sitting Rooms for the Workers in the Home, Bedrooms for Orphans and Workers, a Washhouse and Laundry, Office, and improved sanitary arrangements."[30] The mission now had three main functions: industrial, educational and religious. Money generated from industrial work primarily funded the educational work of the mission though it occasionally supplemented capital improvements to mission facilities. Religious functions were not funded by industrial work, in accordance with Burgess's philosophy of keeping these elements separate.

Burgess's network of philanthropists, businessmen, government consuls, and workers helped her to realize her vision of a self-sustaining mission project. Her large number of contacts and donors included the philanthropists who ordered the goods from Burgess's factory, the middlemen who took them to Britain, and the people who sold the work to supporters in Britain, America, Europe, and locally in Constantinople.[31] Andrew Ryan, a member of the Levant Consular Service at the embassy, helped her get goods through customs while the Friends of Armenia and Friends' Armenian Mission donated money and helped sell goods abroad.[32] At the mission itself, Burgess employed a small but dedicated circle of English and "native" women, as she called them, to help her to run and sustain the day-to-day operations of the mission.[33]

Mission work, as Burgess herself recognized, began to look like a corporation, stretching well beyond Constantinople. "I shall grow into a merchant and missionary in one before I close my career," Burgess reflected. She had "a college trained gentleman of great business experience doing type writing for me and accounts and custom house work and taking journey to buy raw materials from Albania and parts of Greece."[34] The American Bible house in Constantinople served as a storage facility where Burgess had goods held and then shipped to customers.[35] From there, she sent goods to England and America for sale through contacts made through Friends that included the Peckovers and others whom she cultivated while on leave in England. In its 1899 annual report, the Friends of Armenia reported that sales of Burgess's factory goods were doing well in Germany.[36] The most desirable items, artisan rugs, sold for £100 apiece. Even after World War I, when difficulty producing and shipping goods would have strained any business venture, Burgess and her 400 Armenian factory workers were producing and selling over £4,000 worth of "silk and wool rugs and embroidery of the highest quality" to customers in England and America annually.[37]

This industrial work scheme represented what I call self-help philanthropy that cast Ottoman Christians in the role of the deserving poor. Burgess's network of artisanal workers, middlemen and -women, and customers did not write checks or make donations to feed and clothe the destitute but rather expected a material return on their investment in the form of consumer goods. "We were glad to hear that the chair backs gave satisfaction," Burgess wrote in 1903 to Algerina Peckover, the sister of her former employer in Wisbech and a longtime supporter of the mission. "We were pleased with them too. We will send you the remainder of your order next week if possible or the week after. With warm greeting to your household. I love to think of you all!"[38] Peckover served as an able middlewoman in the coming years, facilitating sales between Burgess and her customers in Britain.

The supporters Burgess gathered around her physically at the mission site and virtually through her contacts in England defined humanitarianism in relation to production and consumption. This use of the marketplace to support philanthropic and religious enterprises was certainly not unique to relief work in the Ottoman Empire. The profession of philanthropic work for women that relied on selling goods to raise money, in particular, had deep roots in Victorian culture. As Brian Harrison has argued, "The link between Victorian entrepreneurship, humanitarianism, and philanthropy was close." Charity bazaars often run by female members of church and secular organizations would sell goods to raise money for causes that included education, poverty relief, and supporting foreign missions.[39] Using commerce to benefit society allowed Victorians to reconcile what some historians have considered a deeply ambivalent relationship to the marketplace.[40] The fear that capitalism was undoing the moral fiber of society by enriching the few at the expense of the many led to a doctrine of self-reliance that cast the needy into categories of deserving and undeserving based on their willingness to help themselves through work and discipline.

Schemes like those created so many thousands of miles away from the metropolis by Burgess and the Friends of Armenia connected foreign aid work with the marketplace. Such notions of self-help philanthropy guided the business of relief work among a needy Armenian population with whom Britons had cultivated an imagined kinship. By the early 1900s, Burgess had created a thriving industry that supported over 700 women workers and generated sales between £8,000 and £10,000 a year.[41] She decided first to manufacture toys and received £25 from the British consul in Constantinople for startup costs.[42] "An oriental swing-bed called a 'Salanjack' sold well at first but only proved to have novelty appeal," reported one source.[43] Likewise, knitting stockings proved unsustainable due to the high cost of materials, which made them uncompetitive in the local market.

High-end embroidery, by contrast, had a niche appeal from both a producer and a consumer standpoint. The Near East had long been associated in the minds of British consumers with luxury items such as finished goods including silks and rugs. Consumers in Constantinople and England valued these products as an authentic expression of a regional art form that used quality materials associated with the Near East. Armenian women had engaged in artisanal craftwork for centuries, making it a natural fit for Burgess's project.[44] Ironically, since each region had its own style of embroidery, the women and girls at the factory had to be taught specialized patterns "of fine quality . . . taken from old Turkish, Persian and Armenian needlework" that Burgess believed would most appeal to British consumers.[45] Miss Maud Binns, one of Burgess's English helpers, was responsible for teaching "the older girls one of the Eastern arts, an embroidery called 'Heesab.'"[46] Rug making at the mission followed similar lines.

This attempt to revive ancient patterns no longer produced by Armenian artisans lent the work done in her factory an air of authenticity and rare value. Customers purchased what they believed represented genuine expressions of the art of an ancient people threatened with extinction by a despotic state. In addition, these objects, produced during the height of the Arts and Crafts movement in Britain, had the advantage of seeming disconnected from mass production and thus the perceived evils of urban factory life.[47] The shops that displayed these goods carefully cultivated these consumer desires. "It is no unskilled task this of choosing goods to win the approval of some unknown well wisher," declared the chair of the Friends of Armenia Industrial committee. "Quickly drawers are opened, bales untied—for this one only native materials must be sent that one likes drawn thread on Irish linen; another always wants rich colours typical of Armenia's ancient skill."[48] Of course, the reality of the origins of these consumer products was much more complicated. Not only did the products fail to accurately represent contemporary Anatolian craftsmanship, to produce these goods Burgess set up industrial workrooms in the mission. In the case of rug making, she built an actual factory with looms, regular hours, and an army of

Figure 18. Ann Mary Burgess overseeing Armenian female workers at her factory. Courtesy of the Library of the Religious Society of Friends in Britain, Temp MSS 387/5/9.

workers who produced these goods under the watchful eye of Burgess and her staff (see figure 18).

Self-help philanthropy sometimes unconsciously failed to provide for the immediate wants of those it purported to serve. Burgess's description of the needs of her mission to patrons in the pages of *The Friend of Armenia,* a newspaper published by the organization of the same name, reveals how business and humanitarian interests could work at cross-purposes. "I hope someday the flannelette, stockings, cotton and print, if possible, for overalls for children and underwear for women may come out to us," Burgess appealed to potential donors. "Some of the poor people even suffer disease from want of clean underwear."[49] She then went on to describe the items being made from the fabric on hand for sale: Slipper tops from old materials and toy rabbits, dolls, and donkeys from cotton remnants. Every day Burgess made decisions about whether to use materials to keep women busy working in the factory or for making items that women themselves needed. In this case, she asked donors in England to provide clothing for workers so that materials available on the premises could provide work for potentially idle hands.

The toys, embroideries, and rugs produced by workers found their way to customers through Burgess's business and philanthropic networks in the Ottoman Empire, Britain, and abroad. There were two work depots in Constantinople, one in the old city Stamboul at Mission House and the other in the new city Pera, in the European side of the city. Depots in the North and South of England also sold these products, and the Friends of Armenia distributed them in London, Ireland, and Scotland. However, according to Burgess her most important salespeople came from the "Drawingroom Sales made by the many kind ladies in England who make a display of the work, and invite their friends to come and buy."[50]

Burgess's success inspired others. The mission itself grew into what one supporter called "one of the largest and most successful Industrial Mission centres in the world."[51] The Friends of Armenia came to use this method to fund their work in the villages of eastern Anatolia.[52] Another such factory linked to the mission school was set up in connection with The Church of England's Assyrian Mission in 1902. Management problems meant that the mission factory only lasted for a few years selling carpets made by Assyrian girls to American and British consumers. American missionaries started small-scale industrial work schemes during this time as well.[53] Between 1897 and 1914 the Friends of Armenia started over a dozen industrial work centers in Anatolian villages and set up a permanent shop called "Armenian Industries" to sell these goods at their headquarters at 47 Victoria Street, Westminster.

These organizations shared a common sense of purpose. The Friends of Armenia cast the "Aims of the Society" this way: "With the temporary cessation of widespread massacre the needs of Armenia have changed. What is wanted today is not prompt succor for the wounded and the starving, but such continuous and systematic relief as shall make all who can work self-supporting, and provide for the thousands of helpless orphans. The Friends of Armenia keep this point steadily in view. By supporting industrial centers in many parts of Armenia, and opening a central depot in London for the sale of work, they enable many women who have lost every male relative to provide for themselves and even for their children."[54] In 1909 *The Friend of Armenia* published a manifesto and list of supporters that included British and American missionary organizations.[55] As one appeal for funds asked, "Perhaps you will know of people who will be willing to invest money in such a business (not donate it) for a term of years without interest. If we could get a little capital together for such a purpose, I feel sure we could make profitable use of it for the orphan girls."[56]

IMPERIAL PATRONAGE

The orphans and widows who received aid and worked in the factories and workrooms came increasingly to rely on these institutions for patronage in a world where few other opportunities existed. In some ways, the structure of these industrial work schemes for Armenian women workers and their British women managers mimicked those undertaken by philanthropic-minded Victorian women in England.[57] What most distinguished these schemes from those in England, of course, was that in the Ottoman Empire humanitarianism operated in the midst of social and political instability.

Local women looked to aid workers to fulfill their material needs by providing employment, patronage, and, in times of crisis, physical protection. Although little evidence exists regarding what adult Armenian women factory workers thought of industrial work, both Burgess and the Friends of Armenia recorded the stories of children for the benefit of patrons. The story of the orphan girl Sara Crecorian illustrates how gender and patronage shaped the business of relief work. Crecorian attended the American Mount Holyoke school in the interior village of Bitlis in the early 1900s.[58] Needing funds to continue her education, she contacted the Friends of Armenia for help. This organization, closely associated with Burgess's own enterprise, found in Algerina Peckover a willing patron. In a letter to her "beloved Benefactor" the sixteen-year-old Crecorian declared that Peckover had "fulfilled a parents' obligation for me, an unknown and needy one, bearing in your breast a heart of fatherly tenderness and love for an orphan." Her desire to complete her studies led Crecorian to continue, "I earnestly entreat you not to forget me."[59]

Missionary philanthropists did not limit their advocacy work to girls. Religious education rather than industrial work, however, defined the mission's service to boys. Here, too, the notion of a family structure with Burgess and her single female workers at the shared head pervaded: "Some of our scholars in the Sunday School, who have been attending ever since we began ten years ago, are now grown up. . . . We call these boys, or rather young men 'ours' and they consider they belong to us."[60] Rituals at the mission provided the opportunity to cement these ties in sometimes strange and proprietary ways. During a pageant where children were reenacting the Christmas story, Burgess remarked: "I have been in a hurry to make angels of our school girls" (see figure 19).

This surrogate family structure cast single women aid workers in the role of both mother and father to orphans. Girls like Sara Crecorian

Figure 19. Burgess's orphan "angels" performing at a Christmas pageant. Courtesy of the Library of the Religious Society of Friends in Britain, Temp MSS 387/5/16.

adopted European names and forged new "family ties" to their patrons. For children who had parents still living, usually a widowed mother, work provided for family needs. Widows worked for women missionaries at the mission to provide subsistence for their children. They also sought patrons to support an education that would further a child's status in the mission community. The boys who "belonged" to the mission after attending Sunday School for ten years thus came to rely on the support of their English "mothers and fathers" to offer them work, status, and bread as a sort of birthright.

Similar stories published in the *Friend of Armenia* from those living under this imagined imperial family provide a glimpse of what recipients might have thought of these aid efforts and how they used this assistance. The column "Letters Received from Orphans" connected orphans with their "adoptive mothers/fathers." "Dear Little Mother," started one letter from a child called Vartanoosh living in Van, "We were very hungry, we had no clothing upon us, we had not shoes. We had not fathers to give them to us. God said you to be father and mother for us, and you gave food and clothing to cover our nakedness. . . . We thank you for the orphan house you opened for us."[61] Orphans, while having little power to control how their stories were used, learned quickly how grateful declarations could evoke empathy and keep donations flowing.[62]

Patronage of the kind experienced by Crecorian and others forged new dependent relationships.[63] The *Friend of Armenia* connected orphans with patrons and often included "before and after" photos of orphans helped by aid. For orphans like Vartanoosh, donors provided the necessities like food and clothing but some expected more. Education proved a central motivator. "My Dear Benefactor," started another letter, "I was an orphan and miserable boy. . . . Now I am very happy and am studying in the school Armenian, the Bible and Arithmetic."[64] Some orphans used education to build status and gain entry into European society. "I personally was left an orphan by the massacres of 1895 and was cared for in a missionary orphanage and thus received High School and College education," wrote K. K. Khayiguian from Marseilles, where he served as president of the Armenian Evangelical Churches in France.[65]

"Adoption" for orphans always meant work. The orphanage at Kharpoot in 1900, for example, reported training orphans "in industrial work" to make them "self-supporting." Those with disabilities also found employment; a picture of one orphan, "Blind Mary," appeared in the pages of the *Friend of Armenia* working at a transcribing machine in European-style dress.[66] She had attended the School for the Blind in Urfa. A similar institution existed in Adana. This work, while intended to benefit the child worker in the long term, also brought in income for the institution. "The Reward of Labour" described work for orphan boys that included shoemaking, ironwork, tailoring, and cabinetmaking. "The shop for native shoes is carried on largely for the purpose of teaching our boys the value of time and of having something as an extra trade whereby they could support themselves even if they are not strong physically. This being light work, our smallest boys are learning it, but we believe this in a short time will bring in a little gain."[67] The institution thus used child labor to "reward" the institution with revenue and the child with a skill. No mention of child workers being paid wages appears in the archive.

These relationships clearly opened up the possibility of exploitation. Mission work invited single women like Peckover and Burgess to take a maternalist role in their interaction with the women and children that they served.[68] Evidence suggests that the women and children who worked in the Burgess's factory and those set up by the Friends of Armenia served voluntarily and entered the "family" willingly. However, aid workers' status as privileged British women who had the backing of diplomatic authorities and philanthropic organizations gave women like Burgess an unusual power over their charges. Factory work most often was done in exchange for bread or for educational opportunities. To what extent this labor became a precondition for support is not entirely clear. The Armenian women and children who worked at the handlooms and in the embroidery studio were introduced to a Protestant religious ethic that linked hard work with piousness. For many who survived the earthquake and massacres of the 1890s, their very lives depended on embracing this model.

Authority over Burgess's mission family was strengthened during times of crisis. During the massacres, she refused to take shelter with the British consul, choosing instead to stay at the mission, where she put up a makeshift Union Jack in plain sight. When questioned by Turkish officers on whose authority she acted, she asserted that the flag was there by the command of the British Embassy and that it served as a warning against attacking the Armenians taking refugee at the mission. Several days later, Burgess went accompanied by the British ambassador's dragoman to "every part of the city where Armenians had been slain, and to collect reliable information and statistics" for the British government.[69]

The action of Burgess and her staff during this episode brought her increasing respect from the Armenian community in Constantinople and her supporters at home. It also brought her fledgling mission much needed money. When Sir James Reckitt heard that a packet of his Reckitt's Blue dye had been used to fashion the flag that hung over the mission during the crisis, he was reported to have been so pleased that he "sent the Mission a check for 100 pounds with the message that he believed the product of his firm had never done such a good service before."[70]

GEOPOLITICS AND MISSIONARY PHILANTHROPY

On the occasion of Burgess's "semi-jubilee" at the mission in 1914, a celebration was held and attended by business, political, and religious leaders of the Armenian and expatriate British community. Sir Louis Mallet, the British ambassador, heartily expressed his congratulations and good wishes. A long list of Armenian community leaders further praised what they called Burgess's important work on behalf of Armenians. Even the Armenian patriarch, the head of the Orthodox Church who had actively opposed the efforts of evangelical Protestants to convert Armenians, embraced Burgess's humanitarian efforts. In a prepared statement read by one of his representative, he expressed "the gratitude of his people to Miss Burgess" and prayed for "God's blessing on all of her work."[71]

Although those attending the festivities had no way of knowing it, two new crises were on the horizon: World War I and the 1915 Armenian

Genocide that killed approximately one million Ottoman Armenians and displaced three-quarter million others.[72] Running such a business in a foreign country that served a persecuted minority in peacetime proved difficult at best. The crisis of world war made it almost impossible. By the time World War I broke out in 1914, Burgess had maintained her industrial work scheme for almost twenty years. Her influence in official British government circles led to a reversal of an Ottoman governmental order to leave the country in November 1915. Turkish authorities, however, had commandeered the school for army barracks, leaving Burgess to take refuge in the nearby British Hospital. After the army took over the hospital Burgess moved back to the orphanage, a part of the Friends campus left unoccupied by the Turkish troops.[73]

Her experiences in the wake of the 1896 massacres prepared her, in part, to deal with the coming war. Her status as an Englishwoman and her work on behalf of the Armenians made Burgess particularly mindful of not attracting the attention of Ottoman authorities. At first, she worked with the Red Cross to sustain the day-to-day activities of the mission. When the Armenian Genocide commenced in 1915, however, Burgess again put her factories to work to ameliorate what she called the "sorrow surging round": "In this time of sorrow and poverty, our work has been a great boon. Of course the women can only have enough work given them to cover the cost of their bread, seeing the numbers are so high. At this moment about 400 pounds is required to fill up the deficit of accounts. Of course there is a great stack of work on hand—if ever a way opens for disposing it, even at low prices, we shall be able to go on after the war closes if that happy event ever reaches us."[74] The twin problems of serving those she defined as truly needy (work was given to women literally to earn bread) and selling the goods to her patrons back home led Burgess to rely even more heavily on her network of supporters and unflagging belief in her mission.

As conditions worsened on the ground, Burges did what she could. "Raw materials are so scarce and expensive," one of her American helpers, Hetty Rowe, explained in a letter to a patron. "[Burgess] has even ripped the calico covers off of her mattresses to use. Spool cotton was sold at twenty-five cents and silks for embroidery had greatly increased in value. Fortunately, Miss Burgess had a lot of material on hand. As soon as the work is completed she stores it in large packing boxes at the Bible House."[75] Rather than rely on donations Burgess used all available resources to continue to fill orders for Anatolian-made goods still coming in despite the war. Rowe described the appeal of self-help philanthropy in the midst of war and genocide in almost social Darwinian terms: "Of the various kinds of work among the people, the industrial appealed strongly to me. And when the war broke out, it was more needed than ever before. Gifts of money direct seemed like pampering the people while work gave them new hope and made them more self-respecting."[76] The idea that refugees fleeing persecution were better off working in a factory than receiving direct aid reveals how these twin crises made business, religious, and humanitarian interests almost indistinguishable.

Managing political crisis through humanitarian intervention gave missionary philanthropy a heightened sense of purpose. Burgess clearly took pride in her skills as a businesswoman while embracing her role as humanitarian aid worker. A letter written in 1922 to Algerina Peckover provides a look into how Burgess had come to combine these roles at the mission:

> The sad thing is Armenians in Asia Minor are still suffering worse things than death. We have had a whole week of prayer meetings with a great crowd every night. We are still having Industrial sales we sold £130 worth of toys this last two days. We have a room full of widows and orphans who make dolls, donkeys, elephants, rabbits, etc. all day long. . . . We also have a rug factory and then add on all the religious exercises. Sunday school, bible classes, mission meetings, social gatherings, evening classes and you will see we are not likely to rest and I do not think we shall wear out for some time yet if when we do I trust the work will go on.[77]

Empathy, prayer meetings, and industrial work combined work at a rug factory and in the workrooms with "religious exercises."[78] This business of relief work made it possible for the humanitarian and religious work to "go on."

Burgess's reputation as an honest broker and member of the community allowed her to stay on throughout the crisis and play her part as a humanitarian aid worker along with the Friends of Armenia. The expatriate community living in Constantinople continued to show their support, while well-placed Armenian middlemen made sure industrial goods reached customers in America, Britain, and Europe. In December 1922, in the wake of the burning of Smyrna by Turkish nationalists that eliminated the remaining Armenian, Greek, and Assyrian populations from Anatolia, Burgess moved her operations to Greece with the help of a £500 check from the Friends of Armenia. Taking her factory furniture and industrial goods along with 130 workers, she set up shop on the island of Corfu in "an old Fortress built by the British."[79] There the

Friends' Mission in Constantinople transformed into a refugee camp in Greece where the art of rug making served Ottoman Christians displaced by world war and genocide.

Burgess's story reveals a world of women's philanthropic aid work that joined currents of Victorian evangelicalism, philanthropy, and humanitarian intervention in the Near East. It did so by making relief work an exchange between patron and client. This approach proved influential up through World War I. When the Lord Mayor's Fund set its sights on assisting genocide survivors in 1917 a leader of the Friends of Armenia offered the following advice: "I am certain that the most useful form [aid] can take is the provision of employment especially to women who have no men to aid in their support. Industrial relief has the great advantage over other methods that it does not tend to demoralize the recipients and make them dependent on charity, an effect which the giving of money inevitable produces."[80]

The success of this philosophy, in the case of Burgess's mission in Constantinople, hinged on the ability to fuse missionary religious interests with secular humanitarian and philanthropic concerns. Other aid organizations, including the Friends of Armenia and the Lord Mayor's Fund, would rely on this same formulation. From a missionary outpost in Constantinople, Burgess and her circle engaged Britons in economic, humanitarian, and religious relationships in a region increasingly important to imperial politics. Ultimately the networks created by Burgess during her decades of industrial and religious work tied together a community of unlikely allies that included aid workers, missionaries, diplomats, orphans, widows, and commercial and philanthropic patrons.

Missionary philanthropy like humanitarian diplomacy necessarily conformed to geopolitical realities. The rise of relief work as a business in the service of those who suffered in the late nineteenth century contributed to a sense of proprietorship over the Near East by tying aid workers to their charges in a dependent web of relationships. In this way, humanitarianism developed as a moral ideal driven forward by an evangelical religious imperative and sense of imperial obligation. The challenges faced by Burgess would prove emblematic of the wider difficulties that World War I would pose for those acting on behalf of this Victorian humanitarian ethos during the Armenian Genocide.

5. The Armenian Genocide and the Great War

Allied forces landed at Gallipoli on April 25, 1915. The night before the invasion, the Ottoman government rounded up an estimated 250 Armenian intellectuals and religious leaders in Constantinople on unnamed charges, marking the beginning of the Armenian Genocide.[1] The British soon came to experience World War I on the Eastern Front as a series of military and humanitarian disasters from Gallipoli to the villages of eastern Anatolia. For First Lord of the Admiralty Winston Churchill, defeating the Central Powers' newest ally would check German power in the East. Others cast the war in more ideological terms, raising the possibility that an Allied victory would liberate minority populations. As J. Ellis Barker put it in the *Fortnightly Review*, "The present war is a war against German militarism and a war of liberation. If it should end in a victory of the Allied Powers it should not merely lead to the freeing of the subjected and oppressed . . . in Europe, but also to the freeing of the nationalities who live under Turkish tyranny in Asia."[2]

The unprecedented devastation of the Armenian population along with the Assyrians and Greeks in the Ottoman Empire shaped British perceptions of the Eastern Front throughout the war.[3] Fighting the Ottoman Empire as a member of the Central Powers meant, in part, the liberation of this group.[4] Such concerns solicited a significant political and humanitarian response. By November 1915, widespread reporting of continued civilian massacres led one commentator to conclude: "Avowedly one of the chief objects of the present war is to advantage small nationalities. In this war Armenians are playing no unimportant part."[5]

At end of the war, a more uneven narrative of genocide and "small nationalities" emerged. Massive civilian displacements, massacres, and deportations that occurred under the cover of war revealed how completely humanitarian diplomacy had failed. The inability to stop the Armenian massacres and mitigate the suffering of victims left many disillusioned about Britain's assumed role as a defender of minority interests, which dated back to the Crimean War. Here on the battlefronts and killing fields of the Ottoman Empire, the moral certainty that had guided British foreign policy in the Near East came unhinged.

Historians have argued that Great Power politics had long worked at cross-purposes with humanitarianism in the Ottoman Empire.[6] Britain deployed the image of Armenia as a "victim nation" to provide just cause for the war in the East in the hopes of drawing its American ally into the conflict.[7] This chapter offers a less determinist portrayal of a humanitarian movement that often intersected with and informed the world of high politics during and immediately following World War I. Stories from relief workers, government officials, war crimes tribunals, and the cinema present a view of this tragedy from above and below, revealing the humane and sometimes cynical responses of Britons and their government to war and genocide in the Near East.

BRITAIN'S ARMENIANS

The shocking scale and scope of the Genocide, graphically detailed in the press and by eyewitnesses, raised the stakes for those who understood Britain's obligations to minority Christians as part of a larger humanitarian crusade. Soon after the killings began, organizations stepped up advocacy work, holding public meetings and disseminating a host of publications that made the Armenian cause Britain's cause. These groups had roots in Victorian political culture that had grown up around W. E. Gladstone's untiring support of humanitarian causes that was later taken up by his son. Religious and secular advocacy organizations such as the Eastern Question Association, the Archbishop of Canterbury's Assyrian Mission, and the Anglo-Armenian Association helped sustain this interest.

Advocacy work on behalf of minority Christians merged humanitarian and geopolitical concerns. Activists argued that that war urgently required that Britain honor its diplomatic obligations under the 1878 Treaty of Berlin to better secure ties with Near Eastern Christians and reward those who sided with the Allied cause. James Bryce's Anglo-Armenian Association, for example, cast Armenians as loyal allies in the fight against despotism. The founding of the British Armenia Committee at the end of the Balkan Wars of 1912–13 by group of influential politicians and private citizens with "first-hand knowledge of Armenia and the East" made the case that supporting Armenians bolstered British interests.[8] The committee came out of the 1903 Balkan Committee, which lobbied on behalf of Ottoman minorities. Buoyed by success in negotiating settlements in favor of Balkan Christians after the wars, members turned their attention to Armenia. The chair of the newly fashioned committee, Aneurin Williams, gathered around him members of Parliament, opinion makers, and Armenian representatives in order to pressure the British government to enforce the protections for minorities outlined at Berlin. Williams, a Liberal MP, had a "deeply religious" sensibility and offered a "devoted, almost impassioned service" to the cause of minority protection during his more than ten years of service.[9]

Relief organizations built on the momentum of parliamentary advocacy. Inaugurated in December 1914 in Kensington where "tea and musical entertainment closed the afternoon," the Armenian Red Cross soon attracted a small but loyal base of support by giving lantern lectures and holding other events in private homes.[10] Viscountess Bryce served as president alongside almost two dozen vice presidents that included well-known advocates for Armenia such as the viscountess's husband, James Bryce, Lady Henry Somerset, Lady Frederick Cavendish, MPs Noel Buxton and Aneurin Williams, and the journalist Edwin Pears. The crisis of the massacres brought increased focus to the organization. By summer 1915, the organization began work in two main areas: refugee relief and aid to Armenian volunteers helping the Allied cause.

The Armenian Red Cross made relief work on the Eastern Front patriotic by uniting the humanitarian and military causes. As one appeal put it: "The Armenian Red Cross and Refugee Fund was organized . . . to stem in some degree the torrent of misery caused by the war among the Armenian population of Turkey and Persia . . . and to provide medical necessaries for the Armenian volunteers fighting on behalf of Russia."[11] This heightened sense of purpose cast the Eastern Question as a wartime cause: "Those who are acquainted with Near Eastern affairs know that the horrible massacres, ill-treatment and deportation of the helpless Armenian population of Turkey which occurred in 1915 were brought about indirectly at any rate by the jealousies and intrigues of the Great Powers, Great Britain being prominent among these. This being the case, surely the very least Great Britain can do is to try and make amends to the innocent survivors, who after enduring persecution from their birth, have, from no fault of their own, lost their homes, together with all that made life worth living."[12] In the first year more than 1,800 subscribers raised thousands of pounds for relief work, which the organization sent to the British consul general in Moscow, who then forwarded aid to the head of the Armenian Orthodox Church, the Catholicos at Etchmiadzin, and the mayor of the Armenian-dominated city of Tiflis for dispersal by local relief committees.[13]

Word of the fund got out through newspaper advertisements, sermons, and public lectures. The organization took photos of refugees "being fed by members of the Moscow committee" in order to "appeal to British hearts and consciences more than any words can do."[14] It sent supplies to affected areas via allied transport ships located on the Russo-Turkish border, where most of the refugees had settled. Items included drugs, bandages, and surgical dressings sent via Sweden and warm garments carried free of charge on Russian steamships. Parcels came from "British sympathizers" in places as far away as New Zealand and Japan. British schools, colleges, and working parties also donated materials. Children wrote to say that they "forego coveted treats or prizes that they might send the equivalent for feeding refugees." One woman donor offered to adopt a baby but "had to be told that the difficulties of importing one from the Caucasus were insuperable."[15] Another requested that an "Armenian General" be sent as a companion for a devoted Armenian nurse. Armenian refugees from Belgium came to the organization seeking work, while others wrote asking if the organization could help them find lost relatives.

Emily Robinson stood as the steady force behind the Armenian Red Cross. Her convictions belonged to a Gladstonian age that understood the Eastern Question as a moral and religious imperative. Her father ran the *Daily News* and had sent out correspondents to cover the Armenian massacres during the mid-1890s.[16] Before serving as the secretary for the Armenian Red Cross she published "The Truth About Armenia" in 1913 and later, during the war, published two other short pamphlets, "Armenia and the Armenians" (1916) and "The Armenians" (1918). The latter, priced at threepence, called Armenia "the last rampart of Christendom in the East" and argued that Britain and her allies were fighting the war to secure a "lasting peace" guaranteed "not by a Treaty of Paris, London, Vienna or Berlin but by a consensus of opinion in civilized Europe and the United States." For Robinson and those who advocated the Armenian cause, the aftermath of the war would forge a "new Armenia" as "the centre of civilization and culture in the Near East."

The dual military and humanitarian crises on the Eastern Front required a shift in how advocates represented the cause of Christian minorities. Robinson's brand of nineteenth-century liberal humanitarianism would only go so far with a new generation confronted with the brutality of Total War. The Armenian Red Cross forged moral and strategic arguments on behalf of Christian minorities in a new key. The first strategy equated the Armenian cause with Belgium.[17] "Armenians are our allies as much as the Belgians," one early appeal argued. "The only difference being that whereas Belgium has suffered for seven months, Armenia has suffered for five centuries." The widely reported rape, murder and kidnapping of Armenian girls during the Genocide made the parallel to Belgium more powerful.[18] Ottoman atrocities evoked the outrage over the "Rape of Belgium" that had helped rally the British to war in 1914.[19]

The story of thousands of kidnapped girls further linked the brutality of Germany with that of its ally, the Ottoman Empire. Humanitarian work on behalf of these girls led to the setting up of a special commission after the war by the League of Nations to reunite families torn apart by mass deportations.[20] As Robinson wrote in a letter to the Archbishop of Canterbury about this campaign: "I have been working for the liberation of the Christian women and children forcibly detained since 1915 in Turkish harems. . . . White slave traffic is a crime here and is punished as such in European countries. It seems it has only to be conducted on a wholesale scale and by Turks to be quite permissible."[21] Echoing W. T. Stead's earlier campaign against the white slave trade, Robinson deployed harem slavery as a trope to argue that Britain had a moral obligation to protect and defend women and children in the Near East.

The Armenian Red Cross effectively cast Armenia as both victim and defender of the faith in the wake of the Genocide, raising tens of thousands of pounds for relief work. As "the last stronghold of Christianity in the Near East," the Red Cross argued, Armenians "have ever to struggle patiently and bravely in the face of the greatest privations and sufferings . . . simply because they are consistent Christians."[22] Funds like the Armenian Red Cross further represented Armenians as allies fighting alongside Britain on the Eastern Front. This had little foundation in fact. Spiritual and secular leaders issued a statement at the beginning of the war upon receiving an Allied request for help, declaring that Armenians as loyal Ottoman subjects would not rise up against the empire. However, European-diaspora Armenians and some living across the Russian border did organize. Though effective symbols of British-Armenian unity, the heroes of the Red Cross narrative were little more than an ill-equipped and poorly organized band of international volunteers.[23]

Aid organizations used this small group of mainly Russian national volunteers for propaganda efforts, encouraging patrons to see Armenia as an actual military ally. "If a reason is wanted which will come more nearly home to Britons," a Red Cross report from late in the war declared, "after the disruption and collapse of the Russian-Caucasian Army, Armenian volunteers rushed to Transcaucasia to the rescue from all parts of the world and manfully stopped the breach at fearful sacrifice to themselves thus effectively protecting the flank of the British Mesopotamian army from attack by the Turks." For the Red Cross, "This important service of theirs deserves the highest reward the Allies can give." Contributors to the fund could also do their part by assisting "us in helping a nation which has done so much to help itself."[24] Ironically, although publicizing the Armenian volunteers functioned well as propaganda for the humanitarian cause, it also fueled claims, still made today, that the presence of Russian volunteers justified the Ottoman massacre of over a million civilians from Constantinople to the Russo-Turkish border during the war.[25]

Informally encouraged in their efforts by high-ranking officials at the Foreign Office, the Armenian volunteers were largely supported by private relief funds. The Allies needed to find a way to keep Russia in the war but worried about arming an untested and badly organized force of volunteers north of the Russo-Turkish border. Britain's military leaders saw the Gallipoli campaign rather than the Caucuses as critical to keeping Russia a viable ally, since opening up the Dardanelles would free Russian movement and take pressure off the Western Front.[26] When the Gallipoli campaign seemed doomed to failure by late summer 1915, however, they did not discourage the use of these volunteers to help Russia in the Caucasus.[27] The lack of official support from the British government rendered this international brigade of men of Armenian ethnicity largely ineffective. As one Armenian Red Cross appeal claimed: "There are now more than 8,000 of these volunteers and their number is continually being added to. By the spring it is estimated that there will be between 20–25,000. They have been equipped and are maintained by Armenians all over the world at a cost of £6,000 per day. At the present they have no doctor and there are only five untrained Armenian ladies assisting as nurses."[28] The organization declared that it would split all money raised between four columns of volunteers and the more than 100,000 destitute refugees living just over the Russo-Turkish border.[29]

The seamless link between strategic and humanitarian concerns made relief work part of a common cause during the war. The Armenian Refugees Fund (Lord Mayor's Fund, LMF), founded in October 1915, emerged as the largest of these relief organizations.[30] Started to respond to the humanitarian crisis of the massacres, it defined its purpose in terms of what it called "[t]he wave of indignation and horror that has swept across Great Britain in connection with the treatment of Armenians in Turkish provinces." The fund worked closely with other political advocacy organizations during the war, gaining recognition as the "national fund." The Armenian Red Cross, Save the Children, and Friends of Armenia published appeals on its behalf and even contributed money to the fund. Its leadership, which included politicians, private citizens, and relief workers, broadened the appeal of its work by including other refugee groups. "Though our fund is formed primarily for the relief of Armenian refugees," wrote chairman Aneurin Williams in a letter to the *Times*, "we have laid it down from the first that any others facing the same awful fate should be entitled to share in the relief."[31] The fund cooperated in this task with the well-funded American relief organization Near East Relief, which had a network of missionaries, consuls, and philanthropic organizations on the ground to help distribute aid.[32]

The LMF leadership effectively tied Britain's wartime interests to persecuted minorities. Recognizing the importance of eyewitness accounts for raising money, the organization funded a British Relief Expedition to the Caucasus "to supervise and coordinate the medical and relief work" among Armenian refugees, which was led by a prominent member of the committee, Noel Buxton. A four-page fundraising flyer from December 1916 made the case for immediate intervention. The response to the question of why "Turks attempted to exterminate them" hinged on ethnic hatred, imperial politics, and German intrigue. The Ottoman Empire was "jealous of Armenian energy and ability. . . . The Armenians both by character and religion are impossible to assimilate in Turkey. And moreover they stand as the direct obstacle in the way of the Pan-Turanian ideas encouraged by Germany."[33] This plea for immediate assistance listed the fund's work up to that point, which included founding orphanages, setting up industrial work centers to employ refugees, and starting hospitals and schools.

As a result of these efforts the LMF reported collecting tens of thousands of pounds during its first year of operation from individual small donations made by donors in Liverpool, Manchester, Glasgow, Edinburgh, and London. One fundraising meeting used Buxton's presence in the Caucuses to raise funds for the repatriation of refugees and for rebuilding efforts after the massacres. As Aneurin Williams declared of Armenian and Assyrian refugees in a public meeting, "These people are going back. We are not sending them back (hear, hear) but they are going back to their own districts; and being back, if we can do something to help them to avoid famine in the coming winter, I take it is our duty to do so. (Applause)." The Earl Beauchamp, evoking the 1896 massacres, summed up the purpose of wartime relief work: "English people have always taken an interest in the Armenian nation and the sums of money that have been raised . . . show that the people of this country however great the present needs may be in other directions have not lost sight of such a worthy cause in the face of new needs."[34] A nominal amount of £1,000 did go to displaced Muslims to demonstrate that the fund "drew no distinction of race and religion."

The LMF understood World War I primarily as a war of liberation for "small nationalities" along religious lines. Advocates included Mark Sykes, T. P. O'Connor, and Lady Ramsey, the latter arguing that Armenia was worthy of support as "the first Christian nation." Sykes, at that time engaged in his official capacity in carving up the Near East between Britain and France, introduced the possibility of a national solution. To his mind, "the connection of religion and nationality in Armenian countries is so tied up that their persecution is not exactly or purely a religious persecution."[35]

The appeal on behalf of religious minorities, particularly those displaced by the 1915 massacres, drove relief organizations beyond the war. "The Armenian nation has lost during the war as many lives as the great British Nation," read one 1919 LMF pamphlet.[36] This humanitarian crisis demanded both political advocacy and personal sacrifice. "What ought we do?" asked one appeal: "It is for us 1) To make facts known and to arouse public opinion to support the Government in any relief measures they may propose to undertake 2) To Abstain from every kind of 'luxury foods' in order that more labour, more transport and more supplies may be available for the starving peoples 3) To give generously to the Lord Mayors Fund or to similar Agencies so that the clothing materials and medical supplies which are so desperately needed may be sent out immediately."[37] News of progress was reported to donors in bulletins that provided "recent news from our agents" who distributed aid in Damascus, Aleppo, Constantinople, and other areas where refugees had gathered. Homes for orphans, clothing appeals, and fund-raising for homes for kidnapped women ("[t]he whereabouts of most of them is already known") filled the pages of these reports, assuring donors that they had a role to play in mitigating civilian suffering.[38]

In addition to the organizations discussed above, advocacy groups active during World War I included: The Friends of Armenia, with branches in Ireland, Scotland, Wales and England; the Armenian Bureau of Information; the Lord Mayor's Fund of Manchester; Armenian Orphans Fund (Manchester); The Religious Society of Friends, Armenian Mission; The Armenian Refugees Relief Fund, run by the Armenian United Association of London; and the Armenian Ladies Guild of London.[39] These organizations raised hundreds of thousands of pounds for relief work and thousands more for political advocacy and education programs, keeping the Eastern Front on the minds of Britons during some of the worst years of the war.[40]

Together wartime advocacy organizations shaped both the way officials and the public at large understood the humanitarian crisis in the Near East. So important had this understanding of the Eastern Question become that some worried it overshadowed the grave military situation of the war. The historian J. A. R. Marriott, in "Factors in the Problem of the Near East: Germany," published in the *Fortnightly Review* in 1916, argued that the war necessitated that the public pay greater heed to diplomatic rather than humanitarian concerns. As he concluded:

> To the mass of the people in this country the "Eastern Question" has signified for the last twenty years, the unhappy condition of the Christian subjects of the Sultan . . . This concentration of interest was more creditable to our hearts than our heads. But it is noteworthy mainly because it is essentially symptomatic of our general outlook upon foreign affairs. The Armenian massacres provide a topic on which it is possible to arouse popular passion; it is well adapted to treatment on the platform or in the pulpit. . . . But to follow closely and intelligently the course of diplomacy requires not merely sympathy but knowledge; a real study of foreign affairs demands, not the gifts of the rhetorician but clear thinking and wide reading.[41]

The overwhelming response to the civilian massacres in the Near East opened up a discursive space that made it possible to link humanitarian with military wartime objectives. Marriott's concern stemmed from the increasing attention given to advocacy groups and their power to shape public opinion. In this way, the fallout from the Armenian Genocide proved an important lens through which to view the war in the East. Five months after Marriott warned against fighting a humanitarian war of liberation came a powerful rejoinder that ignited outrage over the handling of the Eastern Question during the war.

BRYCE'S BLUE BOOK

No document had as great an effect on wartime opinion in Britain and other Allied countries as the one published by Lord James Bryce (1838–

1922) in October 1916. *The Treatment of Armenians in the Ottoman Empire: 1915–1916* contained evidence from over one hundred sources that chronicled Turkish atrocities during the Genocide. Issued as a Parliamentary Blue Book, the 733-page document was the most complete set of testimonies to date on the massacre of Armenian civilians that started in the spring of 1915. Although Bryce claimed that it avoided "questions of future policy," the evidence contained in the report drew upon a compelling set of humanitarian arguments that made the case for political intervention.[42] Buoyed in part by the international response to Bryce's report, the campaign on behalf of Armenian victims took shape as a national effort that drove debates over the Eastern Question during the remaining years of the war and beyond.

Bryce's interest in Armenia dated back to a life-changing trek up Mount Ararat that he undertook in 1876. His ascent up the 14,000-foot mountain, considered the resting place of Noah's Ark and the center of historical Armenia, provided the basis for a book and a set of lectures on Armenia. This trip, according to his biographer, marked the beginning of a lifelong career as advocate for Armenian causes.[43] As early as 1878, the "Armenian Community of Constantinople" had written to Bryce thanking him for a Royal Geographical Society lecture he gave "favoring the free development of the Armenian nation."[44] Closer to home, his election to Parliament in 1880 for Tower Hamlets (1880–85) and South Aberdeen (1885–1906) brought his work on behalf of Armenians to the political stage.[45] By the time he founded the Anglo-Armenian Association in 1890 he had secured a network of supporters in Britain and abroad that advocated for the minority reforms first laid out in the Treaty of Berlin. Considered heir to W. E. Gladstone's campaigns on behalf of Ottoman minorities, Bryce stepped up his advocacy on behalf of Armenians as soon as news of the Genocide began to reach Britain.[46]

Immediately after the war started, Bryce, by now a viscount with a seat in the House of Lords, chaired a committee of lawyers and historians investigating reports of atrocities against Belgian civilians by the Germans.[47] His report chronicling the brutal treatment of women and children at the hands of German soldiers was translated into twenty-seven languages and had a tremendous effect on public opinion, serving as a rallying point for the war effort on the Western Front.[48] One year later, when news of the Ottoman massacres began to reach Britain, Bryce and others began compiling evidence from travelers, missionaries, civilians, aid workers and political representatives of atrocities committed against Armenian civilians in the empire.

News of the slaughter reached home by May 2, 1915, when Aneurin Williams wrote to a colleague of "new massacres" committed in Tiflis.[49] Nine days later Sir G. Buchanan informed Sir Edward Grey that the "Minister of Foreign Affairs thinks that we ought to let it be known that we shall hold Turkey responsible at the end of the war for any massacre of Armenians."[50] A joint European declaration of May 24 promised to hold the Ottoman government personally responsible for "new crimes of Turkey against humanity and civilization."[51] Bryce immediately began collecting material documenting the massacres for what would become the Blue Book. By June 1916 Bryce had secured the assistance of lawyers and historians to review the documents and gave the task of editing and organizing to the young Oxford historian Arnold Toynbee.

The Blue Book and Toynbee's other writings on the genocide consolidated a body of evidence on Armenian atrocities collected from observers and victims. In addition to the Blue Book, Toynbee published two long, inexpensive pamphlets: *Armenian Atrocities: The Murder of a Nation* (1915) and *The Murderous Tyranny of the Turks* (1917). Together these texts marshaled a set of arguments that would shape future discourse on the Armenian Genocide. *Armenian Atrocities* made the case for genocide for the first time. In it Toynbee argued that the "exceedingly systematic" nature of the massacres set them apart from nineteenth-century antecedents. Citing evidence taken from fifty different places, Toynbee established a pattern of premeditated mass violence in a chapter entitled "The Plan of the Massacres." Other chapters chronicled deportations and the death toll. The final chapter, "The Attitude of Germany," implicated Germany as an accomplice to the massacres, a role that historians have began to interrogate more closely in recent years.[52] German culpability for atrocities on both the Western and Eastern Fronts, however, went unquestioned at the time.[53] As Toynbee ended the pamphlet: "This shameful and terrible page of modern history which is unfolding in distant Armenia is nothing but an echo and an extension of the main story, the central narrative which must describe the German incursion into Belgium fourteen months ago. . . . What she has done is to bring us all back in the Twentieth Century to the condition of the dark ages. That is the indictment. Let Germany cease to deserve it."[54]

The publication of the Blue Book the next fall, intended as an impartial representation of the facts of the Genocide, inevitably reflected British wartime concerns. A speech given by Bryce in the House of Lords in October 1915, reprinted in *Armenian Atrocities*, summed up his understanding of the motivations behind the killings and deportations. The massacres of 1915, Bryce argued, had political rather than religious origins: "There was no Moslem passion against the Armenian Christians. All was done by the will of the Government and done not from any religious fanaticism, but simply because they wished for reasons purely political to get rid of a non-Moslem element which impaired the homogeneity of the Empire, and constituted an element that might not always submit to oppression."[55] Bryce's emphasis on political over religious motivations, the latter so central to Victorian understandings of the Eastern Question, proved important in the wartime context. Concerns over angering Muslim leaders in the empire animated arguments against intervening in Ottoman internal affairs since the signing of the Treaty of Berlin. A small but vocal constituency had argued that "England is the greatest Mohammedan Power upon earth" and should not alienate Muslim opinion by bowing to "British Christian opinion."[56]

Portraying the massacres as state-sponsored terror dispelled notions that Britain's Eastern policy worked against its own imperial interests by alienating Muslim subjects. The Blue Book charted the systematic nature of the massacres by the government, documenting the presence of concurrent massacres throughout the whole of Anatolia. Organized along regional lines with a map of "affected districts," each of the twenty sections contained multiple eyewitness and secondhand reports, dispatches, news articles, and letters. The appendix cited evidence to refute claims made by Ottoman officials that Armenian disloyalty to the empire justified the massacre of civilians on defensive grounds.[57]

The repetition of evidence in the more than one hundred documents made the case for the systematic nature of the massacres but, according to Toynbee, also made for rather "dull reading." This along with the size of the volume considerably worried Bryce, who first and foremost wanted the Blue Book to be read. Toynbee decided that rather than edit down the documents, a move that would risk calling into question their authenticity, he would provide a guide that highlighted the most important testimonies. As he made the case to Bryce in a letter:

> [I]n publishing a more or less exhaustive collection of material it is almost impossible to make the essential things stand out clearly. I believe the best remedy will be to insert a slip in every copy giving a selected list of the really interesting and important documents and suggesting that readers who cannot digest the whole should turn to these first. I imagine, indeed, that practically no one will read the volume straight through. As to the question of shortening the 5th section . . . cutting down of documents might give the wrong impression; it might suggest that we had omitted or suppressed material in

other places, not merely to save space but to modify the effect of the evidence.[58]

Bryce agreed to a "Reader's Guide," which summed up about one in three documents using one-line descriptive statements at the beginning of the volume. The first item cited, Document 9, simply read, "Letter conveyed out of Turkey in the sole of a refugee's shoe."

Toynbee, in deciding against abridging any of the documents, was not just worried about maintaining the authenticity of the source material. He also drew upon nineteenth-century tropes that cast Armenians as distant kin who shared a common past with his Anglo and American readers. What made the deportations particular hard on Armenians, he argued, was their removal from their homes in a European-like setting: "The Anatolian highlands are physiologically akin to Europe and the Armenians who dwell in them are not only Europeans in their civilization but are accustomed to an essential European climate."[59] Armenians' willingness to help themselves joined geographic with cultural ties. Toynbee made this point to Bryce when asked to take out one set of documents in the interest of space: "the subject of these three consular memoranda is to the point, as it is chiefly concerned with the relief work of the Caucasian Armenians, and it may be well to show that the Armenians are doing things for each other and not merely depending on other people's help."[60] They printed the three reports in their entirety.

In this way the Blue Book served as a source of documentary evidence and a tool for shaping public opinion and future policy. As Bryce concluded his preface to the collection: "It is evidently desirable not only that ascertained facts should be put on record for the sake of future historians, while the events are still fresh in living memory, but also that the public opinion of the belligerent nations—and, I may add of neutral peoples also—should be able by a knowledge of what has happened in Asia Minor and Armenia to exercise its judgment on the course proper to be followed when, at the end of the present war, a political resettlement of the Nearer East has to be undertaken."[61] By raising the specter of the minority question in the postwar settlement the Blue Book effectively politicized future considerations of the Genocide. "Political resettlement" implied something very specific in the minds of Bryce and his supporters. Politicians had touted the idea of a national solution as a panacea for the Near East as early as the Berlin treaty, when the map of the Balkans was redrawn as a series of ethnically and religiously constituted states. The massacres lent a new urgency to calls to recreate an Armenian homeland in eastern Turkey and Cilicia in the south.

In terms of the war itself, the Blue Book served a much more specific purpose. As Akaby Nassibian has shown, the British government used news of the massacres to influence public opinion in the United States and neutral countries like Bulgaria as early as fall 1915.[62] The Blue Book, H. H. Asquith and Stanley Baldwin declared in a joint memorandum published after the war, was "widely used for Allied propaganda in 1916–17 and had an important influence upon American opinion and upon the ultimate decision of President Wilson to enter the war."[63] Bryce's research when placed in the hands of the government could easily transform from a piece of documentary evidence into a propaganda tool. Bryce and Toynbee came to see the benefits and potential drawbacks of publishing the book as a parliamentary document.

Charles Masterman, a politician and journalist in charge of the War Propaganda Bureau, which had published Bryce's "Report on Alleged German Outrages," had a special interest in the Blue Book's propaganda potential. As he wrote to Bryce in June 1916: "I have read through the whole of the proposed blue book on Armenia. It is certainly an amazing work, telling one of the most appalling stories I should think since the beginning of civilization. I am very anxious that it should be published as soon as possible for general reasons connected with the influencing of public opinion, especially in regard to any ultimate settlement in the near East, and am continually urging Toynbee to fresh efforts to get the book through the press." Masterman informed Bryce that the Foreign Office agreed to publish it as "an official blue book" after which "[w]e shall then try and get it the widest possible circulation."[64] The staging of the presentation was important for Masterman, suggesting that the Foreign Office review the documents and that Aneurin Williams ask "a question . . . in the House and the book be laid before the House in answer."[65]

The government paid particular attention to the timing of the release and worried that Bryce's decision to corroborate the facts might cause delay. "As to submitting the documents to historians and Oriental Scholars, I have been talking to Toynbee about it. If you can suggest any names, we will send proofs at once to them. I should only be anxious, however, that the publication of the work should not be delayed by such examination." Even the month of release was carefully considered. Masterman, "in agreement with the Foreign Office," thought that "the next few months of Summer in America it would probably be not much use to send anyone to report upon or to influence opinion there."[66] Instead, he would use one of his contacts in "the United States press" to publish the work concurrently in the United States and Britain as soon as possible in the fall. Parts of the report were reprinted in American magazines as well.[67]

Despite pressure from the Foreign Office to get the book out quickly, Toynbee and Bryce took the time to authenticate their documents during the next five months. Bryce insisted on having the evidence reviewed "by persons of experience" before publication and confirming the original sources.[68] "I have been going through all the documents and find that we have 138 altogether," Toynbee wrote to Bryce in June 1916: "There are still thirty four of which we do not know the authorship, five of these being statements in newspapers of which the ultimate authorship would probably be impossible to unravel. The remaining twenty nine, however, are definite documents by individual witnesses, or people who have had communication with witnesses, and I am going to make a great effort to obtain in confidence as many of these names as possible."[69] Toynbee persisted in authenticating the documents, though expressed frustration when one source prevaricated: "I do not think he quite realizes the importance of being able to say in the preface that the names suppressed are actually in the editor's hands. I am writing to him again." In the end, he sent the collection to scholars in the United States, France, and England for review.[70] Toynbee continued to look for ways to corroborate evidence in the Blue Book after publication. In 1920, he asked the British Armenian Committee to undertake translating and publishing a German book that had recently come to his attention that "remarkably" confirmed the findings of the Blue Book.[71]

While furthering war aims abroad, the Blue Book added momentum to the humanitarian movement at home. Advocacy organizations evoked the Blue Book in meetings held throughout Britain that helped fund relief work. The Armenian Orphans Fund started by the Lord Mayor of Manchester and registered under the War Charities Act of 1916 used evidence found in the Blue Book to legitimate its claims of obligation and friendship: "It is our patriotic duty to do whatever is possible because they have suffered not as Armenians but as friends of the Allied cause. . . . The Armenians volunteered in great numbers for Russia and repeatedly rendered most valuable service to the Allied cause. And it is for these services that . . . the Turks proceeded to wreak on the whole community the vengeance described in the British Blue Book, an authority which does not admit impeachment."[72] The Armenian community in London and abroad understandably took particular notice. Arshak Safrastian, a later leader of the Armenian Bureau advocacy organization, wrote to Bryce from his office at the London School of Economics in March 1917,

"My countrymen in the Caucasus are highly elated over the Armenian Blue Book. The press is full of it."[73]

The publicity surrounding the Blue Book served as a rallying point for the cause of Christian minorities. Although the Ottoman government centrally targeted Armenians for extermination, the minority Greek and especially Assyrian populations also suffered mass violence and massacres throughout Anatolia.[74] The Archbishop of Canterbury drew attention to the massacre and deportation of thousands of Assyrians along the Persian border, leading the Anglican Church to widen the scope of its advocacy efforts.[75] The Archbishop of York wrote in letter from October 1915 that after speaking with Bryce and reading the news accounts of the massacres that he found the whole thing "appalling": "There is, I believe to be a Mansion House Meeting on the subject quite soon and I have authorized Bryce to add my name to those promoting it. Very likely that would be the best time for us to give a little money if we could, and at least we can express our horror at what is going on."[76]

A month and a half after the publication of *Armenian Atrocities* the Archbishop of Canterbury wrote to the Archbishop of York of "being bombarded about the Armenians and indeed the horrors are beyond words." When Harold Buxton, the secretary for the Armenian Refugee Fund, approached him to hold a special collection "for the Armenians throughout all the churches," however, he at first equivocated: "With the Armenians are associated the Assyrians for whom I have some special responsibility and who are in terrible need. The Fund helps both. I have this morning a telegram from Buxton stating that Cardinal ( ) [sic] is going to order Collection in all the Roman Churches on Feb. 6th and urging that we do the same. My own feeling is that we cannot multiply these special Sundays."[77] A year later, the archbishop authorized the inaugural "Armenia Sunday" "for the expression of our common sympathy and earnest prayer on behalf of our Armenians and Syro-Chaldean [Assyrian] brethren." One year later, on February 2, 1917, a second Armenia Sunday was adopted throughout the "Free Churches of Britain," where a two-page brochure on the plight of Assyrians and Armenians was distributed.[78] The years 1918 and 1919 witnessed repeats of the event, with all money collected going toward refugee relief in the Near East.

The publication and subsequent response to Bryce's Blue Book had implications beyond its wartime reception. As a collection of verifiable documents it provided clear evidence of the first large-scale genocide of the twentieth century. The power of its influence, however, rested more in how it was used to serve military and humanitarian agendas. In the hands of the government propaganda machine the book proved a particularly malleable instrument, inciting outrage intended to influence the British and American public in general and the American president in particular. For aid organizations, the publication bolstered the case for humanitarian intervention, helping to raise funds and keep relief schemes in the public eye. Bryce himself had his own agenda, to be sure. Coming out of the Gladstonian liberal tradition, he saw the Armenian cause as both a moral and a political issue. According to his biographer, "Bryce was concerned to establish the facts: but he was still more interested in the moral to be drawn from them."[79]

Toynbee, a generation removed from Bryce (he was twenty-six when he first met the seventy-seven-year-old Bryce), came to question the stance of the Victorian moralist, eventually becoming disillusioned with the advocacy campaign he had helped promote.[80] In his memoir he claimed that "he was unaware of the politics" that lay behind the government's issuing of the Blue Book: "Lord Bryce's concern, and mine, was to establish the facts and to make them public, in the hope that eventually some action might be taken in the light of them. The dead—and the deportees had been dying in their thousands—could not be brought back to life, but we hoped (vain hope) that at least something might be done to ensure, for the survivors, that there should never be a repetition of the barbarities that had been the death of so many of their kinsmen."[81] As Toynbee would come to recognize, the evidence that he painstakingly had readied for publication could not speak for itself. Rather this tragedy of human suffering had already been scripted: a group of innocent civilians aligned with Britain massacred by a despotic state. This narrative, taken from a bygone Victorian era, compellingly intertwined humanitarian and geopolitical interests in a powerful, moralizing vision that linked the defeat of Germany with the liberation of "small nationalities." Eventually, the postwar fallout from the failed campaigns in Gallipoli and Mesopotamia and the Genocide itself would leave little room to remember the story of the Eastern Front as part of the heroic narrative of the Great War.

"CRIMES AGAINST HUMANITY"

Calls to prosecute those behind the Armenian massacres emerged long before the end of the war. "The Armenian race in Asia Minor has been virtually destroyed," Lewis Einstein announced in the *Contemporary Review* in 1917. "England, France, and Russia should, at the proper time, realize what they have suffered as victims of the ill-success of the

Dardanelles expedition."[82] The failed invasion of Gallipoli implicated the Allies in the humanitarian disaster that happened in its wake. For Britain, this responsibility loomed particularly large. Bryce's Blue Book cemented its long-held status as protector of Ottoman minorities. This in addition to the more than one million troops still on Ottoman soil after the conclusion of the war poised Britain from both a humanitarian and military standpoint to take the lead in Allied efforts at a peace settlement on the Eastern Front. This responsibility included the prosecution of war criminals.

At war's end the British had the military infrastructure and the political will to launch an inquiry into the massacres. Initially, they placed hopes in the time-tested but ultimately futile course of humanitarian diplomacy. "Everyone in Constantinople is discussing sweeping measures of reform," approvingly declared the *Times* shortly after the signing of the armistice. The prosecution of "those responsible for the massacres would come as a matter of course" out of fear of harsher measures "imposed by the Allies."[83] News of continued massacres and pressure from humanitarian organizations at home in the following months convinced Britain to take action.[84] The Constantinople War Crimes Trials, a historically unprecedented court martial set up to prosecute Turkish officials for the Armenian massacres, was the result.[85] By spring 1919, the Ottoman government, under intense British pressure, arrested over 100 high-profile suspects, including government ministers, governors, and military officers.[86]

The ultimately short-lived series of four trials resulted in the execution of three minor officials for "crimes against humanity," a term deployed for the first time in reference to an international proceeding to describe the Armenian Genocide.[87] The failure to fully prosecute those responsible for the genocide revealed the muddled sense of mission that accompanied this early attempt at human rights justice. Understood by historians as a turning point that refused to turn, the Constantinople War Crimes Trials had limited success due in part to the broad application of the new category of "war crimes" to British military and Armenian civilian populations.[88] Specifically, the plan to prosecute Ottoman leaders for the massacres emerged alongside another wartime outrage that long had worried officials: the treatment of British prisoners captured on the Eastern Front. Ambassador Louis Mallet directly linked these concerns in a letter to Sir R. Graham after the armistice: "It will be necessary to provide for the punishment of any Turks who can be proved to have been responsible for the perpetration of instigation of 1) Armenian massacres 2) outrages committed on any other subject races, Greeks, Nestorian Christians etc 3) ill-treatment of prisoners. On the latter point I am writing to the Prisoners of War Department who have kept a black list."[89] No such "black list" existed for those accused of the massacres. This left prosecutors to rely on the Ottoman government to conduct its own investigations. Faith was placed in officials who demonstrated a willingness to arrest alleged perpetrators. One new governor appointed at Angora reportedly had fifteen suspects arrested. The "Situation Report" by a British officer charged with tracking arrests sounded a cautiously hopeful note: "I believe the Vali has arranged for a Court Martial to be sent here from Constantinople in order to try all those in the Vilayet who were implicated in the Armenian massacres. If this is correct it will be a very good thing."[90] Such uncertainties about both who was being prosecuted and what they were being prosecuted for plagued the trials from their initial conception until the end.

Attention inevitably turned to Britain's enemy Germany, further complicating the prosecution at Constantinople. Laying the blame for the massacres at Germany's feet had proved a useful tactic during the war and continued during the trials. This added another level of difficulty to gathering evidence and getting the trials off the ground. In making the case for the Armenian massacres as a war crime, Admiral Calthorpe, the High Commissioner at Constantinople and a key force in the proceedings, argued that German officers should also be held responsible: "If Allies decide to bring to trial those guilty of crimes against humanity during late war I desire to point out that name of Liman von Sanders should be borne in mind." The long list of crimes listed by Calthorpe included the charge that in his role as inspector general of the Ottoman army, a post he held starting with the end of the Balkan wars, von Sanders used his "autocratic power as Military dictator" to order the mass deportation of Armenians and Greeks. Another of his "crimes against humanity," as Calthorpe captured the phrase, included his ordering of a "trench system deliberately cut through British cemeteries at Gallipoli."[91] Calthorpe did not deal with the question of where or under which jurisdiction, the German or Ottoman war crimes tribunals, von Sanders should be tried. Eventually, von Sanders was arrested and later released.

Following through with the maze of prosecutions for those accused of massacring civilians and mistreating prisoners of war put pressure on officials to manage public opinion while applying pressure on Ottoman officials. In relating an interview with one such official the British high commissioner turned to "the question of the Armenian massacres and the treatment of British Prisoners":

> I said that the released prisoners were now arriving in England
> and were relating their experiences, and that the same indigna-
> tion which I had felt myself was already showing itself as prevalent
> throughout public opinion in England as evidenced by the news
> telegrams which were reaching this country. . . . With regard to the
> Armenians, knowledge of what had happened was only now becom-
> ing really known. In this case also, the signs of public indignation
> were perfectly clear. I was certain, speaking as a private Englishman
> and without any instructions, that there were matters on which His
> Majesty's Government had an inflexible resolve: the authors of both
> would have to be punished with all rigour.

The official, Rechid Pasha, responded with assurances that the Ottoman
government planned to punish those responsible: "He said that he himself
was insisting on the infliction of proper punishment and that he would
resign from the cabinet if this were not done."[92] Calthorpe remained
skeptical, leaving the interview with a strong message: "what we looked
for was more than good will; it was for actual results. . . . I warned him
again that the question of the prisoners of war and of the Armenians
were most important and that he would do well to devote to them his
utmost attention."

Such admonitions proved as ineffective after World War I as they had
after the signing of the Treaty of Berlin. By the end of January Calthorpe,
frustrated that the Sultans "timorous" behavior had prevented the arrest
of sixty men on the minister of interior's list of war criminals, declared
in a telegram to the Foreign Office marked "Very Urgent": "It is of course
high time that action should be taken; there has already been too much
delay."[93] Four days later news of the escape of a key suspect hit Calthorpe's
desk. He immediately sent his representative, the long-time Levant
Consular Service agent Andrew Ryan, to visit the vizier, who informed
him that Calthorpe "took gravest possible view of incident which was
a direct challenge not only to his government but to Entente Powers."
Ryan, in a confidential memo, attempted to mollify Calthorpe, claiming that both the vizier and minister of interior understood the gravity
of matter and that they promised to try to recapture the prisoner. Still,
Ryan worried that there were still so many other criminals at large that
the "present unsatisfactory situation cannot be allowed to continue."[94] A
series of subsequent releases of accused prisoners by the Ottoman government in May forced a response. On May 28, 1919, all of the prisoners
awaiting trial at Constantinople were transferred to British custody in
Malta.[95]

By taking the prisoners into custody Britain tried to salvage what already seemed a doomed effort. Without access to official Ottoman records and a reluctant sultan frightened by a looming nationalist backlash, the trials had little hope of going forward. The invasion of Smyrna by the Greeks in May 1919 galvanized anger toward the Allies, further limiting the possibility of Ottoman cooperation.[96] Yet officials pressed on, citing British honor and prestige as a factor in this decision. As Calthorpe argued, "It was pointed out to the Grand Vizier that when the massacres became known in England British statesmen had promised the civilized world that persons concerned would be held personally responsible and that it was firm intention of His Majesty's Government to fulfill this promise."[97] Ultimately, the glacial pace of the peace settlement with the Ottoman Empire, still four years away, and the drawing down of troops in Anatolia began to throw doubt on the entire enterprise. Turkish prisoners languished in British jails as the War Crime Trials came to an abrupt halt. By summer 1919 the British reduced its force in the region from 1,000,000 to 320,000.[98]

Eventually something would have to be done. The resolution of territorial adjustments and the signing of a peace treaty with the Ottoman Empire hung in the balance. Two years after the transfer of prisoners to Malta, now War Secretary Winston Churchill stepped in with a proposal intended to satisfy a war-weary population: a prisoner exchange. Although a number of protests were heard from within the government most came around, however reluctantly, to the idea that Britain would exchange all but the worst offenders of the prisoners at Malta for a group of twenty-nine British soldiers recently captured by the Nationalist Army, which was gaining strength in Anatolia.[99] An "all for all" exchange ultimately took place. The Foreign Office justified this about-face by maintaining "that it is vastly more important to save the lives of these British subjects than to bind ourselves by the strict letter of the law as regards the Turkish prisoners at Malta."[100]

The exchange, set for fall 1921, incited public outrage. The *Times* asked why the "eight war criminal accused of the gravest offenses" were not tried when the evidence was fresh in 1919 and argued that it was still not too late to gather evidence as was done in the case of German war criminals.[101] A letter to the editor by an advocate for prisoners of war argued against a prisoner exchange due to the terrible crimes of the accused.[102] At the root of this criticism lay the issue of British prestige, which some believed an unconditional release of men accused of war crimes would diminish: "Our dawdling, hesitating, ambiguous Near Eastern policy has involved us in no greater humiliation than this. Our prestige is evaporating in the futility of our councils. Throughout the East our assertion of right and not mere force of arms has been our strength. If by such a pitiful surrender we abandon this weapon how shall we cope with the growing dangers?"[103]

The high-profile campaign for the release of Colonel Alfred Rawlinson gave a face to the story of the twenty-nine soldiers exchanged with the Ottomans in November 1921. Rawlinson, the younger brother of the commander of the British forces in India, had been captured in Anatolia shortly after the war. While a prisoner he witnessed the horrific treatment of Ottoman civilians and prisoners of war.[104] He himself suffered at the hands of his captors, given few rations and confined in dirty, miserable conditions. In 1923, he published a popular memoir, *Adventures in the Near East*, in which he offered a nihilistic view of Britain's historical treatment of the Eastern Question:

> It appeared to me, also, that there is nothing new to be found in the bad treatment of their prisoners by the Turks, or in their traditional persecution of the Christian minorities who have so long and with such difficulty contrived to exist in many of the districts under Turkish rule; and that unless we were in a position to back up any agitation with respect to these matters by not only a display, but by an application, of force, which would be capable of being followed up, if necessary by serious and active military operations, it would be to the last degree unwise to bring such question forward at all.[105]

Britain remained unwilling during the war, as it had in the past, to stop the "traditional persecution of Christian minorities" through military force. Legal prosecution had also failed. Despite his own experiences as a prisoner of war Rawlinson told his readers that Britain should maintain good relations with Turkey and worried that evidence of his ill treatment would help fuel the humanitarian argument in favor of continued intervention. Rawlinson had other more immediate things to worry about, as it turned out. About to have his meager government pension cut off, Rawlinson's book opened with an appeal to the public by Admiral Sir Percy Scott for adequate compensation to men "who have readily given all they had to give for the service of their country."

Somehow the war of liberation had gotten off track. The collapse of the Constantinople War Crimes Trials in the face of a rising tide of Turkish nationalist sentiment opposed to Allied intervention offered little hope for justice for genocide victims.[106] In terms of prestige, the British could only watch as the men who perpetrated civilian massacres and crimes against their own soldiers were set free. By the early 1920s a war-weary population that understood humanitarianism as intimately tied to geopolitics began to question the moral certainty of the prewar generation.

ATROCITY ON FILM

While the storm over the War Crimes Trials brewed in Constantinople and Whitehall, the British went to the movies. The screening of the graphic atrocity film *Auction of Souls* in October 1919 created a sensation. Over the course of the following year the book of the same title went into at least twenty-six printings as the film found its way into provincial and urban theaters from London to Belfast. The book and film told the story of a teenage girl, Aurora Mardiganian, who survived the Armenian massacres. In 1917, she made her way to the United States, where appeals published on her behalf to find her brother caught the attention of a Hollywood writer and producer. Harvey Gates maneuvered to become Mardiganian's guardian, translated her story, published it under the title *Ravished Armenia* in 1918, and made it into a feature film with that same title that same year. This Hollywood production came to Britain from the United States on a wave of publicity that promised audiences a real-life drama of the 1915 massacres.

Auction of Souls, as it was called in Britain, straddled the unsteady divide between history and entertainment. It offered viewers a visual spectacle of wartime atrocity while at the same time claimed authenticity as a historical document, starring Mardiganian in the lead role. This "carefully orchestrated commercial production," according to Anthony Slide, exploited the story of the Armenian massacres and Mardiganian herself for financial gain. Although most viewers in the United States treated the film "with respect and dignity" due to "its subject matter that made it above reproach," one critic condemned the "cheap sensationalism" surrounding the film, claiming to be "heartily sick of the screen's exploitation of atrocities under any guise."[107]

In October 1919 a series of private screenings in London introduced the film to British audiences. The initial reaction reinforced the combination of horror and sympathy for massacre victims expressed by advocacy groups and the public during the war. An invitation-only event at the premises of the film's British distributor, the General Film Renting Company in Soho, drew a notable crowd that included a number of religious and secular leaders. "I wish that this finely set up film might be seen by all thinking men and women in this country," remarked Rev. F. B. Meyer after the screening. Rev. Bernard Vaughan offered his opinion to those present when he took to the stage after the presentation: "We have followed this picture with agonizing interest, but awful as were the atrocities depicted I am very sorry to have to say that they fall far short of the realities." The dozens of journalists who attended a subsequent press screening at the London Coliseum gave the public its first glimpse of the film through movie review columns. Reviews in the urban and provincial press called the film "enthralling and terrible" while using the opportunity to throw blame on Germany for the Genocide and even going as far as to call for the "urgent need for the independence of Christian Armenia." A final private showing at Queens Hall on October 29 included "a number of prominent public and private people," including James Bryce, H. J. Gladstone, and Church of England bishops and other members of the clergy. When asked his opinion of the film, Lord Gladstone replied, much as his father might have, "Most excellent, just the film to create and army of Crusaders."[108]

The last thing the government wanted in 1919 was a crusade. Worries over the film surfaced when the distributor set the film for general release. "This film must be stopped," declared one Home Office memo.[109] The considerable buzz surrounding a film that only a select group of people had as yet seen coupled with plans to release it in over fifty provincial theaters triggered a response by the British Board of Film Censors (BBFC). Despite its name, the board served only an advisory function and did not have the power to censor a film outright. Rather, this industry-appointed body gave its seal of approval by issuing a certificate. Having offices a few doors down from the distribution company on Wardour Street in Soho allowed the board to keep a particularly close eye on the distribution of the film. A handful of public showings in November and December of that year already had alarmed members of the board. The Middlesex County Council took action against the Gaiety Cinema, Twickenham, for showing the film in November 1920 without a certificate from the BBFC.[110] A month later, *Auction of Souls* played to a capacity audience at the Carlisle Theater in an edited form approved by the Carlisle police that "slightly curtailed" a scene that depicted a woman being dragged to death behind a horse. In December, the board decided to withhold its certificate for the edited version of the film.[111]

Unease over the potential effect of *Auction of Souls* on the public drove this controversy. Two issues topped concerns: indecency and the question of prestige, particularly in the British Empire. When the Criminal

Investigation Department of New Scotland Yard visited Sidney Arnold, the proprietor of the General Film Renting Company, in January 1920 they informed him that *Auction of Souls* constituted an "indecent exhibition." Arnold demurred, arguing that it had been shown without objection in the United States and that stopping the release of the film would cost him £25,000: "On Monday next posters would be coming out on the trams and buses . . . throughout London." Having just rented the Albert Hall the following week at the cost of £5,000 per showing, he hoped to sell out at the price of £1 per ticket. To defend his position Arnold produced testimonials speaking to the value of the film and readily agreed to any changes that the Home Office might require.[112]

The charge of "indecency" rightly surprised Arnold. He soon came to understand that the government clearly did not want the film shown at all. Concerned that the withholding of the BBFC certificate would not curtail "the indiscriminate public exhibition of the film," it sent the case to the Foreign Office for review. Prosecutors concluded that the Obscene Publications Act of 1857 gave the government the authority to charge Arnold with a misdemeanor for displaying a movie that threatened public morals by depicting naked, crucified girls. Eventually they brought the Ministry of Health into the discussion, claiming that sexual content in the film raised questions about venereal disease. The state of undress of the American actresses stood at the crux of the government's case. "The most horrible incident is the display of a long line of crosses bearing the crucified bodes of stark naked young girls. This I believe was true to fact, but was none the less distressing to look upon on that account: the fact that the originals of this picture were not dead Armenians but live American girls exposed thus to the operators' camera hardly improves matters."[113]

The inability to prove that the actresses were truly naked, despite the repeated close scrutiny of Foreign Office moviegoers, threatened to derail the prosecution's case. Scotland Yard worried that with only one scene in question they would not be able to assure a conviction. Even that scene upon closer examination did not seem to meet the criteria of indecency. As one official put it, "the renters told us at the close of the exhibition that when photographed the girls were entirely covered by tights fitting very closely to the contours of the skin. Superintendent Thomas said that this was a common device and that he had noticed certain wrinkles when the picture was shown. I did not notice any wrinkles on the two occasions on which I saw the picture, and I do not think any ordinary person seeing the film would think there was any covering; but no doubt the covering was there."[114] In the end, Arnold agreed to delete the scene, wrinkles and all, succumbing to police pressure rather than face prosecution.

The crucifixions troubled the Foreign Office for another reason. The image of young girls nailed to crosses symbolized the oppression of Christian minorities by the Muslim majority. This evocative scene suggested that religious, not political, motives stood behind the massacres. This idea had been one that officials and humanitarian groups had tried to counter during the war in order not to alienate Muslim public opinion in the wake of the recent Amritsar Massacre in India. As one Foreign Office official put it: "The film is neither vulgar nor—in the strict sense—immoral but of necessity it abounds in horrors and as it stands is calculated to offend the religious feelings of any Moslem. We may not be inclined at this moment to consider unduly the susceptibilities of the Turk, but our Indian and Egyptian dominions contain many Moslem subjects (at present far from contented) and it is here that the religious danger—if any—lurks."[115] Representatives of the Muslim community, to whom the Foreign Office attached "much importance," wrote objecting to the film on the grounds that it would incite "anger and indignation . . . among His Majesty's Muslim Subjects."[116] Objections continued even after the decision to remove the crucifixion scene was made: "Should permission, however, be granted for such exhibition my Committee entertains serious apprehension of disturbances."[117] The timing of the film had special significance, according to another source, threatening to cause tensions after the war between Christians and Muslims at "such a critical hour."[118]

Accusations of indecency ultimately proved cover for imperial concerns. When the India Office became involved in early January, Lord Curzon argued that the Foreign Office and the BBFC should use any means necessary to get the film stopped if alterations were not made:

> Lord Curzon understands that some of the letter press dwells unduly on the religious aspect of the Armenian massacres and is calculated to give offence in India. In view of the apparent intention, as indicated in the enclosed letter, to exhibit the film without suppressing the passages referred to above or making the alterations in the film itself deemed essential by the British Board of Film Censors, Lord Curzon would suggest that the Home Office be asked to take the necessary action in order to prevent on the ground of public morals, the appearance of the film unless the producers are ready to submit to censorship.[119]

Articles in the *Times* followed the controversy, presenting the government line to the public and chronicling "police objections," "alterations," and "exhibitions."[120] The politicization of the film diminished the power of calls to hold the perpetrators of the Genocide accountable due to religious considerations. The indecency charge, used for purely political purposes, cast a long shadow over representations of the massacres as mere cinematic sensationalism.

In the end, the Foreign Office agreed to let the film, in its edited form, be shown under certain conditions. In addition to removing the crucifixion scene, officials excised all references to "Christian" from the subtitles in order "to give them a political rather than a religious aspect."[121] This altered the meaning of some parts of the film very little, such as removing "Christian" before the word "missionaries." Removing Christian from one subtitle, "I intend to kill every [Christian] man and woman and every child over three," however, erased any sense of motive for the massacre that ensued in the subsequent scene.[122] The film distributors agreed to a limited engagement at the Royal Albert Hall, two shows a day for three weeks. Some argued that its humanitarian message would not be diminished by the cuts: "Few lengths of the 8000 feet of which the film consists would survive the censors' shears if this were a film produced in the ordinary way for recreation of the public. It is here that the censors are in difficulties. The film is not . . . put forward in the ordinary way: it is one that is put forward to the purposes of propaganda in a good cause: it is largely backed by honest and reputable societies and individuals. The religious crux can be overcome."[123] The film's support among "reputable societies and individuals" eventually dissipated the government's purported "moral and religious concerns." The Foreign Office had sought in vain to get Bryce's and Gladstone's approval when it started efforts to suppress the film. The Archbishop of Canterbury had written the Foreign Office wanting information on the film's suppression. Emily Robinson also lobbied on behalf of the Armenian Red Cross for its showing.

As the terms of the debate over the film were set, the British public began to take sides.[124] "I would like (as a mother) in the name of the womanhood of the country," wrote Lady Baird to the Home Office, "to protest against the revolting exhibition now proposed to be held at Albert Hall."[125] A reviewer for *Evening Standard* disagreed: "Every Englishwoman should make it her business to see Auction of Souls, the film depicting a percentage of the least revolting atrocities practiced on the Armenian Christians as soon as it is released."[126] One man wrote that he "should like to take my wife to see it."[127] Another correspondent argued that showing the film constituted "an affair of Empire," since showing the film would anger Muslim opinion and thus assist Britain's enemies.[128] Erin Johnson from the London Bridge YMCA believed the film sent a different message: "What an awful charge lies at the door of the British Government for upholding the Turkish Empire all these years and thereby passively permitting such inhuman actions. It made me feel like getting a club and starting out for Downing Street. I hope the film may be sent out to all the colonies so that the whole Empire can see for themselves what 'Defender of the Faith' really means. I was sitting next to two ladies and I was so mad I started swearing. When I apologized to them, they replied, 'We feel the same way.'"[129]

The film continued to draw heated responses after the end of its Albert Hall engagement. Subsequent screenings of the film concerned one official who wanted to know if the Home Office "was aware that film called the 'Auction of Souls,' reinforced by pamphlets and books on the same subject is being exhibited in this Country; and whether the attention of the Censor should be directed to the matter in view of the Peace Treaty not yet concluded with the Ottoman empire."[130] The Home Office secretary sent a brief reply: the government did not censor films. Some mistakenly believed Armenian advocacy groups to be behind the film. One official wrote to Lord Bryce questioning whether he and Lord Gladstone had been involved in the production and claiming that "the film had been prepared under the auspices of the Armenian Relief Committee." Bryce quickly disavowed him of his suspicions, claiming to have had no involvement with its production or promotion. Sponsorship by the League of Nations Union, an organization with the patronage of government officials and prominent citizens, added to the further politicization of the film. An editorial in the *Times* claimed that the League showed it in Albert Hall rather than in cinemas both to overcome objections that the film did not constitute suitable "entertainment" and because "the film which leaves little to the imagination will be the best possible argument in favour of a League for the protection of weak countries."[131]

The controversy over the release of *Auction of Souls* painted the story of the massacres with a jaundiced face, allowing a censored and sensationalized film to masquerade as history. Advertisements for the film promised that it represented "the Great Exposure of Turkish Atrocities in Armenia" based on the Mardiganian's book and Bryce's Blue Book, and was supported by the League of Nations Union. A crucified girl under a black crow served as a titillating symbol in the ad, even though the scene itself had been cut from the British version (see figure 20). A pocket version published by Odhams replaced the hard-to-find privately published American version of the book, which was timed to coincide with

TO-DAY AT 3 & 8.30.

ROYAL ALBERT HALL

& FOR 3 WEEKS. Twice Daily—3 & 8.30.

Auction of Souls

AUCTION OF SOULS

The Great Exposure of Turkish Atrocities in Armenia shewn on the Largest Screen in the World. Founded on the book " Ravished Armenia " and the Report of Viscount Bryce's Commission. Presented by The League of Nations Union by arrangement with The General Film Renting Co., Ltd.

FULL SYMPHONY ORCHESTRA
AND CHOIR OF SOLOISTS

Popular Prices: 12 - to 1 3. Hall & Usual Agents.

Nearest Underground Station: South Kensington. Buses Nos. 9, 33, 33a, 46, 46a, and 73 pass the door.

THE LEAGUE OF NATIONS UNION, 22, Buckingham Gate, S.W.1.

Figure 20. Advertisement for *Auction of Souls,* depicting the cruci-fixion scene deleted from the censored version of the film. *Times,* January 26, 1920.

the release of the film in British theaters. The "first large impression" was reported to have sold out on the first day.[132] By the time a new edition appeared in 1934 over 360,000 copies of the book already were in circulation. A lecture tour planned for Mardiganian offered, in the words of one reviewer, another "fillip" to the film.

The controversy also influenced the film's reception by critics and the public. A reviewer for the *Universe* claimed that the "realistic fidelity of the film" made it worth seeing: "While the film altogether is of the highest merit, it possesses an added interest in the fact that the persecuted Christian heroine Miss Aurora Mardiganian portrays thrilling scenes and incidents in which she took personal part during the massacres—a very rare combination to imagine."[133] "We repeat this is a dreadful drama of real life, of real happenings in our own time, which every thinking person should make a point of seeing." The "thrilling scenes" may have made *Auction of Souls* more interesting for the above reviewer, but the sensationalism also blurred the line between history and fiction, a point not lost on the film's critics. One Muslim community leader argued that it was "a work of fiction acted by Americans" and therefore should not be shown to British audiences.[134]

Some critics blamed the medium. The *English Review* saw the movies as a "new form of illusion," calling *Auction of Souls* a work of propaganda and blasting what it called "bestiality" at the heart of a film that claimed to be "presented to the public on behalf of 'Christianity.'"[135] For the reviewer Sidney Low of the *Fortnightly Review, Auction of Souls* was part of a group of "political films which failed to convey the lesson intended. The spectator who went into the Albert Hall with a shudder came out with a yawn. A performance which might have been intolerably painful turned out to be rather dull; it assuredly did not evoke that fever of pity and resentment which it was, I presume, designed to arouse." The book he considered not much better but at least it conveyed the desired effect: "Nobody who has gone through its pages will regret that the Allied Council insists on bringing Enver and Talaat to trial." However, "in the *Auction of Souls* film the crusading spirit evaporates. The attack on Turkish oppression misses fire. To the majority of the audience the licentious pashas and beys and the persecuted Christians are only characters in trite fairy tale, like the wicked noblemen and virtuous poor folks of the serial novel. It is just a story; not as I have said, in this case a good story. But how is it possible to impose a sense of reality if your medium compels you to satisfy a craving for sensational incident and familiar cheap sentiment?" The effect was worse than denying that the tragedy happened; it erased it from history. Any lessons from the massacres, as Low put it, were "reduced to triviality or passe[d] by unnoticed."[136]

In this changed postwar landscape the moral outrage that had rallied Britons to the cause of a small group of persecuted peoples during the time of Gladstone and Stead failed to solicit the same response. The storm over *Auction of Souls* eventually passed. Only bits of the film have survived in private archives, including the powerful and controversial crucifixion scene.[137] A large file catalogued under the innocuous title of "Entertainments: Objectionable Films: 1916–1920" at the National Archives that contains newspapers articles and reviews serves as the only evidence of its existence. With the film seemingly best forgotten as a piece of postwar sensationalism, the nation soon got on with the business of piecing things together at home after a devastating war.

War on the Eastern Front offered humanitarianism its greatest challenge to date, leaving the memory of the Armenian Genocide as one of its most lasting victims. Before the failure of the Constantinople War Crimes Tribunals, victory in the East was cast as a moral and military victory. This notion drew upon an almost century-long obsession with British claims over the Near East as its protector and heir. The humanitarianism that emerged as a language of the Eastern Question, however, faltered when it came to doing something to stop and later prosecute the war crimes on the Eastern Front. Wartime leaders like David Lloyd George showed little leadership on this count, tepidly embracing W. E. Gladstone's moralizing foreign policy only to use it to further their own political ends.[138] "Four years of a World War altered the Eastern Question out of all recognition," wrote the redoubtable historian R. W. Seton-Watson in 1935.[139] The ineffective response to the humanitarian crises of the war had not a little to do with this transformation.

Wartime discussions of the Eastern Question on the surface replicated old debates over Britain's engagements in the Near East. One side understood defeating the Ottoman Empire as a matter of empire while the other urged immediate involvement on behalf of persecuted Christian minorities. The war, however, had changed the tenor of these debates by entangling the moral, political, and religious issues at a moment when the resolution of military questions seemed most pressing. In the end, the brutality of the crimes committed during the conflict temporarily brought home the inhumanity of modern war that made civilians victims. This reading of the war reveals the marginal place of the Eastern Front in considerations of the human costs of Total War.[140] New massacres committed at Smyrna in 1922 would place Britain's long-standing geopolitical priorities and humanitarian commitments to persecuted minorities in the Near East on even more uncertain ground.

6.   Smyrna's Ashes

I wonder how many Britishers were at the evacuation of Smyrna?
If there were any they will hear me out in any statements set
below and having emerged safely from that hell make them
realize whether this was a horrible nightmare or reality, when we
arrived on Sunday 3rd September 1922.

C. J. HOWES, chief petty officer, HMS Diligence

Civilization in 1922 is a mockery!

LIEUTENANT C. S. B. SWINLEY, HMS Curacoa,
letter to his mother, September 30, 1922

Howes and Swinley, along with hundreds of other military men stationed along the Smyrna quay in September 1922, witnessed the final
chapter of the war in the East unfold with the destruction of the Ottoman
Empire's key commercial Mediterranean port city along with its entire
population of non-Muslim inhabitants. "It was not long after our stay
in Constantinople with our Fleet that we had a sudden call to sail to
Smyrna where the Turks were raiding and devastating the City," one
sailor recalled while stationed on the hospital ship, *Maine*. "The carnage
and cruelty to the Greek civilians was indescribable. We saw from where
we were just off the shore the Turks bayoneting bodies, men, women and
children through the windows of their homes. Hundreds of Greek civilians as well as troops hanging over the dock water side and the Turkish
soldier coming along and deliberately severing the victims' arms result-
ing in hundreds of bodies falling to their deaths in the sea."[1] "Fire has
broken out in the Armenian quarter of the town, aided by strong wind is
spreading rapidly," recorded another eyewitness stationed in Smyrna on
September 13 (see figure 21).[2] The fire spread westward to the Greek and
European quarters, making it to the American settlement of "Paradise,"
leaving only the Turkish quarter untouched. "The stench of human flesh
burning was appalling and the streets were stacked with dead, men,
women, children and dogs," Howes wrote. His commander, Sir John de
Brook, concluded: "The spectacle was magnificently terrible."[3] Within a
matter of days, one of the most cosmopolitan and multiethnic cities of the
Ottoman Empire had disappeared from the map.

Figure 21. Smyrna ablaze, September 1922. Reproduced from film footage
of the Smyrna fire from the Sherman Grinberg Film Library, courtesy of the
Armenian Film Foundation.

The men who watched Smyrna's destruction from their ships moored
in the harbor could do little to stop the slaughter. While life got back to
normal in Europe after the signing of the Treaty of Versailles in 1919,
Smyrna offered a terrible reminder that World War I continued in the
East. Here on the Smyrna quayside civilians and military men witnessed
the last act of the Ottoman Empire's solution to the minority problem.
The Allies' ill-conceived response to the rising tide of Turkish nationalism, coupled with a wait and see attitude to the events at Smyrna,
exacerbated the humanitarian crisis unfolding in the Mediterranean.[4]
Eventually, many did take a turn as heroes by participating in rescue
efforts. This helped ease the suffering of civilian victims while revealing other uncomfortable truths about the reality of Total War on Eastern
Front.

The international crisis of the 1920s that would displace over one
million Greek, Armenian, Assyrian, and European inhabitants of the
Ottoman Empire put in sharp relief the failure of humanitarian diplomacy in the face of genocidal nationalism.[5] It also marked a symbolic

end to the connection between British humanitarianism and Eastern Christians. The peace settlement signed at Lausanne in summer 1923 codified a vision of the Near East mapped along ethnic and religious lines. With the final elimination of the Christian population from the region, the burning of Smyrna dramatically erased the impetus for protection of subject minority populations that had made foreign policy when it came to the Eastern Question a matter of conscience.

Allied ships called to the Smyrna harbor in early September 1922 included American, French, Italian, and British destroyers, battleships, and aid vessels with orders of strict neutrality. "Our duty is to watch the pier and landing places for refugees, and if British to bring them off," one sailor recorded in his diary.[6] The British consul at Smyrna, Sir Henry Lamb, initially sounded the alarm, requesting that evacuation ships be sent as soon as word reached him of the Greek defeat in the interior at the hands of Turkish nationalist forces. Greece had occupied Smyrna since their 1919 invasion, supported by David Lloyd George's government. Reports of Greek atrocities against Muslim subjects during the occupation fueled an already tense postwar situation, one made worse when victorious Turkish nationalist forces replaced the retreating Greek army in 1922.[7]

The forces of the nationalist leader Mustafa Kemal, operating outside the sanction of the Ottoman government at Constantinople, fully controlled the city by early September. The "inability of Greek army to defend town from invasion" according to a Foreign Office telegram, prompted orders for the "Evacuation of the British Colony at Smyrna" on September 2.[8] Lord Curzon proposed the "[c]omplete evacuation of Asia Minor" the next day. "His Majesty's Government are ... anxious to terminate disastrous warfare and to avoid further shedding of blood," wrote Curzon to a British official in Constantinople, and "will gladly take any steps in conjunction with their allies to secure these objects." Curzon cautioned that the government must also "consider political conditions under which evacuation will take" place, which included, he believed, the "Protection of Christian populations."[9]

By September 4, however, plans had been secured only for the evacuation of British nationals, whom the government would provide with food for the voyage but no accommodation upon arrival in either Malta or Cyprus.[10] When the *Iron Duke* arrived in the Smyrna harbor on September 4, it had the charge of collecting approximately 1,200 refugees from 4 designated locations along the coast. Heavily armed soldiers in "Khaki fighting kit and shrapnel helmets" would ensure the prevention of "any but British subjects from embarking."[11] The order of strict neutrality excluded assisting or taking any non-British nationals onboard ships. This placed military men in an unenviable position of having to turn away desperate civilians marked for elimination by Turkish nationalists.

Even before the fire started the sailors who arrived in Smyrna in early September realized that this would not be a routine evacuation. The presence of regular Turkish cavalry and armed irregulars called "chettes" increased the tension among an already nervous populace in a place where Greeks, Armenians, and Europeans historically dominated.[12] Anxious residents already filled the harbor when the first British ships arrived. Those stationed on the HMS *Tribune* watched the scene from its mooring on the Custom House wharf: "Ferry boats crowded with terrified Greeks—one passenger not understanding our neutrality and evidently disappointed at us taking no action, shouted out at us as the ferry passed, 'Thank you very much, kill us like lot chickens'—this was accompanied by the suggestive motion of drawing the hand across the throat." This comic gesture found its tragic counterpoint in the scene on shore where the crew witnessed a series of brutal murders in broad daylight.[13]

Many suspected that the violence would get worse, but few anticipated that the nationalist army would set fire to the city. Eyewitnesses reported seeing Turkish soldiers deliberately starting the fires that would leave the city in ruins. Howes recorded the fate of refugees who had taken cover in an Armenian church: "an American eye-witness declared that the regular Turks set fire to the church and then surrounded it."[14] Numerous other sources corroborated these observations. Members of the Smyrna Fire Brigade testified in a trial against the Guardian Assurance Company after the war that they witnessed barrels of petroleum unloaded by Turkish soldiers and purposefully set ablaze.[15] By September 14 arson had spread to the port offices. "Eyewitnesses from the HMS *Cardiff* state that these offices were deliberately set on fire by Turkish soldiers who were going round the building with torches," reported one sailor who believed the fires had been set "to cover up traces of more massacred Armenians."[16]

In the days preceding the fire, British ships, like their American and Italian counterparts, remained "fully occupied" evacuating their own nationals. "Most of us of my vintage were used to evacuations," Captain Swinley of the HMS *Curacoa*, a ship stationed in the Mediterranean, later recalled.[17] Disturbing signs, however, suggested that this one would be different. "At noon a dead body appeared, in an upright position (tied in a sack, which was evidently weighted at the bottom) and floated to the ship's side, where it remained owing to the direction of the wind. A second body appeared an hour later, and as there was no prospect of these floating away, they were weighted and sank." Those refugees who made it to ship alive fared little better. "At 2330 a man was seen swimming towards the ship he hailed us with 'I am a Greek officer' we were unable to assist him but he clung to our cable for an hour and a half, eventually swimming off and we hope succeeded in reaching the shore again."[18] By following orders of neutrality, the British only added to what Officer Drage described as a "very muddled evacuation." The outbreak of the fire added to the confusion, driving an estimated half-million refugees to the two-mile-long Smyrna quayside. A day after the fire devastated the Armenian and Greek quarters of the city, sailors reported that "scores of people were swimming round the ship imploring to be saved, some of them holding the ship's side after we had got under way."[19] Sailors, Officer Drage related in an interview after the war, had orders to do all they could to "take off refugees." This included "beating women over the head to stop them from swamping my whaler."[20]

Suddenly, on September 14 "a signal was made by the Commander in chief—'away all boats'" and the mission transformed into a rescue effort (figure 22).[21] Although the record of the original order has disappeared from the National Archives, the recollection of observers and news reports tell a story of an ad hoc rescue mission executed in response to circumstances on the ground, not orders from London. When Admiral de Roebuck gave the order to start evacuating non-British refugees, he did so by arguing "that the agreement not to take any refugees on board British ships could no longer be binding."[22] Duncan Gardner Wallace, a member of a prominent Levantine family called up as a reservist officer in the Royal Navy at the outbreak of the war, served on the *Iron Duke* at the time of the fire. "The situation was obviously horrifying for the crews and those in command of the British ships," his son remembered his father saying, "particularly in the light of our own country's political and moral responsibility for what was happening."[23] Wallace, having lived and worked in Smyrna, implored the Admiral to abandon the policy of "strict neutrality." "Whether or not assisted by press or diplomatic reports which were probably now reaching allied governments of developing events," Wallace recalled, "the orders were at last changed and British ships authorized to take off refugees of all nationalities who were in danger." Soon after, the admiral gave Wallace a small landing party to evacuate a makeshift hospital of evacuees set up in the European area of the city.[24] The coordination of this effort extended beyond the military, with the Board of Trade helping to organize transportation for the evacuees

Figure 22. Smyrna harbor patrolled by Turkish soldiers on shore, with Allied ships waiting. Reproduced by permission of D. W. Vereker. Private collection.

"to suitable destinations where supplies will be available."[25] Not long after Wallace's own family disembarked in Alexandria "as penniless refugees."

The humanitarian crisis caused by the fire turned others of the dozens of Allied ships in the harbor from observers into participants.[26] For many victims, however, the rescue effort came too late. One of the ships moored along the dock described the scene: "Thousands must have been saved by the fleet. Owing to the roaring of the fire, the cries of the people, and the crashing of falling beams, rescue work was very difficult. A horse caught fire and galloped madly into the crowd—its end was not seen."[27] The ships' decks heaved with refugees who later were forced to disembark on nearby Karnac. The uncoordinated nature of the effort made the response inadequate at best. "There are still large numbers of refugees ashore, and the French and Italians are continuing the embarkation of their subjects. If we still need a reminder of what has taken place, we get it in the corpses that constantly float past the ship. Men, women and children drift past and we are thankful they do not hang round the ship as they did when we were secured to the wall."[28] Those serving at Smyrna described the task of evacuating hundreds of thousands of refugees as overwhelming. Initially sent to evacuate 1,200 British nationals, they found themselves ill-equipped to deal with the crisis (see figure 23). Officer Drage remembered during this tumultuous time pulling an infant from the water, shocked that it had survived the scene. This often led to half-measures including picking up and leaving refugees anywhere that would take them. Drage's rescued baby ended up at a nearby monastery.[29] Immediately after leaving Smyrna, Howes wrote, "as hard as our boats and sailors worked during the night in rescues we didn't seem to make much impression in diminishing the crowd. Old women of 80 and upwards had all the household goods they had managed to rescue on their humped backs, cripples were staggering along the burning beach, and were dropping on the way. Skeletons and remains of crutches testifying to their fate."[30]

In the absence of a coordinated effort by officials on the scene and in London the humanitarian mission faltered. This had important political implications. As the Allies struggled to gain control of the refugee situation, Mustafa Kemal's hold on the city tightened. Kemal informed the Allies that all evacuations would cease on October 1 and Turkish commander Nourredin Pasha claimed, according to Rear Admiral Tyrwhitt, that after that date "any refugees remaining after that date would be massacred."[31] According to one newspaper report, "No reply has been given to the request made to the Turks for an extension of time, but the work was still proceeding and was not stopped on September 30 as threatened by

Figure 23. Smyrna refugees awaiting their fate. Young men were deported to the interior, while others were transported to various destinations in the Mediterranean on Allied ships. Reproduced by permission of David Vereker. Private collection.

the Turkish authorities." Greek ships under American control and British ships took part in evacuating 177,000 "refugees of all nationalities," with most of the majority, 146,700, taking place between September 26 and 29.[32] Having "completely cleared the town of Greeks and Armenians," one official wrote, "The Turks claim to have solved the problem of minorities. Large numbers left by sea, but many thousands of males especially have been marched to the interior."[33]

The "problem of minorities," however, continued for the Allies. Lt. Swinley described the scene of the rushed evacuation under Kemalist dictates from his vantage point on the HMS *Curacoa* in late September:

> The town appeared quiet except for smoke rising from two smoulder-ing fires. . . . On the 26th the evacuation commenced. Every avail-able hand in the ship was landed and arrangements were made for dealing with the baggage and were sorted out by the Turkish Guard who kept back men of military age. . . . Many of these unfortunate refugees, chiefly Greeks and Armenians, were in a pitiable state and several died on board or fell exhausted on reaching the gangways . . .

Families became separated and the shrieking and crying of women and children whose husbands and fathers had been seized by the Turks at the barriers was truly pitiful. Each ship was crammed and there was hardly room to move on deck.[34]

After four-and-a-half days of loading rescue ships, "the flow suddenly ceased and we learned that the evacuation was to all intents and purposes finished."[35] Those who made it on board were taken to Mitilini on the Greek island of Lesbos while the men of "military age" separated from their families were deported into the interior where many were killed or died of exposure or starvation. The Foreign Office reported that the HMS *Cardiff* and HMS *Curacoa* evacuated approximately 30,000 per day (it was "impossible to give exact figures"), and that by the end of September "there is no apparent diminution in the numbers clamoring for admission to the embarkation jetty."[36]

The Allied position in the East continued to deteriorate in October and November, though one official reported that "[w]hile openly rejoicing in the disappearance of the Armenians and the departure of the Greeks, certain Turkish officials continue to deplore the absence of the British in their capital."[37] Conditions in Smyrna, however, suggested that the British might not be welcome either. In October, Acting Vice-Consul Urquhart reported to Sir H. Rumbold in Constantinople that along with Greek churches being "systematically razed to the ground" the "British cemetery at Bournabat [a Smyrna suburb] had been entered and the graves defiled." Urquhart concluded: "It is becoming increasingly clear that the military are out of hand."[38] For those who wanted to come back to reclaim their property Urquhart had little to offer. "So far as trade is concerned the outlook is perplexing. . . . The conclusion is that the Turks have no commercial or fiscal policy whatsoever," he wrote to Rumbold.[39] By mid-November Rumbold informed Curzon that the "Situation is less satisfactory. Military attitude increasingly aggressive. . . . Seriously considering both advising British subjects to leave Smyrna and preventing others landing."[40] Urquhart agreed. He himself had faced harassment by Turkish soldiers who took his diplomatic pass away and threatened him with violence when he tried to embark on a ship to communicate with his superiors. By the end of November only a handful of Britons and Maltese nationals who refused to leave remained in Smyrna.

Confrontations with Kemalist forces over the civilian evacuations made it clear that peace on the Eastern Front hinged on letting the nationalists resolve the minority question their way. Such a capitulation showed how little purchase a once self-confident humanitarianism, which drove nineteenth-century foreign policy, held after the disaster at Smyrna. Within a matter of months, Britain was forced to the table to renegotiate the ill-fated Treaty of Sevres. This first attempt at peace with the Ottoman Empire contained strong protections for Christian minorities. The "strained but absentminded" arguments of the Lausanne conference, as one historian characterized the negotiations that would ultimately revise Sevres, led to a new treaty that weakened minority protection provisions.[41] With Britain's pro-Greek policy in ruins with its architect, Lloyd George, and his coalition government out of office, nationalists considered the signing of the Lausanne Treaty in July 1923 "the greatest diplomatic victory" in Turkish history.[42] In the end, the haphazard humanitarian relief effort weakened the effect of the military victory over the Central Powers on the Eastern Front while doing little to stem the chaos of the refugee crisis.

The total devastation of Smyrna and the subsequent evacuations indicated that the price of enforcing the dictates of a foreign policy that pledged to protect minorities would be continuing a war that no one wanted to fight. As Howes concluded the chronicle of his days in Smyrna in September 1922, "Although the British navy landed with arms but did not fire, and so plunge England into the War the greatest credit is due to them for the splendid way the controlled themselves whilst these atrocities were committed all round them."[43] The atrocities offered another sailor a different lesson. As he left Smyrna for Constantinople less than a week after the fire began, he concluded in his journal that it would "be a long time before we forget the experiences of the last few days, and above everything else we are thankful that we were not born Armenians."[44]

THE ROAD TO SMYRNA

The events of September 1922 marked the lowest point in more than three years of clumsy military and diplomatic maneuvering that had failed to bring peace to the Near East. Fear of continued violence between Christians and Muslims informed early discussions of the peace settlement with the Ottoman Empire. The Allies decided that Greece should take over the Christian-dominated west coast of Anatolia. On May 11, 1919, Foreign Secretary Balfour sent a secret dispatch from Paris outlining Allied plans for the protection of Smyrna's Christian inhabitants: "with a view to avoiding disorders and massacres of Christians and its environs, the occupation of the town and forts by Allied Forces has been decided upon by President, P.M. and M. Clemenceau. Greek troops are on their way to Smyrna and Turks will be summoned to hand over forts to a landing party." This plan, put into action within forty-eight hours' time, was not revealed to either the Turkish or Italian delegation.[45] Lloyd George's support of the invasion had at its core the belief that leaving the administration of Christian minorities to the Greeks would best serve minorities and British imperial interests.

The Greek invasion and massacres committed by the Greek army against Muslim civilians after landing, however, emboldened Turkish nationalists, who blocked the implementation of the Treaty of Sevres signed in August 1920. Significantly, the failure of Sevres meant that fighting between the Allies and the Ottoman Empire on the Eastern Front continued well beyond the signing of the Armistice at Mudros in October 1918. Military confrontations included not only the Greek invasion of Smyrna and subsequent reconquest by Turkish troops led by Mustafa Kemal but also the Allied offensive in Cilicia, the historic site of Armenia in southern Anatolia that the Allies failed to reconstitute after two years of French occupation, and the maneuverings of Britain's "Hush Hush army," which had a mission to check Russian ambitions and win the support of minority populations living in eastern Anatolia.

These years of continued fighting and sectarian violence fueled worries over instability in the region. "Turks have shown themselves incapable of governing," wrote one nervous British resident early in 1919 who did not believe that the Greeks would do much better. Smyrna stood at the center of these discussions due to its position as an important outlet and center for global trade. One Foreign Office report cited that the majority of shipping interests historically had rested in British hands, as did the cloth and carpet making industries. A representative for the British Chamber of Commerce in Smyrna confirmed this and asked that the government help safeguard commercial interests.[46] The presence of Allied troops did not satisfy some who hoped that Britain, France, or the United States would take charge of the city. In the end, the high commissioner at Constantinople, Admiral Calthorpe, best summed up the situation in Smyrna, claiming that conflicting interests among the Greek, British, French, American, Italian, and Ottoman forces meant that "[g]overnment is rendered almost hopeless by uncertainty."

International mandates supported by the League of Nations led to more uncertainty when it came to the question of minorities. An important part of Allied efforts to resolve the war in the East centered on finding a diplomatic solution to the problem of Muslim-Christian violence. As

Bruce Clark has shown, the postwar treaties set out to solve the divisive issue of religion by using "religion as a criterion" in the peacemaking process.[47] At the center was the League of Nations and the negotiation and enforcement of so-called Minority Treaties, provisions to protect "those elements of the population who differ from the majority of their countrymen in race, creed, or tongue" within individual treaties negotiated between the powers after the war.[48] Sevres and Lausanne both contained minority provisions. Transnational commitments to the protection of minority rights after the war required the consent of individual nations to treaty agreements legitimated by the League. Even though the League of Nations covenant included no mention of minorities itself it would eventually be left to the League, not Britain, to enforce internationally agreed-upon provisions that protected minorities living in disputed territories.[49]

Post–World War I minority treaties, like their nineteenth-century predecessors including the Treaty of Berlin, promised much and delivered little. Regardless, postwar negotiators viewed such agreements as the best hope to resolve the ongoing problem of sectarian violence. As one analysis of these agreements concluded in 1925, "The idea underlying the minority treaties is clearly the child of another period. It was conceived in the throes of the world struggle, amidst the destruction which brought about the war, which the war condemned but which the peace has unfortunately revived." Nevertheless, it was concluded, "These treaties are, with the League itself, the main hope of Europe and the world."[50] Between 1920 and 1923 the Allies held over two dozen conferences throughout the capitals of Europe touting an outmoded treaty system as the solution to resolving the ethnic and religious hatred exacerbated by a protracted world war.

Although the rise of the League of Nations would eventually internationalize the minority question, Britain initially took its traditional leadership role as guarantor of minority rights after the signing of the armistice with Turkey. Considerations of these questions fell to the "Eastern Committee" first set up by the War Cabinet in March 1918. Here Lord Curzon, Robert Cecil, General Smuts, Sir Louis Mallet, and other Eastern Question veterans coordinated British policy on the "Eastern Front," an extremely broad category that included any "enemy movement or action in the Black Sea, the Caucasus, and Trans Caucasus, Armenia, Persia, the Caspian, Transcaspia, Turkestan, Afghanistan, Sinai, Palestine, Syria the Hejaz, Arabia, Mesopotamia, the Persian Gulf."[51] When discussions in this catchall committee of Near Eastern affairs turned to the Ottoman settlement in December after the armistice, Curzon opened the meeting by citing Britain's obligation to Christian minorities in the Treaty of Berlin. His plan to create an Armenian state in Cilicia came out of strategic considerations, as he believed it would serve as a barrier to the spread of a nationalist-driven Pan-Turanism. Other committee members wanted a bigger Armenian state set up in eastern Turkey that would include more territory beyond that of the historically Armenian-dominated vilayets in Anatolia.[52]

These discussions kept a keen eye on public opinion. As Robert Cecil acknowledged to his Eastern Committee colleagues at the December meeting: "This question of Armenian relief is one which excites a great deal of feeling."[53] Concerns over the rising power of the United States also came into play. Cecil's support for an American proposal for humanitarian aid that he claimed "can do no harm" met with immediate objections. This aid, some argued, would lead America to set up a "commercial enterprise" in the region that would challenge British trade interests. In the end, the committee decided that it had little choice but to cooperate with the relief effort and to send money and ground support, leaving the Americans to supply food aid through organizations like the U.S.-based Near East Relief.

The maze of political and humanitarian interests governing the peace settlement generated confusion as the Treaty of Sevres unraveled, shaking the moral certainty that had guided nineteenth-century treaty negotiations with the Ottoman Empire. In a 1921 letter to Lord Curzon, Montagu at the Foreign Office expressed his frustration with the ongoing war between Turkey and Greece: "I am so very much at sea as to what exactly is the position with regard to the Turkish treaty that I do not know how to answer it. Are we still awaiting a reply from the Greeks and the Turks to the offers finally made to them? Are they to be left to stew in their own juice? Are we to allow fighting to go on forever? What is the end of this business? If you could find time to suggest an answer to this letter, it would help me very much."[54] The minority issue, in particular, clouded attempts at a settlement. The politician T. P. O'Connor wrote Curzon on Christmas Eve that he believed that despite signs of waning interest, public opinion remained "unanimous" in favoring the liberation of "every Christian race from the dominion of Turkey."[55]

HUMANITARIANISM AND THE EASTERN SETTLEMENT

O'Connor's observation that Britons still understood Near Eastern Christian minorities as their special responsibility found expression in humanitarian advocacy work. Activists from religious and secular relief organizations continued to lobby the government and provide aid to civilian victims after the war including the Lord Mayor's Fund (LMF), the Friends of Armenia, and the British Armenian Committee (BAC). To bolster support for their cause, these organizations used reports from representatives sent to the Caucasus to do relief work, the media, and fund-raising appeals.[56] Political pressure groups hoped that talk of an American mandate for Armenia would come to pass and ease Britain's sense of moral and financial responsibility. The BAC put pressure on the government to encourage the American mandate while organizing efforts to increase pledges of aid for refugees.

The attempt to find a political solution rallied humanitarian efforts uniting national and international aid organizations like the LMF, the BAC, and American philanthropic groups. Joint public meetings and deputations to the Foreign Office and House of Commons by the LMF and BAC had become commonplace as early as 1918 and continued through the early 1920s.[57] The BAC also encouraged meetings held by Free and Established Churches advocating for a favorable postwar settlement for Armenia.[58] The formation of the Armenian Bureau of Information, a publishing arm run by prominent London-based Armenian advocates, that same year kept the work of these committees before the public. BAC members also relentlessly pursued press coverage of Armenian issues in the American and British press. In August 1920 the BAC reported in their weekly meeting that they had placed stories and letters to the editor in over a hundred newspapers in order "to gain more sympathy for Armenia" from "the British public."[59] Pledges of financial support came in from individual contributors, the Armenian communities in London, Manchester, and Liverpool and aid organizations abroad.

Advocacy efforts continued throughout the crisis. As late as the 1930s some philanthropists still maintained that "[t]he Armenians are really our national responsibility."[60] The Assyrian cause, supported by the Archbishop of Canterbury, achieved greater visibility after the war despite their smaller numbers and the lack of a significant Assyrian community in Britain itself. Greeks also had advocates in Britain. The most notable "Philhellenes," of course, had been W. E. Gladstone himself and later Lloyd George, whose support of the Greek invasion of Anatolia caused his downfall in October 1922. The Greek nation, some believed, would best represent the interests of Pontic, or Ottoman, Greeks. Yet advocates also maintained that Britain bore responsibility for this group as well. "The Greek military disaster in Asia Minor, followed by the burning of Smyrna, led to a general flight of Greek inhabitants from Asia to Greece," wrote one aid worker in the *Fortnightly Review,* and "the suffering of these helpless multitudes might well strike a note of pity in our languid hearts. England, through her politicians, has too much responsibility for encouraging the Greeks on their desperate Asia Minor adventure for the national conscience to be without burden on this matter."[61] The Archbishop of Canterbury encouraged the government to loan money to Greece for refugee resettlement.[62] During the early 1920s, the Anglo-Hellenic League and BAC issued a pamphlet on the deportations in Asia Minor in an attempt to make the case of persecuted minorities one.[63]

For skeptics, the Smyrna disaster served as a warning against further humanitarian intervention, one that called into question Britain's historical role as a defender of minority rights. One writer for the *Saturday Review* called the minority problem a sad case, yet implored, "is the whole world to go to war again because of that misfortune?"[64] E. N. Bennett in the *English Review* sounded a siren against sympathizing too much with Ottoman Christians, claiming that "religious bigotry, faked atrocity films, and reckless newspaper propaganda" would help drive "our debt-burdened, war weary nation into fresh campaigns and heavy expenditure."[65] At the same time pro-Ottoman organizations like the Near and Middle East Association mobilized on behalf of cultivating stronger commercial relations with the region by supporting Muslim interests in the peace settlement.[66]

Probably the most prominent critique came from Arnold Toynbee, the co-author of the Bryce Report, who claimed that his earlier work later made him "lean over backwards" to give the Turkish case a hearing.[67] In 1921 he served as a correspondent for the *Manchester Guardian* in Anatolia, taking pains to represent himself as an "impartial observer" of Eastern affairs. Toynbee argued that "the ineptitude of Western diplomacy" brought the current refugee crisis and war to a head and ultimately resulted in a fire that could have been prevented by keeping the Greeks out of Anatolia in the first place. "The blood of their slain and the smoke of their burning cry out to Heaven and the Recording Angel has certainly entered these items against the names of Mr. Lloyd George and his French and Italian colleagues."[68] At the root of this analysis rested Toynbee's belief that the humanitarian disaster at Smyrna, which included both Muslim and Christian victims, only exacerbated political tensions at home: "Who indeed would have believed beforehand that the tragedy in Anatolia would become good copy for a newspaper stunt or that the Conservative Party in Great Britain would be able to turn it to account for getting rid of Lloyd George?"[69]

Peace negotiations with the Ottoman Empire put new pressure on the old question of British responsibility for the protection of Near Eastern Christians. The government keenly understood the difficulty of answering to a public that both continued to give generously to the LMF, Friends of Armenia, and other aid organizations and wanted the war to end. Political lobbying organizations like the BAC tried to square the circle by supporting a national solution enforced by Britain that offered protection for minority populations within ethnically organized nation-states. In 1921 Aneurin Williams wrote to Lord Curzon in support of this plan, but Curzon dismissed it as naïve: "You cannot expect this country (or indeed any other) arbitrarily to select a portion of Turkey, to eject all other races, to concentrate within a ring of British bayonets a large number of destitute refugees and so to organise an Armenian national existence at immense expense to the British taxpayer." As Curzon patronizingly concluded, "You really must trust the government who are just as humane as you are, to do their best. Quite the worst thing, I am sure, is to despair either of your own country or of the race in whose fate you have always shown so devoted and passionate an interest."[70]

REVISING THE PEACE

Lausanne put Curzon's "humane" Near Eastern policy to the test. The failure of Sevres made a new treaty inevitable, a process that languished until after the burning of Smyrna. Less than two months after the last fires died out the Allies were back at the table with the new nationalist-led Turkish government and ready to make the necessary concessions for peace. The final agreement reflected the new reality. "Though Turkey had shared the final defeat of the Central Powers, the nationalists had never ceased fighting," one commentator observed. "In peace conferences there should be a victor and a vanquished, but at Lausanne the vanquished had become victorious and the partner of the former victors had been woefully defeated."[71] The powerful position of the new Kemalist government, on the heels of its victory over Greek forces, meant that Britain occupied a much weaker position than it had at the time of the 1918 Armistice. Over the seven months of negotiations at Lausanne the entire Sevres agreement came under scrutiny, particularly the minority treaty section. The ending of the Allied occupation of Constantinople and the so-called freedom of the Straits, which sought to keep open key shipping waterways that connect the Black Sea to the Mediterranean, also topped the agenda. On the eve of the opening of the Lausanne Conference, one newspaper headline summed up the British position: "Constantinople must not be allowed to be a second Smyrna."[72]

Key to the revision process was sorting out claims and defining the status of Christian minorities in the Near East. The experiences of two consular officials who worked on the minority provisions reveal how Britain came to define this responsibility. Sir Andrew Ryan and Sir Robert Graves came of age in the early days of the Levant Consular Service. Graves, a member of a prominent Anglo-Irish family, was part of a first generation of Levant trainees. After completing a student-interpreter training course in Constantinople in 1879 he served under Henry Layard at Constantinople and later in the consulates at Sofia and Erzeroom. Ryan, the son of an Irish candle maker, entered consular service twenty years later, attending Queen's College in Cork and Kings College London before being sent by the Foreign Office to Cambridge in April 1897 for further language training.[73] He moved from dealing with the woes of the British and Maltese colony at Constantinople, which he called a "chronicle of trifling affairs," to service at the embassy in 1907, serving under Sir Gerald Fitzmaurice. Though Ryan described his tasks as "still non-political" they put him in touch with "the affairs of the numerous British churches, schools and charitable institutions in the Turkish Empire." Eventually, Ryan came to spend more and more time at the seat of Ottoman government affairs at the Sublime Porte.[74]

The war offered new challenges for these two old hands. Graves served as an interpreter for the army at Gallipoli and later came to join the Constantinople staff at the time of the Greek landing in Smyrna in 1919. Meanwhile, Ryan waited for an opportunity at Constantinople in his new post at the Foreign Office, which had taken on more responsibility coordinating the war effort. The defeat at Gallipoli forced Ryan to wait his time out in London. The signing of the Armistice with Turkey brought this period to an "abrupt end" and that day he found himself on his way to Constantinople. "We had fancy titles to mark the fact that Great Britain was still in a state of war with Turkey," he recalled of his early days at the embassy.[75] Affairs in Constantinople after the Armistice continued in a state of flux. Allied diplomats descended on the scene, adding to the confusion: "There were large numbers of Allied warships in the port. The presence of so many authorities was all the more confusing as their position in relation to each other and to the Turkish Government had still to be defined."[76]

Ryan was assigned to a special section of the High Commission designed to "deal with the affairs of Armenian and Greek victims of persecution." As Ryan understood his role, "The Greeks had suffered greatly before the war and probably during it, though anything they suffered from 1915 to 1918 was overshadowed by the persecution of the Armenians, most of whom had been deported or massacred. We had in the British High Commission an Armenian and Greek section for the purpose of redressing their wrongs."[77] Graves upon his arrival in 1919 joined the Armenian and Greek Section (AGS), as it came to be called, as a military attaché with special responsibilities that included the "rescue of Armenian and Greek women and children who had been forcibly converted to Islam from the Turkish houses and institutions into which they had been taken, and also obtain the restitution of their rights to owners of Christian properties which had been arbitrarily confiscated." The AGS also employed "Relief Officers with knowledge of the country and the languages" to report "on the condition of the native Christians who had remained in the interior, and in ministering to their needs as far as they were able."[78] Ryan took part in similar efforts; corresponding with relief workers and taking part in British and American efforts to repatriate Armenian girls.[79]

This work deeply involved these two relatively minor officials in treaty negotiations over the minority question. Graves had witnessed the opening drama of the Constantinople War Crimes tribunals in May of 1919, when the British "arrested and deported to Malta . . . the leading members of the Committee of Union and Progress."[80] In July, after being put in charge of the AGS he exercised influence over responses to U.S. President Woodrow Wilson's scheme for Armenia and Kurdistan. Graves "was not a little pleased to find that Admiral Webb concurred entirely in my views on a subject with which I had been familiar for more than a quarter century and to know that they went to Paris as his own considered opinion."[81] Ryan, too, took a role in Sevres. As he claimed of his own motivations regarding the minority issue: "We were dealing with a country which under its then rulers, had stabbed us in the back in 1914 which had shown hostility to foreign interests, which seemed unlikely to be able to work out its own financial and economic salvation, and which above all (in my view) could not be trusted with the fate of its minorities, to judge by the merciless persecution of the Armenians during the war. Rightly or wrongly, these were the ideas which inspired all discussions in responsible Allied circles."[82]

Focus on the minority question as a problem of reform ultimately failed to sustain Sevres just as it had the Treaty of Berlin a generation earlier. Graves remembered that as early as 1919 that "[o]wing to the reduction of relief funds things were going badly with the Armenian and Greek Section and reports from our Relief Officers told of growing insecurity in the interior and difficulties in obtaining the release of Islamized women and children and the restitution of confiscated Christian property."[83] By the end of the year, the Supreme Council of the Allies had rejected appeals from the Armenian and Greek patriarchs for relief funds just as word of new massacres in Cilicia reached the embassy after a visit from the Bishop of Gibraltar and two American aid workers. "The year 1919 had ended with the rejection by the Supreme Council of the Allies of an appeal from the Armenian and Greek Patriarchates for an advance of funds for their distressed communities," Graves remembered. "I began the New Year with a sense of depression and the fear that the hopes which I had founded on our victory in the East were in danger of being disappointed."[84]

Under these changed conditions, Graves continued his work on the minority sections of Sevres: "[I]n my capacity as head of the Armenian and Greek section I drafted proposals for the protection of Minorities and the restitution of confiscated Christian property in Turkey as well as for the exemption of the properties of Christian Ottoman subjects in the territories of the Allied Powers from seizure and liquidation for the payment of reparations." Graves was informed that his proposal had been recommended for inclusion in the treaty. His memoirs, like Ryan's, show a keen connection to the work that he performed for the AGS. Later he reflected that he regretted turning down a post in Bulgaria (a country that he "retained a lingering sympathy for"), having thought that he "might yet do useful service in the work which had been the chief interest in my life for so many years, namely the protection of the Christian minorities in Turkey."[85]

Peace negotiations started at Sevres had little hope for going forward as the new nationalist government took hold of the city of Ankara. Meanwhile, the Allies shuffled top diplomatic posts in far-off Constantinople in the futile hope of regaining influence.[86] The failure of the London Conference in February 1921 between the Turkish nationalist government and Allied representatives made the British give up on the possibility of leading the charge in brokering a settlement regarding the minority question. Disappointment with the outcome of the conference coupled with budgetary constraints "marked [the AGS] for suppression at the end of the year 1921." It also ended Graves's more than forty years of continuous service with the Foreign Office.[87] After retirement he worked with the LMF and later joined Ann Mary Burgess at Corfu, where along with his sons he supported her rug factory and work with Armenian and Greek refugees.[88] During the mid-1920s he served on the Greek Refugee

Settlement Commission. Ryan, however, remained a steady presence in peace negotiations through to the Lausanne Conference. His role as a delegate made him "mostly occupied with questions concerning minorities and the position of foreigners and their interests in Turkey." In one of his final acts in Constantinople he served as interpreter to the last sultan in a meeting with Rumbold immediately before the two men departed for Lausanne on November 15.

At Lausanne, diplomats led by Lord Curzon kept pressure on the minority question. Historians have focused on Curzon's obsession at the conference with grabbing hold of the administration of oil-rich Mesopotamia, which according to G. D. Clayton paved the way for "a new British Middle Eastern empire . . . between the Mediterranean and the Persian Gulf."[89] This certainly played a role in British perceptions of its role in the region. Curzon's understandings of the minority question at the conference also loomed large. Determined to serve as the conference's president, Curzon provided the moral argument for what he called the "unmixing populations" that he claimed would protect survivors of the Genocide and Smyrna disaster. The dividing of states along religious lines he argued would also best serve British political interests in the "changed conditions in the Near East."[90]

Lausanne was Curzon's conference, but it was the League of Nations that had the final say regarding minorities. In a changing geopolitical order international bodies like the League would eventually supplant the British Empire's historical leadership on the issue of minority protection. Curzon dedicated three sittings of the conference to the problem of minorities although, according to Harold Nicolson, he fully realized that Turkish negotiators would not agree to outside interference, British or otherwise, regarding how to deal with the remaining Christian population.[91] The League of Nations' High Commissioner for Refugees Dr. Fridtjof Nansen offered Curzon a way out that fit neatly with Curzon's own geopolitical and ethnographic world view. Nansen proposed a population exchange between European Muslims and Ottoman Christians. His plan ultimately would be responsible for displacing approximately 1.2 million Orthodox Christians and 400,000 Muslims. The plan called for Christian and Muslims to switch places, with Christian minorities going to Greece and Muslim minorities going to Turkey.[92]

This proposal reflected a subtle but important difference in how Lausanne categorized minorities. In the Lausanne Treaty the category of "Moslem and non-Moslem" replaced a more diverse characterization of minority communities embodied in Sevres that favored the use of the term "racial minorities" and "non-Turkish" as categories over specifically religious characterizations.[93] These new categorizations drew upon timeworn Victorian understandings of ethnographical difference. At the same time Lausanne's architects refined categories of difference to make religion distinct from ethnicity. Understanding the conflict in the stark terms of Muslim versus non-Muslim obscured the referent that had animated British humanitarianism in the Near East starting in the Crimean War. The Armenians, Assyrians, and Greeks became part of a catchall category of minority victims defined in opposition to Islam.

After arriving in Constantinople early in 1923 Ryan remarked that "[w]e found the city greatly changed. The Allied occupation still continued in theory, but, apart from the presence of troops and warships, it had little life in it." Back in Britain, a similar sentiment pervaded. In July 1923, the *Daily Express* caricatured the conference in a cartoon entitled "The Woman of No Importance." The image depicted "a dejected goddess carrying a cage in which was a dove shedding copious tears through the wires."[94] Peace with Turkey excited little interest at home with the exception of those who, like Ryan, worried that the price of ending the war at Lausanne was the "final death-blow" to the possibility of coexistence between Muslims and Christians in the Near East. "We took home peace without great honour," Ryan concluded, "Still it was peace, after close on five years of armistice."[95]

Back in Smyrna, one British observer watched the Turkish buildup of arms along the coast: "Tomorrow will see the end of the Allied Occupation and we shall have a division moving in on the 5th and 6th.· The Christians are, as you can imagine very anxious as to what will happen to them."[96] By this time, however, the vast majority of Turkey's Christian inhabitants had succumbed to deportations, massacres, and the fire at Smyrna. The remainder faced a new life as refugees exiled by a peace treaty that legitimated the nationalist solution to the minority problem enacted by a dying Ottoman Empire.

DISPLACED PEOPLES

The more than one million Greek, Armenian, and Assyrian refugees that flooded Greece from the Ottoman Empire served as a grim reminder that the minority question still lingered as a humanitarian and political problem. After Smyrna, "Christian Minorities," according to one observer, "became synonymous with the word refugees." Greece willingly took in all refugees expelled from the Ottoman Empire as a condition of the Lausanne negotiations but now faced its own crisis, with twenty percent of its population during the mid-1920s holding refugee status.[97] Greece and the League of Nations looked for help mainly from Britain, France, and the United States, countries with strong ties to these new stateless peoples. The British government accepted relatively few refugees from this category and funded even fewer projects related to resettlement. The public, however, continued to give. Private charities like Save the Children, the Lord Mayor's Fund, and the Society of Friends Relief organization scrambled to fund projects that served a population of displaced civilians scattered outside of the boundaries of the Near East.

Described as a "problem of colossal dimensions," the postwar process of what Curzon had called the "unmixing populations" officially commenced in January 1923.[98] The uncertain status of Armenians and Assyrians made theirs a particularly difficult case long before that date.[99] The virtual elimination of the entire Christian population in Anatolia after Smyrna put pressure on the surrounding regions at a time when the Armenian national question remained unresolved.[100] In addition to Greece, Armenians and Assyrians found their way to British-mandated territories in Mesopotamia, settlements in Erivan, the core of the eventual Soviet territory of Armenia, and French-mandated territories in Syria. Strict immigration controls meant that few ended up in Britain itself. The founding of an Orthodox Armenian church in Iverna Gardens in Kensington in 1922 offered a token symbol of London's small Armenian community.[101] The tightening of immigration restrictions before the war accelerated in the postwar period further confined the settlement of refugees to the regions bordering the former Ottoman Empire.[102]

This closed-door policy left officials desperate to find a solution that diffused blame for the refugee crisis and cost taxpayers as little as possible.[103] When Aneurin Williams accused Curzon of not providing a safe haven for Armenians massacred at Cilicia after the French withdrawal in 1921, Curzon shot back: "What would you have us do? It is a practical impossibility to accommodate them in Cyprus, Egypt, Mesopotamia or Palestine ... Further there is no money to defray accommodation were it available."[104] Another answer was to transfer responsibility to Commonwealth countries. New Zealand, Australia, and Canada previously had expressed a desire to take refugees willing to work the land. After Smyrna, the Foreign Office put pressure on these countries to take new refugees. As one official phrased the appeal to Commonwealth countries, "many of these Christian refugees are industrious people accustomed to pastoral and agricultural pursuits and constitute desirable immigrants."[105] The Australian government objected: "[T]he migration policy of the Commonwealth is confined to British people under the Empire Settlement Act . . . . The High Commissioner regrets that the suggestion for the absorption in Australia of a number of Armenians cannot be considered at present." Other Foreign Office appeals yielded a similar response. New Zealand was "prepared to consider individual applications" but refused to take a large number of Greek, Armenian, or Assyrian refugees.[106] Canada eventually relented and took a group of orphan children.[107]

In the end, many seemed satisfied to turn to charity appeals rather than face the potential flood of immigrants at British ports. The LMF declared that Britain would join her allies "in taking the first steps toward the liquidation of Allied obligations to the Armenian People" by helping in resettlement efforts abroad.[108] In a June 1920 advertisement in the *English Review,* Save the Children appealed for funds to serve the "5 million children starving in Central Europe and Near East." Another paper dubbed Save the Children part of "The New Army of Helpers" in the fight to help refugee children. The BAC launched numerous campaigns between January and March 1920 in the *Times* on behalf of "Near East" aid organizations. Appeals continued throughout the 1920s. The Bishop of London joined with the LMF in taking up the cause of rescuing kidnapped "slave girls."[109] A Friends of Armenia appeal in the *Saturday Review* read, "The Refugee—and an opportunity," calling for support of an agricultural relief work scheme for Armenian refugees "who were the first nation to embrace the Christian faith" in French-mandated Syria.[110] Another appeal asked, "What are you doing for Armenia?"[111]

A difficult question indeed. The geographic scope of the refugee crisis spread private and government relief efforts thin. Charities like the LMF began to oversee several relief efforts initially funded by the British government.[112] In 1922, refugee relief efforts were grouped together under the heading of the British Relief Mission.[113] One of the earliest and largest government-initiated programs was the refugee camp established thirty miles northeast of Baghdad at Bakuba in December 1918.[114] Lt. Dudley Stafford Northcote, a Cambridge graduate and grandson of the Earl of Iddesleigh, recorded in a series of letters home his three-year experience running the camp. Northcote, untrained in relief work, left his regiment after the signing of the Armistice with Turkey to find himself in charge of 1,300 Armenian and Assyrian refugees from eastern Anatolia (mainly Urmiah and Van) with the help of five British soldiers.

Northcote's new job assisting the repatriation of refugees, he admitted in a letter to his mother, was "quite a change from soldiering."[115] By spring 1919, the camp's population had swelled to house 30,000 Assyrians and 15,000 Armenian refugees. Northcote settled into his role, learning Armenian, participating in the daily life and rituals of the refugees, and even playing tennis on the newly built courts at Bakuba.[116] His early assessment of the situation, drawn from Reuters news reports, made him cautiously optimistic. He believed that his temporary position would continue until peace negotiations decided "which great Power is going to take the regions to which the refugees have got to be repatriated."[117] The repatriation process began in August 1920, as refugees were moved to Nahr-Umar, intended as a transitional camp outside of Basrah.

Contrary to Northcote's belief, the awarding of the Mesopotamian mandate to Britain had done little to help refugees at Nahr-Umar. For the Assyrians, the unraveling of Sevres coupled with resistance from local inhabitants to resettlement activities slowed the process of repatriating them around Mosul.[118] Private, public, and League of Nations interests all got involved in the resettlement process. The British continued to participate in the scheme on the grounds that the Assyrians had helped the Allies and consequently suffered brutal massacres during the war.[119] As one aid worker put it, Britain would "never abandon a friend."[120] With funds administered by the LMF, private appeals met the need of £6,000 to supply three months of relief measures. Regular reports to the Treasury chronicled how money was being spent.

The LMF soon ran out of money, forcing the fund to appeal to the government for help in anticipation of growing need. A population of around 15,000 Assyrians scattered throughout the Mediterranean had requested help settling in the British mandated territory in Mesopotamia.[121] According to one Foreign Office official, the government, while in sympathy with the plight of the Assyrians, denied the possibility of the use of public funds but claimed that "the Archbishop of Canterbury is being asked whether money can be raised privately."[122] As one official concluded, "there is no prospect of funds being provided by His Majesty's Government for the repatriation or maintenance of these unfortunate people."[123] The government, however, continued its arms-length involvement with Assyrian humanitarian efforts. In the end, the British and Iraqi government and philanthropic organizations together would contribute £300,000 to resettlement efforts.

Resettling Armenians from the camp proved equally difficult. The League of Nations under High Commissioner Nansen and U.S. President

Wilson recognized the unstable region of Erivan, precariously situated between Turkey and Russia, as a national homeland for Armenians. Proposals for an Allied mandate for the region were initially put forth at the San Remo conference in April 1920. Eventually negotiators rejected the mandate and supported establishing an Armenian state outside of the region of historic Armenia where few Armenians currently lived. The founding of Armenia on a small, 11,500 mi^2 piece of land on the border of the Ottoman Empire further distanced Britain from Anatolian concerns. After a brief period of independence as a republic, in 1922 this region became the Soviet Republic of Armenia and is today the independent Republic of Armenia.[124]

Logistical problems around the transporting of refugees from Basra to Erivan meant that by July 1921 Northcote found himself in charge of 13,000 Armenian refugees with nowhere to go.[125] The government announced plans in summer 1921 that it would close the camp on the grounds that it had already cost British taxpayers too much. A small food ration was offered to refugees willing to leave voluntarily. Northcote, having lived with the refugees for almost three years, refused along with his staff, as he put it, to send "women and children out of their tents" into the desert. Upon hearing of the plan, the BAC contacted the Colonial Office on behalf of the refugees, arguing successfully for more time. The group also worked to get Northcote's message out to the public that the £1.5 million spent on the Armenian refugees would be thrown away with little to show for humanitarian efforts.[126]

The public campaign that ensued led to a compromise that put the LMF in charge of administrative functions that later brought the refugees to Erivan. Northcote, now an employee of the LMF, agreed to stay on and take the refugees to Erivan with the fund's secretary, Rev. Harold Buxton. The government reluctantly continued its involvement. Steadily deteriorating conditions in Erivan due to famine and the overwhelming flow of refugees (more than 1,000 persons per day from all over the region) meant more appeals from the LMF.[127] Eventually, the government High Commission granted £35,000 that Buxton and Northcote administered through the fund to close the final chapter on Nahr-Umar. Meanwhile, Save the Children donated another £10,000 for this work as Northcote raised additional funds by selling refugee lace work in Britain until the mid-1920s.[128]

By this time, the settlement of refugees from the former Ottoman Empire had become a global rather than regional problem. As Nansen put the case in January 1923, "the presence in Greece of such a vast number of refugees for whom no livelihood can be found constitutes a problem with which the Greek government cannot hope to deal unless its efforts are supported by the outside world. Capital is needed for the settlement of these refugees and is needed at once."[129] Although the British offered relatively little in terms of cash, a network of consular officials, civil servants, and private citizens were hard at work.[130] Britain's *chargé d'affaires* in Athens, C. H. Bentinck, helped coordinate the aid efforts of the British Red Cross in Athens and oversaw camps on the outskirts of Athens for the more than one million refugees "scattered in large and small groups" and speaking over half a dozen languages who had come from "Smyrna, Syria, Armenia, Eastern Thrace and areas bordering the Black Sea."[131]

Eager to end temporary camps and see the permanent settlement of refugees, aid workers understood that "extraneous relief must sooner or later come to an end." To this end, organizations began to appeal "to the philanthropy of the people of our Empire to help." The need, however, continued to overwhelm aid efforts. In late 1922 13,000 refugees had landed in Corfu alone, with the total number in Greece growing to 868,186, with another 52,000 expected to arrive shortly thereafter.[132] Fear of epidemics setting in with the arrival of hot weather led to a number of stopgap measures that did little to stem the overall crisis. Outside of Athens the Stringos Camp, New Phalerum, held 4,000 refugees under the care of the British Relief Committee; its unhealthy conditions worried Bentinck.[133] In February 1923 he tried to get his counterpart in Cyprus, Malcolm Stevenson, to admit around forty Armenian Orphans to the Adventist Mission School by assuring him that the mission and not the government or the community would support the children.[134]

When Save the Children pulled out of Greece during the mid-1920s one of the things that worried Bentinck most was the thought that the British would not get credit for all of the work it had done on behalf of refugees.[135] An assessment of this role came in the form of the refugee survey done by the Royal Institute of International Affairs in the late 1930s. Britain had earned a "prominent role" in "international work for refugees" based largely on the work of private relief societies, according to the report. The LMF, the Society of Friends, and Save the Children all received praise, as did the efforts of individuals including Lord Robert Cecil and Lord Cranborne in connection with the League of Nations. British loans to Greece and Bulgaria through the League and money given to help in the settlement of Assyrian refugees also received mention. In the final assessment, however, Britain no longer held claim to the leadership role it once had regarding minority protection in a newly reconfigured East. As the report concluded: "It is doubtful, however, if this international work, largely personal and periodic is a sufficient contribution when measured by the stand of those made by other countries."[136]

KITH AND KIN IN THE FORMER NEAR EAST

The postwar crisis opened up a new category of refugee that further tested bonds with the people of the Near East. Refugees who claimed British citizenship and lived in the Ottoman Empire, included in the broad category of "Levantines," faced a particular set of challenges after Smyrna. Levantine inhabitants of the Ottoman Empire strongly identified with Britain. Though many had never stepped foot in England they held British passports and expected the government to help them during the crisis. After all, the government sent ships to Smyrna in the first place to assist in the evacuation of this Levantine population. Soon the plight of displaced Levantines began to mirror that of the Greek, Armenian, and Assyrian refugees. When it came to British subjects claiming asylum, officials found themselves stuck between a largely haphazard refugee policy and the demands of distressed individuals claiming citizenship rights.

A notice posted at the four points of embarkation around Smyrna in early September 1922 defined the limits of the government's responsibility for Levantines. Since the decision to leave was voluntary the government would not provide maintenance for any refugee after they disembarked: "nor will you be entitled to claim any compensation against the British Government for any damage to your property or losses sustained in consequence of your departure" (see figure 24).[137] British refugees found themselves scattered in settlements throughout the Mediterranean after the evacuation of Smyrna. Cyprus and Malta proved the most obvious stopping points due to their connection with the Empire, though some Levantines also ended up in Athens.

Support did eventually come from the government, but as a series of letters to the British legation at Athens from Smyrna refugees revealed, the allowance was "hardly enough to keep body and soul together."[138] A letter signed by "ONE OF THE MANY UNFORTUNATE SMYRNA REFUGEES" angrily countered suggestions that the evacuees find jobs instead of asking for help from the government, attesting that "we are not beggars. . . . All we ask for is fair play and we are not getting it and you are aware of the fact. Hoping you will do your best for us and I trust that you will if *you* are *British*."[139] Word that their allowance would be

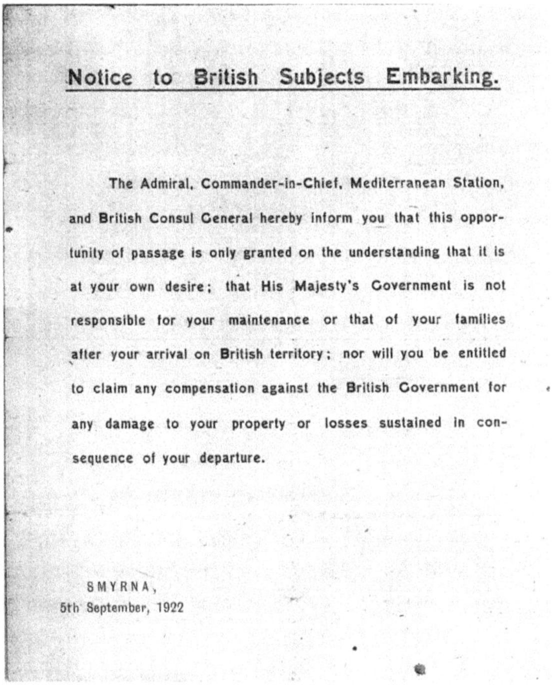

Notice to British Subjects Embarking.

The Admiral, Commander-in-Chief, Mediterranean Station, and British Consul General hereby inform you that this opportunity of passage is only granted on the understanding that it is at your own desire; that His Majesty's Government is not responsible for your maintenance or that of your families after your arrival on British territory; nor will you be entitled to claim any compensation against the British Government for any damage to your property or losses sustained in consequence of your departure.

SMYRNA,
5th September, 1922

Figure 24. The voluntary evacuation order from Smyrna for British subjects. S. L. Vereker Papers, IWM, 75/87/1.

totally stopped reached the colony in early December. *"A BRITISH LADY SMYRNA REFUGEE"* pleaded their case to Athens and London, calling the action "most unfair. We cannot find work here and we have lost everything through no fault of our own."[140] These appeals left the legation scrambling for an answer. London had the final say and Bentinck could do little to hurry their decision even though his staff believed that cutting the allowance "would involve hardship."[141]

Those with more ambiguous claims on British citizenship joined the hundreds and thousands of stateless refugees throughout the Mediterranean desperate to find a new home country. When Nicholas Sanson and Henry Martin applied for passports from the British Consul at Smyrna in late September 1922 they had little to attest to their citizenship status apart from their Anglo-sounding names. The fire had made them into undocumented refugees, emergency passholders number 84 and 90, respectively, dependent on foreign aid supplied by the British government and relief organizations. One a clerk claiming Maltese citizenship and the other a shoemaker with a British father, Joseph James Martin, they eventually solicited the help of the consul, who protested the denial of their application to Foreign Office officials. Both had Greek mothers and had been granted emergency passes and a small allowance in local currency to help them in get to Malta. There they met up with Sanson's English-speaking cousin, who traveled with them to London. Authorities turned away these men at Dover because they did not have passports or speak English. They were refused passage back to Malta on grounds that they could not produce proof of British citizenship. The two men "languished" at Calais during the winter of 1922 as officials tried to sort things out.[142]

Bentinck intervened on the behalf of these two men since he initially had granted the passes while working with the Smyrna consulate after the fire. "They could not produce to me absolute proof of nationality and that is why I gave Passes and not passports," Bentinck claimed, "but I feel pretty certain that with names like theirs they must really be British subjects." He made the case for their citizenship by arguing that "the character and composition of the late British colony at Smyrna consisting largely of what are known locally as 'Levantines' must be fully understood at the Foreign Office. These unfortunate people have no particular connection with any other part of the world. Smyrna was their home in every sense of the word as refugees they are unwelcome wherever they go, but it seems particularly pathetic that they should actually be prevented from setting foot on English soil."[143] Levantines had enjoyed British nationality as a result of the capitulations with Turkey and their connections with the Levant Company, he argued, even though many had intermarried. After checking with local sources he claimed that the names of Sanson and Martin were still well known in the Levantine community alongside Whittall, Patterson, and other prominent families. Later, the then acting consul at Smyrna questioned this assertion, claiming that he could find no evidence of employment or citizenship.[144]

The case of Sanson and Martin appealed to Bentinck. Eager to defend his granting of the passes in the first place, he also held a larger concern for the Levantine community, which he believed held legitimate citizenship claims. "The case in point appears to me is to be a particularly hard one," he wrote to his superiors at the Foreign Office in January 1923. "These people bear English names and the presumption is that their claim to British nationality is a true one. In the circumstances in which the flight from Smyrna took place, it seems more than probable that their papers, like their clothing and all their worldly goods were lost. There would surely appear to be no justification for allowing them in the face of the evidence produced to be stranded in France or in Greece, countries to whose hospitality they could produce no possible claim." In this line of thinking Sanson and Martin were British by association if not blood. As Bentinck concluded, "I trust your lordship may be able to obtain permission for these people to set foot upon the soil of the only country in the world to whose protection they can lay claim."[145] The fire had exposed the unusual status of the Levantine community, a not-quite British mixed-race element that now showed up on England's shores claiming citizenship rights. The controversy continued through April, with Bentinck defending the claims of Levantines above other refugees like those from Bolshevist Russia who "bore far less respectably British" credentials.[146] For Bentinck the historic status of Levantines trumped the problem of their mixed origins and questionable citizenship status.

For Lord Curzon, this case tested his own ambivalence regarding Britain's moral responsibility for this population. He intervened in November, asking that immigration authorities demonstrate "leniency" regarding Sanson and Martin. Curzon insisted "that refugees from the Near Eastern theatre of war, whose claim to British nationality appears doubtful to the immigration officers, might be given the benefit of the doubt unless there are very special reasons to the contrary."[147] He ultimately failed in his appeal. One Foreign Office official expressed fear that such a policy "would expose this country to the flood of refugees from Smyrna." This led to a policy that demanded "prima facie evidence of British nationality."[148] Britain's "excessively cautious post-War immigration policy" led some in the international community to question why a country that had traditionally served as a place of asylum had not in this moment "shown a braver record as a country of sanctuary."[149] As individuals of mixed race, half Greek and half British, Sanson and Martin existed in a space between two worlds, stranding them in Calais, where their story disappears from the historical record. On one side they belonged to a once-prosperous European community that had for centuries dominated commercial life in the Levant. On the other, they bore the mark of a persecuted, displaced group of Christian minorities, a stigma that would ultimately deny them a home in Britain.

The disaster at Smyrna and the seemingly unsolvable postwar refugee crisis further blurred the lines between humanitarianism and foreign policy in a much changed world. Historians have tried to understand why postwar policy and sentiment that continued to favor the special treatment of persecuted minorities resulted in half measures that contributed to the growing refugee crisis after the war.[150] What has been read as a gradual disengagement from Turkish affairs after the 1923 Kemalist revolution explainable by postwar political expediencies, the thirst for oil, and declining British power should also be understood as part of a longer story of failed humanitarian diplomacy that attempted to solve the problem of sectarian violence through the redrawing of the Near East as a patchwork of religiously and ethnically homogenous nation-states. In this context, Curzon's support of the League of Nations' proposal of a Muslim-Christian population exchange at Lausanne that ultimately legitimated the nationalist vision of "Turkey for the Turks" made sense.

After Smyrna, the moral certainty that guided humanitarian considerations of the Eastern Question before the war offered little comfort to those displaced by this vision of the East starkly divided between Muslims and Christians. Seemingly reconfigured to fit postwar geopolitical realities, the new map would nevertheless hold the indelible mark of the Victorian mapmaker who first imagined and charted these divisions. Ultimately, the ethnographic and religious world view that informed nineteenth-century understandings of the Near East found expression in a toxic nationalism that further sharpened divisions based on religion, ethnicity, and creed in a new Middle East.

Epilogue

From Near to Middle East

Looking back on his time as an interpreter in the Levant Consular Service after World War I, Laurence Grafftey-Smith reflected on how much the Victorian map of the world that he had grown up with had changed: "The perpetual kaleidoscope of Time, gently making nonsense of dynasties and institutions and established circumstance, confuses even the gazetteers. Where do the younger generation look to find Fashoda, Christiania or Mesopotamia, and who of my generation can recite the states and capitals of independent Africa? There was once a Near Eastern Question, but where today is the Near East? The Middle East, remote sixty years ago, now encroaches on the Mediterranean."[1] This book has traced the birth of the Middle East in Western imaginings through a rather long and circuitous route. From its origins in the invention of the idea of the Near East after the Crimean War to its entry into common usage after World War I, the Middle East, as Grafftey-Smith's nostalgic narrative map suggests, historically has been read through the lens of contemporary concerns. The Eastern Question offered a way of ordering and understanding the Near and, later, Middle East as a geographic idea in relation to the West. Over the course of the nineteenth and early twentieth centuries mapmakers, diplomats, politicians, travelers, and missionaries participated in the invention of the Middle East as a cultural marker that helped define its relationship to both the British Empire and Europe.

Ultimately, the historical imprecision of the term "Near East" allowed for the expansion and contraction of its geographic and political reach. Its elasticity as a geographical descriptor had its final test during World War I, which forced the British to rethink their relationship to a waning Ottoman Empire. The military disaster at Gallipoli, coupled with the wartime genocide against Ottoman Armenians that the Allies were unwilling and unable to stop, made the Near East seem distant. Indeed, the Western Front overshadowed the Eastern Front both during the war itself and in the peace negotiations with the Ottoman Empire, which did not see final resolution until the Treaty of Lausanne in 1923. The postwar refugee crisis and new international alignments further strained historical connections with the land and people of the Near East as Britain struggled to deal with displaced peoples from the region after the war.

The Near East, however, had always refused easy incorporation into a religious ideal that had its roots in Victorian debates over the Eastern Question. Being made up of a string of "Debatable Lands," in the words of D. G. Hogarth, meant that the Near East and the people that inhabited it kept a temporal and geographic distance from Britain itself. The failure of projects like those spearheaded by the Church Missionary Society demonstrated the difficulty in making the kinship metaphor between Orthodox and Anglican Christians securely manifest. Part of the problem was the marginal status of mission work in the Ottoman Empire. Unlike Africa and India, two regions that received the majority of missionary attention, Near East missions continued to struggle for recognition and status. A lack of conversion among Muslims and Orthodox Christians in the region further hampered efforts to put this region at the center of evangelical thinking.

Rather than abandon this project, missionaries offered more expansive ways of seeing the Near East. On the eve of the war the Church Missionary Society offered supporters a "graphic sketch" of the "Near East" "written by one of our missionaries at work among Moslems in an Oriental land within the Turkish Empire."[2] Here the Near East is reintroduced to readers geographically as Asia Minor, Syria, and "Turkish Arabia" and culturally as one inhabited by Muslims. The subtext of the decline of the Ottoman Empire suggested that the Near East again proved ripe for missionary intervention. At the end of the war, missionaries reasserted the idea of the Near East as the Holy Land that stretched from the Mediterranean to the borders of India. "The Near East, although in a sense the oldest mission field of the Church, has not hitherto attracted much attention from the rank and file of the supporters of Christian missions," one missionary journalist proclaimed. "The lands which lie between the Mediterranean and the frontier states of India were the cradle of our race and of our faith . . . the war has now drawn the world's attention to these regions, and Christian people are opening their eyes to the strategic importance, from the missionary point of view of the lands of the Bible.[3] The war had

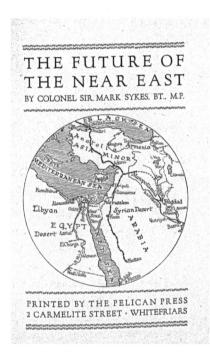

Figure 25. Mark Sykes's map sketch on the cover of his pamphlet "The Future of the Near East" (London: Pelican Press, 1918), depicting his religious and geopolitical vision of the Near East.

brought the project of defining the Near East within the sphere of British geographical, cultural, and religious interests full circle as the granting of Britain the mandate over Mesopotamia and Palestine formalized its control over the "Holy Land."

For Mark Sykes, the integrity of the idea of the Near East also revolved around its location as the birthplace of Christianity. His pamphlet "The Future of the Near East" (1918), published just after the war, defined the Near East as encompassing those regions within an "800 mile radius centered on Jerusalem" (figure 25). Sykes argued that peace in Europe depended on two things: preventing Turkey from "dividing Europe against itself" and "redeeming from bondage the Asiatic peoples whom the Turks have oppressed." A month after the signing of the secret Sykes-Picot agreement, which divided up the Ottoman Empire between Britain and France, a memorandum entitled "The Problem of the Near East" argued that success on the Eastern Front held the key to Allied success in the war. Sykes's twin narratives of the Near East serve as a reminder that a religious conception of the Near East had its counterpoint in an imperial and commercial narrative first conceived of after the Crimean War.

This capacious vision of the Near East would not last long after the war. While Sykes was formulating his vision of a Near East centered at Jerusalem, other commentators began to revive the idea of the Middle East to describe these territories. The "middle east" had been used as a general descriptor of parts of the Ottoman Empire as early as 1876, but it was only given its geographical integrity and important capital letters in the early twentieth century. Valentine Chirol used the term specifically to refer to "those regions of Asia which extend to the borders of India or command the approaches to India."[4] The idea of a "Middle East," however, had lain dormant until after the war. Between April 1919 and May 1921 Robert Machray published a series of three articles in the *Fortnightly Review* that reintroduced the Middle East: "The New Middle East" (April 1919), "The New Middle East in the Making" (October 1919), and "The Situation in the Middle East" (May 1921). By 1921, Machray offered his own definition after admitting "that the expression itself is one of convenience rather than of geographical correctness." For Machray the Middle East in 1921 consisted of "Caucasia, Armenia, Cilicia, Syria, Palestine, Arabia, Mesopotamia, Kurdistan Persia, Transcaspia, and part of Turkistan." He had argued in an earlier piece that the new nations of the Balkans, once considered the beginning of Britain's Near East were now "European nations." This expansive definition left little room for a Near East that seemingly disappeared at the borders of a Turkish rump state. An invention of the twentieth century, the overlapping territories of Britain's Middle East would replace outmoded Victorian traces of a region once so closely associated with the Eastern Question in the minds of the British.

New visual postwar representations of the region further indicated that the Near East had begun to lose its usefulness as a political category. Harmsworth's "New Atlas" of 1919 adopted the motto, "The World Remapped." Its use of new lithograph techniques and inclusion of a "pictorial gazetteer" that used photos to tell stories made this an atlas targeted at the general reader. These were specifically English maps that did not follow in the tradition of German mapmakers who tended to include every name of every place. Though German maps might be more accurate, they were, according to the editor, "unreadable." Large maps of Arabia and Persia were included alongside a thematic map entitled "Oriental Industries" that might have looked familiar to those who purchased Harmsworth's earlier edition (figure 26). This map had originally appeared titled as the "Near East" in the 1909 atlas, with some important exceptions. Consul stations, railway lines, cables, canals, steamship lines, and now wireless stations were designated much as they were ten years earlier as were products, industries, and natural resources. Missing in Harmsworth's new rendering was any reference to this region as the "Near East."

Two other major atlas projects of the interwar period showed only shadowy outlines of the Near East. The massive three-volume *Times Atlas* published in 1922 designated the region as "Persia" (figure 27). The "Near East" appeared in shaded type at the front of the Persia plate as in the index. Similarly, A.K. Johnston's 1931 *Atlas of World History*, published for use in British classrooms, contained forty-nine thematic historical maps with only one reference to former Ottoman lands: "The Expulsion of Turkey from Europe," a small inset map attached to a larger map of Europe.[5]

Still, the Near East lingered in the British imagination. Cecil Beaton was sent by the Ministry of Information at the beginning of World War II to take pictures and inform on the situation in Cairo, Alexandria, Iran, Iraq, and Syria. In his memoir entitled the *Near East* he drew a muddled and romantic portrait of the overlapping worlds of Middle and Near East: "I have discovered how 'out of touch' with their homes the men in the Middle East seem, it may be that, in spite of the ceaseless newspaper reports and countless books on the subject, the Near East is still, to many at home, a world apart, remote and mysterious. If so, it may not come amiss to give the immediate impression of an ordinary individual arriving in this utterly different atmosphere."[6]

The idea of the Near East survived until World War II in part because it was a useful tool for explaining why Britons would care about the distant suffering of a small, persecuted minority living on the edge of Europe. By offering a face to the Eastern Question Christian minorities gave humanitarianism its subject. As that vision of a persecuted minority under the protection of the British Empire came under strain, the result of war and genocide, the Near East faded into the "utterly different atmosphere" of a new Middle East. Born out of debates over the Eastern Question, the idea of the Near East enabled Victorians to organize their world in terms of religious identities, which in turn shaped a generation of leaders who helped remake the region after the war. These men, many of whom had come of age in an era of Gladstonian moral certainty, participated in the most extensive redrawing of the map to date, a process of erasure and invention that had the power to determine which things

Figure 26 *(overleaf)*. A Near East map now retitled "Oriental Industries," from J.A. Hammerton, ed., *Harmsworth's Atlas of the World* (London: Amalgamated Press, 1919).

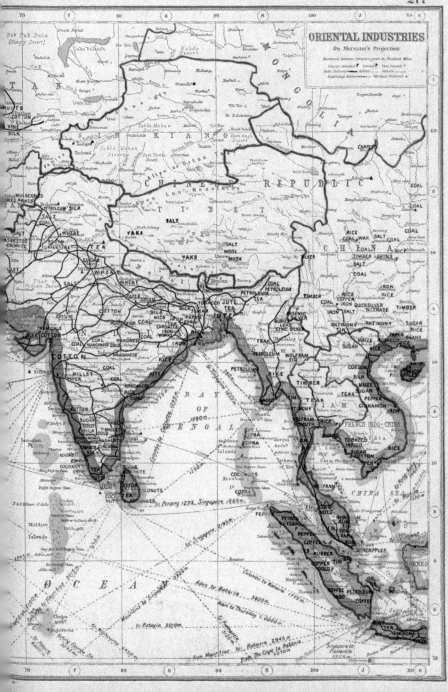

ORIENTAL INDUSTRIES

On Mercator's Projection

PERSIA

The Shaded Area on Index Map shows the extent of this Plate

INDEX TO SECTION MAPS OF THE NEAR EAST
ON SCALE OF 1 : 4,000,000

Figure 27. "Map of Persia," shaded plate with reference to the Near East. *Times'
Survey Atlas of the World* (London, 1922).

would be remembered and which forgotten. Choosing to remember the
Eastern Question as primarily a set of geopolitical concerns while forget-
ting the humanitarian ethos that it inspired has rendered events like the
Armenian Genocide and the burning of Smyrna as forgotten footnotes in
the story of the Great War.

One of the latest maps with the designation "Near East" that I have
located was published in 1939 (figure 28). Tucked away in the back of John
Hope Simpson's book *The Refugee Problem,* the map illustrates a freshly
minted Near East with its boundaries drawn by the Treaty of Versailles
and the Mandate Commission. Here the Near East is depicted at the center not of the British Empire but of a world humanitarian crisis brought
on by war, genocide, and a peace settlement that ossified the divisions
between a Muslim East and Christian West. The authors of the report

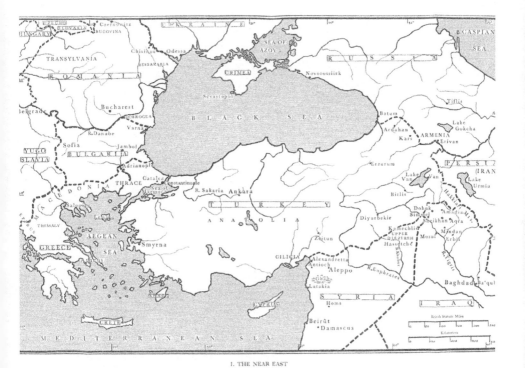

1. THE NEAR EAST

Figure 28. New postwar map of the Near East depicted as part of the worldwide refugee crisis. Reproduced from John Hope Simpson, *The Refugee Problem: Report of a Survey* (London: Oxford University Press, 1939), by permission of the publisher.

wondered why Britain, though generous with private aid relief, refused to follow other European capitals and accept destitute refugees from the Near East. With a new crisis on the horizon the peoples of the Near East were no longer distant kin but potential harbingers of a larger problem of decline. The problems of the Middle East, as this region would now be known, would be left for a new generation of politicians to solve.

Notes

1. Dora Sakayan, trans., *An Armenian Doctor in Turkey: Garabed Hatcherian, My Smyrna Ordeal of 1922* (Montreal: Arod Books, 1997), 38.

2. Bruce Clark, *Twice a Stranger* (Cambridge, MA: Harvard University Press, 2006), xii.

3. Sakayan, *My Smyrna Ordeal of 1922*, 47, 49.

4. Valentine Chirol, *The Middle Eastern Question, or Some Political Problems of Indian Defence* (London: John Murray, 1903), 5. Chirol's notion of a Middle East drew on Mahan's use of the term, which he used in an article in the *National Review* in September 1902. Chirol popularized this notion among a British audience in the *Times* in a series of nineteen anonymous dispatches starting in October 1902, with the final article, "The Middle Eastern Question," appearing in April 1903. These dispatches were immediately published in *The Middle Eastern Question*. Mahan's use of the term is discussed in Karl E. Meyer and Shareen Blair Brysac, *Kingmakers* (New York: Norton, 2008), 37–38.

5. My survey of nineteenth-century German and French bibliographies, encyclopedias, and dictionaries yielded these results and included: Johannes Klatt and Ernst Kuhn, eds. *Literatur-Blatt für Orientalische Philologie*, vols. 1–4 (Leipzig: Otto Schulze, 1883–85); Karl Friederici, *Bibliotheca Orientalis: Vollständige Liste der vom Jahre 1876 bis 1883 erschienenen Bücher, Broschüren, Zeitschriften, usw. über die Sprachen, Religionen, Antiquitäten, Literaturen und Geschichte des Ostens* (Leipzig: Otto Schulze, 1876–83); and *Brockhaus' Conversations-Lexikon: Allgemeine Deutsche Real-Encyklopädie* (Leipzig: F.A. Brockhaus, 1887). For more recent German uses of the term see Todd Kontje, *German Orientalisms* (Ann Arbor: University of Michigan Press, 2004), 179–81.

The French use of "Levant" dated from 1694. They also used the term "Orient," which dated from 1606. The term *extrême orient* was in use as early as 1852. ARTFL-Frantext database, http://artfl-project.uchicago.edu, accessed April 2, 2010; Dictionnaires d'autrefois database, http://artfl-project.uchicago.edu, accessed April 2, 2010.

6. George N. Curzon, *Persia and the Persian Question*, 2 vols. (London: Longman, 1892).

7. Britons came to imagine the Ottoman Empire over the course of the nineteenth century, as Nancy Stockdale has suggested, through a set of lenses colored by the popularly held belief in "the region's singular status as the 'Holy Land.'" *Colonial Encounters among English and Palestinian Women, 1800–1948* (Gainesville: University Press of Florida, 2007). On nineteenth-century English perceptions of Palestine, see Eitan Bar-Yosef, *The Holy Land in English Culture 1799–1917* (Oxford: Clarendon, 2005).

8. James Scott, *Seeing Like a State* (New Haven: Yale University Press, 1999). See also Ricardo Padron, *The Spacious World* (Chicago: University of Chicago Press, 2004); Henri Lefebvre, *The Production of Space*, trans. D. Nicholson-Smith (Oxford: Blackwell, 1991).

9. Missionaries from the United States, Germany, and France soon followed. Mary Taylor Huber and Nancy Lutkehaus, eds., *Gendered Missions: Women and Men in Missionary Discourse and Practice* (Ann Arbor: University of Michigan Press, 1999); Mary Mills Patrick, *Bosporus Adventure: Constantinople Womens College, 1871–1924* (Stanford, CA: Stanford University Press, 1934); Julius Richter, *A History of Protestant Missions in the Near East* (New York: Fleming H. Revell, 1910); Rhonda Semple, *Missionary Women: Gender, Professionalism, and the Victorian Idea of Christian Mission* (Suffolk: Boydell Press, 2003); Maria West, *Romance of Missions: or, Inside Views of Life and Labor in the Land of Ararat* (New York: Randolph, 1875).

10. Missionaries historically had focused their efforts on Eastern Orthodox Christians, in part due to laws that made the conversion of Muslims to Christianity a crime punishable by death. Formal efforts started with the founding of the Church Missionary Society's "Mediterranean Mission" in the early 1800s. Though short lived, it provided a foundation for establishing the presence of British Protestant churches in the region that lasted through to the twentieth century. Richter, *A History of Protestant Missions*, 104–80.

11. Bruce Kuklick, *Puritans in Babylon*, (Princeton, NJ: Princeton University Press, 1996); Tom Davis, *Shifting Sands* (Oxford: Oxford University Press, 2004).

12. R. W. Seton-Watson, *Disraeli, Gladstone, and the Eastern Question* (1935; reprint, New York: Norton, 1972); Richard Shannon, *Gladstone and the Bulgarian Agitation 1876* (London: Thomas Nelson, 1963); Richard Millman, *Britain and the Eastern Question, 1875–1878* (Oxford: Clarendon, 1979); Ann Pottinger Saab, *Reluctant Icon: Gladstone, Bulgaria and the Working Classes, 1856–1878* (Cambridge, MA: Harvard University Press, 1991); H. C. G. Matthew, "Gladstone, Vaticanism, and the Question of the East," in *Studies in Church History*, vol. 15, ed. D. Baker (1978); Harold William Temperley, "The Bulgarian and Other Atrocities, 1875–78," *Proceedings of the British Academy* (1931), 105–46.

13. On humanitarianism in Africa, see Kevin Grant, *A Civilised Savagery: Britain and the New Slaveries in Africa* (New York: Routledge, 2005).

14. H. C. G. Matthews, *Gladstone, 1809–1898* (Oxford: Oxford University Press, 2001), 262–71.

15. Donald Bloxham, *The Great Game of Genocide: Imperialism, Nationalism, and the Destruction of the Ottoman Armenians* (Oxford: Oxford University Press, 2005), 29–44; Akaby Nassibian, *Britain and the Armenian Question 1915–1923* (London: Croom Helm, 1984), 33–44.

16. Arnold Toynbee, "Armenian Atrocities: The Murder of a Nation," (London: Hodder and Stoughton, 1915).

17. Gary Bass contends that this period witnessed the rise of a secular and broad-based humanitarianism only tangentially linked with nineteenth-century religious revivalism. *Freedom's Battle* (New York: Vintage, 2008), 19–24.

18. Samantha Power, *The Problem from Hell* (New York: Harper, 2007).

19. These include: Jo Laycock, *Imagining Armenia* (Manchester: Manchester University Press, 2009); Billie Melman, *Women's Orients: English Women and the Middle East, 1718–1918* (Ann Arbor: University of Michigan Press, 1992); Maya Jasanoff, *Edge of Empire* (New York: Knopf, 2005); Priya Satia, *Spies in Arabia: The Great War and the Cultural Foundations of Britain's Covert Empire in the Middle East* (Oxford: Oxford University Press, 2008).

20. See for example, Edward Ingram, ed. *Anglo-Ottoman Encounters in the Age of Revolution: Collected Essays of Allan Cunningham,* vol. 1 (London: Frank Cass, 1993); Joseph Heller, *British Policy towards the Ottoman Empire, 1908–1914* (London: Frank Cass, 1983); M. S. Anderson, *The Eastern Question, 1774–1923* (London: Macmillan, 1966); J. A. R. Marriott, *The Eastern Question: A Study in European Diplomacy,* 4th ed. (Oxford: Clarendon Press, 1940). On British diplomacy and the question of the Armenian Genocide, see Bloxham, *The Great Game of Genocide;* A. D. Kirakossian, *British Diplomacy and the Armenian Question from the 1830s to 1914* (Princeton, NJ: Gomidas Institute, 2003); Manoug Somakian, *Empires in Conflict: Armenia and the Great Powers, 1895–1920* (London: I. B. Tauris, 1995).

21. This typology has been critiqued by scholars, including Karen Barkey, *Empire of Difference: The Ottomans in Comparative Perspective* (Cambridge: Cambridge University Press, 2008); Caroline Finkel, *Osman's Dream* (New York: Basic Books, 2005); Laycock, *Imagining Armenia;* Meyer and Brysac, *Kingmakers;* Diane Robinson-Dunn, *The Harem, Slavery and British Imperial Culture* (Manchester: Manchester University Press, 2006).

CHAPTER 1

1. "Mr. Gladstone on the Armenian Question," *Times,* September 25, 1896.

2. "The Armenian Massacres," *Times,* September 26, 1896. Statistics on the massacres come from contemporary estimates of numbers killed "directly and indirectly" between 1894 and 1896. Donald Bloxham, *The Great Game of Genocide* (Oxford: Oxford University Press, 2005), 51.

3. *Times*, October 8, 1896, cited in the entry for "October 20, 1896," in H. C. G. Matthew, ed. *The Gladstone Diaries* (Oxford: Clarendon Press, 1994), 13:427.

4. Margaret Anderson, "Down in Turkey, Far Away: Human Rights, the Armenian Massacres, and Orientalism in Wilhelmine Germany," *Journal of Modern History* 79, no 1 (March 2007), 80–83; Sean McMeekin, *The Berlin to Baghdad Express: The Ottoman Empire and Germany's Bid for World Power* (Cambridge: Harvard University Press, 2010), 14–15.

5. "Lord Beaconsfield at Aylesbury," *Times*, September 21, 1876.

6. As Thomas Laqueur argues, "creation of sympathy of the ultimately distanced person" rests on "the central question of why the moral franchise is extended at any given time to one group but not another." "Bodies, Details and the Humanitarian Narrative," in *The New Cultural History*, ed. Lynn Hunt (Berkeley and Los Angeles: University of California Press, 1989), 202–4.

7. "Communications with the Far East," *Fraser's Magazine* 54, no. 323 (November 1856), 574. "Fraser's Magazine," in *Dictionary of Nineteenth-Century Journalism*, ed. Laurel Brake and Marysa Demoor (London: Academia Press/British Library, 2009), 229–30.

8. The decline of the "taxes on knowledge" in the mid-1850s brought the war home to a wider reading public by making periodicals a central feature of British political life. According to M. S. Anderson, the press played an important role in drumming up sentiment for this "wildly" popular war, in the words of one contemporary observer, even before the official war declaration was made against Russia on March 28, 1854. See Anderson, *The Eastern Question, 1774–1923* (London: Macmillan, 1966), 128–35; and Stefanie Markovits, "Rushing into Print: 'Participatory Journalism' during the Crimean War," *Victorian Studies* 50, no. 4 (summer 2008), 561.

9. According to the Oxford English Dictionary, this definition of "Levant" came into its earliest usage in the fifteenth century. Its most general use appeared in the mid-eighteenth century, when one commentator designated the Levant as "any country to the East of us." www.oed.com, accessed June 1, 2010.

10. "Communications with the Far East," *Fraser's Magazine* 54, no. 323 (November 1856), 580.

11. Ibid., 574.

12. David Fraser, *The Short Cut to India: The Record of a Journey along the Route of the Baghdad Railway* (Edinburgh: Blackwood, 1909), 13–46.

13. On the controversy over the building of the Baghdad Railway see McMeekin, *Berlin to Baghdad Express*; H. J. Whigham, *The Persian Problem: An Examination of the Rival Positions of Russia and Great Britain in Persia with Some Account of the Persian Gulf and the Baghdad Railway* (New York: Charles Scribner's Sons, 1903); Edward Mead Earle, *Turkey, the Great Powers, and the Baghdad Railway: A Study in Imperialism* (New York: Macmillan, 1923); and Maybelle Kennedy Chapman, *Great Britain and the Baghdad Railway, 1888–1914* (Northampton, MA: Smith College, 1948).

14. "History of Eastern Church," *Edinburgh Review* 107 (April 1858), 356–57. Christ Church in Istanbul now is part of the Anglican Diocese of Europe.

15. "The Eastern Church: Its Past and Its Future," *National Review*, July 1861, 61.

16. "The Russo-Turkish Question," *Fraser's Magazine* 48 (December 1853), 718.

17. These conceptions of Jews often were figured in a negative rather than positive light. See David Feldman, *Englishmen and Jews* (New Haven: Yale University Press, 1994); Anthony Wohl, "'Dizzi-Ben-Dizzi': Disraeli as Alien," *Journal of British Studies*, 34, no. 3 (July 1995), 375–411. On the importance of Christians along the proposed Anatolian Railway line see Fraser, *Short Cut to India*, 298–307.

18. "Correspondence Respecting the Rights and Privileges of the Latin and Greek Churches in Turkey: Presented to both Houses of Parliament by Command of Her Majesty," *Edinburgh Review* 100 (July 1854), 43.

19. "The Eastern Question," *London Quarterly* 29 [1867?], 405.

20. The data from 1876 to 1885 largely correspond with the finding of Paul Auchterlonie in "From the Eastern Question to the Death of General Gordon: Representations of the Middle East in the Victorian Periodical Press, 1876–1885," *British Journal of Middle Eastern Studies* 28, no. 1 (May 2001), 5–24.

21. R. W. Seton-Watson and a generation of historians who followed argued for the importance of the controversy generated over the Bulgarian Atrocities in shaping liberalism during the late 1870s. R. W. Seton Watson, *Disraeli, Gladstone, and the Eastern Question* (1935, New York: Norton, 1972). Those writing in this tradition include David Harris, *Britain and the Bulgarian Horrors of 1876* (Chicago: University of Chicago Press, 1939); Richard Shannon, *Gladstone and the Bulgarian Agitation 1876* (London: Thomas Nelson and Sons, 1963); Richard Millman, *Britain and the Eastern Question, 1875–1878* (Oxford: Clarendon Press, 1979); and Ann Pottinger Saab, *Reluctant Icon: Gladstone, Bulgaria and the Working Classes, 1856–1878* (Cambridge, MA: Harvard University Press, 1991).

22. These reforms harkened back to failed attempts starting in 1839 to modernize Ottoman government from within. In 1856, then British ambassador Stratford Canning was central in negotiating a liberalization of Ottoman policies toward non-Muslim subjects in the Treaty of Paris. For a contemporary account of the treaty negotiations, see George Douglas Campbell Argyll, *The Eastern Question* (London: Strahan, 1879), 1:1–35. See also Bloxham, *Great Game of Genocide*, 31–33; and Vahakn Dadrian, *The History of the Armenian Genocide*, 6th ed. (New York: Berghahn, 2003), 14–20.

23. "Derby at the Meeting of Conservative Working Men, Edinburgh," *Times*, December 17, 1875.

24. No official numbers exist, leaving a wide range of possible statistics. David Harris quotes numbers given by a Turkish tribunal, a British consular agent, American investigators, and Bulgarian historians ranging from 12,000 to over 100,000 dead. *Britain and the Bulgarian Horrors*, 22.

25. Between September 1 and December 1876 Derby received 455 memorials and petitions on the subject. Shannon, *Gladstone and the Bulgarian Agitation*, 148.

26. On Gladstone and the Bulgarian question, see: H.C.G. Matthew, "Gladstone, Vaticanism, and the Question of the East," in *Studies in Church History* 15, ed. D. Baker (1978), 417–442; Seton-Watson, *Disraeli, Gladstone and the Eastern Question*; Harold William Temperley, "The Bulgarian and Other Atrocities, 1875–78," *Proceedings of the British Academy*, 1931, 105–46.

27. H.C.G. Matthew, *Gladstone, 1809–1898* (Oxford: Oxford University Press, 2001), 158, 265, 629, 635.

28. Those in attendance included the Duke of Westminster; the Earl of Shaftesbury; Sir G. Campbell, MP; the Bishop of Oxford; Anthony Trollope; Mr. Fawcett, MP; Sir T.F. Buxton; Mr. S. Morley, MP; Mr. Trevelyan; Mr. Cowper-Temple; Rev. Canon Liddon; Rev. W. Denton; E.A. Freeman; Lord Waveney; and others who included "Ladies . . . accommodated in the gallery." "The Eastern Question Conference," *Illustrated London News*, December 16, 1876, 575.

29. Paul Auchterlonie, "From the Eastern Question," 5–24.

30. Seton-Watson, *Disraeli, Gladstone, and the Eastern Question*, 570.

31. Millman, *Britain and the Eastern Question*, 183–84.

32. Eastern Question Association, *Papers on the Eastern Question* (London: Cassell Petter and Galfin, 1877).

33. "The Eastern Church," *Edinburgh Review* 107 (April 1858), 165.

34. Shannon, *Gladstone and the Bulgarian Agitation*, 69–78; Patrick Joyce, *Democratic Subjects: The Self and the Social in Nineteenth Century England* (Cambridge: Cambridge University Press, 1994), 207.

35. Shannon, *Gladstone and the Bulgarian Agitation*, 73, 78.

36. W.T. Stead, *The MP for Russia: Reminiscences and Correspondence of Madame Olga Novikoff* (New York: Putnam, 1909), 1:ix.

37. Stead, "Relations of the Press and the Church," *Christian Literature and Review*, 1894.

38. Harris, *Britain and the Bulgarian Horrors*, 110–11.

39. Wohl, "'Dizzi-Ben-Dizzi,'" 375–76.

40. Stead's association with Madame Novikoff, a spokeswoman for Russian causes in England and a close friend of Gladstone, influenced his pro-Russia views and were magnified in *The MP for Russia*, his two-volume tribute to her.

41. W.E. Gladstone, "Paths of Honor and Shame," *Nineteenth Century*, March 1878, 593.

42. "What Is the Eastern Question?" *St. Pauls* (1878), 279.

43. E. Bosworth Smith, "The Eastern Question: Turkey and Russia," *Contemporary Review* 29 (1876), 148.

44. John Probyn, "The Eastern Question in 1878," *British Quarterly Review* 67 (1878), 519.

45. Gladstone, "Paths of Honor," 594.

46. Edward Freeman, "The True Eastern Question," *Fortnightly Review* 24 (December 1875), 756, 759, 762.

47. W. R. W. Stephens, *The Life and Letters of Edward A. Freeman*, 2 vols. (London: Macmillan, 1895), 479.

48. The W. T. Stead Resource Site, http://www.attackingthedevil.co.uk.

49. On the Boers, see W. T. Stead, "Are We in the Right?" (London, 1899), 15. See Judith Walkowitz, *City of Dreadful Delight* (Chicago: University of Chicago Press, 1992), 94–98, for a discussion of "white slavery."

50. Dorothy Anderson, *The Balkan Volunteers* (London: Hutchinson, 1968), 19–20, 208.

51. The "philo-Turkish" faction of public opinion, centered largely in London, kept its distance from the agitation. Shannon, *Gladstone and the Bulgarian Atrocities*, 160–70.

52. Gladstone to Newman Hall, October 12, 1878, as quoted in ibid., 162.

53. E. A. Freeman, "The Eastern Church," *Edinburgh Review* 107 (April 1858), 353.

54. Ibid., 183.

55. E. A. Freeman, "The Geographical Aspects of the Eastern Question," *Fortnightly Review* 27 (January 1877), 76.

56. Stead, *Northern Echo*, July 5, 1876.

57. Freeman, "True Eastern Question," 760.

58. Freeman, "The English People in Relation to the Eastern Question," *Contemporary Review* 29 (1877), 490.

59. Stead, *Northern Echo*, July 13, 1876.

60. Shannon, *Gladstone and the Bulgarian Agitation*; David Harris, *Britain and the Bulgarian Horrors*.

61. Malcolm MacColl, "Are Reforms Possible under Mussulman Rule?" *Contemporary Review* 40 (August 1881), 279.

62. Seton-Watson quoting Gladstone, *Disraeli, Gladstone and the Eastern Question*, 545–46.

63. Athelstan Riley, "Christians and Kurds in Eastern Turkey," *Contemporary Review* 56 (September 1889), 452–68.

64. Rev. Malcolm MacColl, "Full Report of Conference of Anglo-Armenian Association," November 27, 1894, Bryce Collection, Bodleian Library.

65. J. W. [Julia Ward] Howe, "Shall the Frontier of Christendom Be Maintained?" *The Forum* 22 (November 1896).

66. Goldwin Smith, "England's Abandonment of the Protectorate of Turkey," *Contemporary Review* 31 (February 1878), 615.

67. Gladstone, "Paths of Honor," 600.

68. "The New Eastern Question," *National Quarterly Review* 11 (January 1880), 149.

69. Feldman, *Englishmen and Jews*, 36–47.

70. Humphrey Sandwith, "How the Turks Rule Armenia," *Nineteenth Century* 3 (February 1878), 319–25.

71. Isabella Bishop, "The Shadow of the Kurd," *Contemporary Review* 59 (May 1891), 643.

72. Bloxham, *Great Game of Genocide*, 51–57.

73. Robert Zeidner, "Britain and the Launching of the Armenian Question," *International Journal of Middle East Studies* 7, no. 4 (October 1976), 479.

74. Forty-eight of these articles dating from August 1890 to January 1897 are reprinted in Arman Kirakossian, ed., *The Armenian Massacres, 1894–1896: British Media Testimony* (Dearborn: University of Michigan, 2008).

75. Bloxham, *Great Game of Genocide*, 53.

76. "Sultan Abd-ul-hamid by an Eastern Resident," *Contemporary Review* 67 (January 1895), 48.

77. E. J. Dillon, "Armenia: An Appeal," *Contemporary Review* 69 (January 1896), 19.

78. "The Two Eastern Questions," *Fortnightly Review* 65 (1896), 193.

79. E. J. Dillon, "The Condition of Armenia," *Contemporary Review* 68 (August 1895), 183.

80. Quoted in Lillian M. Penson, "The Principles and Methods of Lord Salisbury's Foreign Policy," *Cambridge Historical Journal* 5, no. 1 (1935), 100. This policy shift demonstrated Salisbury's keen consideration of public opinion in making his decisions.

81. Zeidner, "Britain and the Launching of the Armenian Question," 480.

82. H. F. B. Lynch, "The Armenian Question," *Contemporary Review* 69 (February 1896), 272.

83. William Watson, "The Turk in Armenia," in *The Purple East: A Series of Sonnets on England's Desertion of Armenia* (London: John Lane, 1896), 16.

84. George W. E. Russell, "Armenia and the Forward Movement," *Contemporary Review* 71 (January 1897), 25.

85. P. W. K. Stride, "The Immediate Future of Armenia: A Suggestion," *The Forum* 22 (November 1896), 312.

86. Ghulam-us-Saqlain, "The Musselmans of India and the Armenian Question," *Nineteenth Century* 37 (June 1895), 926.

87. R. Ahmad, "A Moslem View of Abddul Hamid and the Powers," *Nineteenth Century* 38, July 1895, 158.

88. Akaby Nassibian, *Britain and the Armenian Question 1915–1923* (London: Croom Helm, 1984), 61.

89. The organization intended to streamline the distribution of funds for relief efforts and included "representatives of all the Societies in Great Britain, and Ireland which are working for the relief of Armenian distress." The Duke of Westminster served as president; James Bryce as chairman of the conference, and the fifteen vice presidents and four honorary secretaries included representatives of secular and religious based organizations involved in coordinated relief efforts.

90. A. Bradshaw, "Deserted Armenia," *Our Sisters* 2, no. 114 (1897), 52.

91. "The Condition of Armenian Women," *Women's Penny Paper*, November 15, 1890, 57.

92. For example, a biography of the Swiss activist Madame Thoumaian in the *Woman's Herald* (August 10, 1893) dubbed her "A Heroine from Armenia." See also letter to the editor from Lucy Thoumaian, *Woman's Signal*, June 6, 1895, 416–17.

93. Lady Henry Somerset, "A Cry from Armenia.' Response to a Letter from Armenian Women of Constantinople to Lady Henry Somerset," *Shafts* 3, no. 9 (1895), 132.

94. "Armenia: What Is Best?" *Shafts*, [1896?].

95. Somerset, "Annual Address," *Woman's Signal*, June 25, 1896, 405.

96. *Woman's Signal*, May 21, 1896, 331.

97. *Woman's Signal*, April 22, 1895, 121; lead editorial, August 29, 1895, 487; "Foreign Troubles," October 10, 1895, 232.

98. Editorial, *Woman's Signal*, September 26, 1895, 528.

99. "Armenians at Hawarden: Mr. Gladstone and the Refugees," *Woman's Signal*, April 25, 1895, 264–65.

100. Ibid.

101. Letters to the editor, *Woman's Signal*, February 27, 1896, 189.

102. "Armenian Atrocities," *Woman's Signal*, May 9, 1895, 302.

103. "Lady Henry Somerset's Efforts for the Armenian Refugees," *Woman's Signal*, October 15, 1896, 246.

104. "Lady Henry Somerset's Letter of Thanks," *Woman's Signal*, March 18, 1897, 172.

CHAPTER 2

1. Larry Wolff, *Inventing Eastern Europe: The Map of Civilization on the Mind of the Enlightenment* (Stanford, CA: Stanford University Press, 1994), 148–55.

2. P. J. Marshall, *The Making and Unmaking of Empires* (Oxford: Oxford University Press, 2005), 6–9.

3. Sir Charles Moore Watson, *Fifty Years of Work in the Holy Land: A Record and Summary, 1865–1915* (London, 1915), 3–4. A survey of the index of the magazine *Royal Geographical Society* shows sustained growth in references to maps of the "East" starting in 1893 and continuing through to the 1920s.

4. The British sent representatives to officially survey the western regions of the Ottoman Empire after the signing in 1878 of the Treaty of Berlin, which set up new boundaries in the region today known as the Balkans as described in Lady Ardagh (Susan Countess of Malmesbury), *The Life of Sir John Ardagh* (London: John Murray, 1909). By the 1890s, the mapping of the Ottoman Empire, particularly along the border with Russia, was considered important as a "theatre of future war," according to Captain F. R. Maunsell's confidential *Military Report on Eastern Turkey in Asia*, vol. 1 (London: Harrison and Sons, 1893), 17.

5. The War Office's official project to map "Eastern Turkey in Asia" contin-

ued from 1901–20. A. Crispin Jewitt, *Maps for Empire: The First 2000 Numbered War Office Maps, 1881–1905* (London: British Library, 1992), xii.

6. Cox to [Curzon?], June 29, 1907, and March 20, 1907, Cox Papers, Royal Geographical Society (RGS).

7. Robert Latham, *The Varieties of the Human Species* (London: Houlston and Stoneman, 1856), 305–6.

8. Latham first introduced this idea in his study of European ethnography. Though he casts the Turk as an invader who is "Asiatic rather than European," he concludes that "The Turk is European, as the New Englander is American; ie not strictly so." *The Ethnology of Europe* (London: John Van Voorst, 1852), 6, 221–37.

9. British Library Map Collection. Johnston had helped make the atlas an affordable consumer luxury and published the first mass-market atlas in 1859. By the late nineteenth century, even the War Office began to rely on private firms, including Johnston, to publish material when it needed a map done quickly and cheaply. Jewitt, *Maps of Empire*, xvii.

10. "The Eastern Question Conference," *Illustrated London News*, December 16, 1876, 578.

11. "I was anxious to get up a little map . . . to show roughly the distribution of the principal Christian races in European Turkey," Campbell wrote in his introduction. "The Mahommedans are so scattered and intermixed throughout the country that I found it impossible to give them without going into greater minutiae than is practicable in the time and on so small a scale; so I beg it may be understood that I have not taken on myself to expel the Turks from Europe before their time, but have only relegated them to the letter-press and given in the map the areas in which Christian races are found." George Campbell, *A Handy Book on the Eastern Question* (London: Murray, 1876), ix–x.

12. Campbell claims that "[t]here is no reliable census of the population of European Turkey. The best estimates put it at about 8 or 9 million excluding the tributary states. I should think that, including Constantinople it is probably more. The Mahommedans are better counted for military purposes than the Christians, and their relative numbers are, I believe exaggerated. The excess of population over the usual estimate is probably among the Christians. The estimates would give about 3.5 million Mahommedans and 5.5 million Christians in a population of 9 million" (ibid., 24). Campbell regrets that his map of Christians in Europe does not including the Christians of Asia Minor due to the current "degraded" state of these once "rich, populous and luxurious kingdoms" that were "the seat of the earliest and most flourishing Christian Churches" (ibid., 4-5).

13. Ibid., 48.

14. W. Denton, *The Christians of Turkey: Their Conditions under Mussulman Rule* (London: Dalday, Isbister and Co., 1876), 46–47.

15. Ibid., 196.

16. On the history of Greek independence, see Richard Clogg, *A Short History of Modern Greece* (Cambridge: Cambridge University Press, 1986).

17. Lady Ardagh, *The Life of Sir John Ardagh*, 54.

18. Ibid., 64–66. Members included representatives from Russia, Turkey, France, Germany, Austria, Italy.

19. Ibid., 94.

20. One of the villages in question, Djuma, was burned while the commission was doing its work. Ardagh reported that similar difficulties were faced by the commission in establishing the new Greek frontier in 1881 where surveyors had an escort of 400 men. Ibid., 106.

21. Ibid., 119.

22. William Miller, *Travels and Politics in the Near East* (London: Unwin, 1898), xiii.

23. Ibid., xi.

24. Maunsell, *Military Report on Eastern Turkey*, vol. 1.

25. Kiepert's original map, "Ethnographische Übersicht des Europäischen Orients" (1876), is held in the British Library map collection.

26. In addition to the British and German maps already cited in this chapter, see Élisée Reclus, "Poulations de la Turcuie d'Europe" (1876); and Karl Sax, "Ethnographische Karte der Europäischen Turkei" (1877). Russia was also engaged in ethnographical investigations in western Russia and the Caucasus during this period. See P. Chubinsky, "Book of the Ethnographic Statistical Expedition to the Western Russian Region," Imperial Russian Geographical Society (1874); L. P Zagursky, "Ethnographical Classification of Caucasian Races" (1888), and V. L. Seroshevsky, *Yakuts* (1896); RGS Map Collection.

27. Marion Newbigin popularized this idea in *Modern Geography* (London: Williams and Norgate, 1911). Newbigin claims that "modern geographical science" began in 1859 with the death of Humboldt and Ritter, "two great geographical pioneers," and the publication of Charles Darwin's *On the Origin of Species.*

28. Newbigin's books, which went into multiple printings, staunchly advocated the serious study of human geography in all levels of education and continued to be popular up through the 1920s. See for example, *Modern Geography; Geographical Aspects of the Balkan Problems in Their Relation to the Great European War (with a Coloured Map of South-Eastern Europe and Sketch Maps)*, 2nd ed. (London: Constable and Co., 1915); and *The Mediterranean Lands*, 4th printing (London: Christophers, 1928). On the rise of human geography see Glenda Stuga, *The Nation, Psychology, and International Politics, 1870–1919* (London: Palgrave, 2006), 22.

29. Newbigin, *Mediterranean Lands*, 204.

30. Peter Mentzel, *Transportation Technology and Imperialism in the Ottoman Empire, 1800–1923* (Washington, DC: American Historical Association, 2006), 31.

31. David Fraser, *The Short Cut to India: The Record of a Journey along the Route of the Baghdad Railway* (Edinburgh: Blackwood, 1909), 302–4.

32. Maunsell, *Military Report on Eastern Turkey,* 17–19.

33. Maunsell was elected to the RGS in 1891, published regularly in its *Geographical Journal,* and contributed photographs of "Asiatic Turkey" to its collection until his death in 1936. Obituary, *Times,* December 8, 1936, Times Digital Archive, accessed May 28, 2010.

34. The first category listed "Russians, Greeks , Georgians, Armenians, Assyrians (Nestorians), Chaldeans." In separate categories came "Iranians," "Turanian," and "Semetic" groups. RGS, Percy Cox files, GSGS, 2901.

35. Jewitt, *Maps for Empire.*

36. Josef Altholz, *The Religious Press in Britain, 1760–1900* (New York: Greenwood, 1989), 123. See also Anna Johnston, *Missionary Writing and Empire, 1800–1860* (Cambridge: Cambridge University Press, 2003); and Anna Johnston, "British Missionary Publishing, Missionary Celebrity and Empire," *Nineteenth Century Prose* 32, no. 2 (fall 2005), 22–25.

37. Eugene Stock, *History of the Church Missionary Society* (London: Church Missionary Society, 1899), 1:38.

38. Julius Richter, *A History of Protestant Missions in the Near East* (New York: Fleming H. Revell, 1910).

39. Stock, *History of the Church Missionary Society,* 1:222. Kenneth Craig argues in "Being Made Disciples–The Middle East" that the Church Missionary Society (CMS) believed that working through Eastern Orthodox Christian communities would be "the means, even the *raison d'être,* of reaching Muslims." In Kevin Ward and Brian Stanley, eds., *Church Mission Society and World Christianity, 1799–1999* (Richmond, Surrey: Curzon Press, 2000), 126.

40. The *Gleaner* first appeared in 1841 and ran until 1870. It was later revived in 1874, continuing publication until 1921. It was started in 1841 as an official organ of the CMS to promote mission work. Priced at twopence, the organization gave away many more than it sold of this heavily subsidized chronicle of society reports and records. According to its editor, Eugene Stock, high production costs, dull content, and a general decline in "missionary zeal and interest" led the CMS to drop the periodical in 1870, a move not "lamented by anybody." Stock helped revive the *Gleaner* in 1874 as a sixteen-page, quarto-sized "popular magazine" under the guidance of the CMS secretary, Rev. Henry Wright. In the place of unreadable reports Stock introduced a "new *Gleaner*": sixteen pages in length with illustrations, serialized stories, and a two-column format that imitated popular mainstream periodicals. These innovations worked and by the 1890s the monthly circulation reached its peak of 82,000. *Gleaner,* January 1, 1918, 5.

41. *Gleaner,* May 1874, 1.

42. Though interest in Persia dated back to the CMS's early beginnings when it translated a version of the Bible into Persian, "the stern law of the Koran, which condemns to death a Mohammedan changing his religion" and a "deficiency in funds" had prevented the CMS from establishing an actual missionary outpost. It took Bruce's initiative while on leave from his work in India in 1869 to get the mission started. Bruce found a way to convince hesi-

tant church officials regarding the establishment of this mission by drawing on familiar markers that connected the region geographically and historically to the mission project. Settling in the minority Christian Armenian quarter in Julfa outside of the historic Persian capital of Ispahan, Bruce maintained that he could minister to Orthodox Christians while gaining a foothold among the majority Muslim population. His school for Armenian boys also included some Muslims and his relief work during the "Persian famine" of 1871–72 "bound him more closely than ever to the country." By 1876, when the mission was approved, Bruce's work had expanded the reach of the CMS in the Near East beyond the Mediterranean to Persia. *Gleaner*, May 1876, 76.

43. *Gleaner*, January 1894, 6.

44. On Victorian notions of the Aryan, see Tony Ballantyne, *Orientalism and Race* (New York: Palgrave, 2002); George Stocking, *Victorian Anthropology* (New York: Free Press); and Robert Young, *The Idea of English Ethnicity* (Oxford: Blackwell, 2008).

45. *Gleaner*, December 1896, 122.

46. *Gleaner*, January 1898, 4.

47. *Gleaner*, November 1877, 122.

48. "Epitome," *Gleaner*, January 1879.

49. *Gleaner*, February 1877, 21.

50. Ibid., 22.

51. "Islam and Christian Missions," *Gleaner*, May 1892, 68.

52. "Editorial Notes," *Gleaner*, April 1895, 60.

53. Rev. R. Bruce, "Persia and the Persia Mission," *Gleaner*, January 1894, 3.

54. "From the Home Field: The Moslem Box," *Gleaner*, February 1910, 32.

55. George Curzon, *Problems of the Far East*, 3rd ed. (London: Longmans, 1894), xi–xii.

56. Ibid., xii.

57. Verney Cameron, *Our Future Highway: The Euphrates Valley*, 2 vols. (London: Macmillan, 1880).

58. A. S. Goudie traces Curzon's influence on the Royal Geographical Society in "George Nathan Curzon: Superior Geographer," *The Geographical Journal* 146, no. 2 (July 1980), 203–9.

59. Curzon quoted in Peter King, *Curzon's Persia* (London: Sidwick and Jackson, 1986), 8.

60. King, *Curzon's Persia*, 1. Denis Wright claims that Curzon's attachments to the region were "romantic" and "imperial" and did not arise from any "great admiration for the Persians as a people." "Curzon and Persia," *The Geographical Journal* 153, no. 3 (November 1987), 347.

61. E. A. Reynolds-Ball, *Practical Hints for Travellers in the Near East* (London: E. Marlborough, 1903).

62. "The Near East," *Gleaner*, January 1913; "Editorial Notes," *Gleaner*, September 1918.

63. Rev. R. Bruce, "Persia and the Persian Missions," *Gleaner*, January 1894.

64. Valentine Chirol, *The Middle Eastern Question, or Some Political Problems of Indian Defense* (London: John Murray, 1903), 17.

65. William LeQueux, *An Observer in the Near East* (New York: Doubleday, Page and Co., 1907), 306.

CHAPTER 3

1. Stratford de Redcliffe, "The True Meaning of the Eastern Question," May 16, 1876, reprinted in his *The Eastern Question* (London: John Murray, 1881), 17.

2. Stratford de Redcliffe, "Suggestions for the Settlement of the Eastern Difficulty," November 1876, in ibid., 29.

3. The decree reinforcing the 1839 Tanzimat reforms came in 1856 and was later mentioned in the Treaty of Paris that ended the Crimean War that same year. Donald Bloxham, *Great Game of Genocide: Imperialism, Nationalism, and the Destruction of the Ottoman Armenians* (Oxford: Oxford University Press, 2005), 31–34.

4. This was the largest number of consuls ever employed by Britain in the region since the service began in 1592 under the Levant Company. Thirty-two consular outposts had shrunk to eleven by the time the government took over for the Levant Company in 1825. John Dickie, *The British Consul* (New York: Columbia University Press, 2007), 61–63.

5. Elridge cited in D. C. M. Platt, *The Cinderella Service: British Consuls since 1825* (Hamden, CT: Archon, 1971), 134.

6. C. M. Kennedy in a dispatch to Lord Granville, Cairo, February 10, 1871, cited in ibid., 153.

7. Ibid., 132–33.

8. Lord Palmerson, May 7, 1855. Commons, *Hansard Parliamentary Debates*, 3rd series, 138, co. 216.

9. Dickie, *The British Consul*, 63–64.

10. *Quarterly Review*, April 1903, 610, quoted in Platt, *Cinderella Service*, 130.

11. Lord Strangford, "Chaos," in Lady Strangford, ed., *A Selection of the Writings of Viscount Strangford* (London: Richard Bentley, 1869), 1:65.

12. *Dictionary of National Biography*, 1882, and *Dictionary of National Biography*, 2004, 467–68.

13. A. Vambery to editor of the *Times*, Beaufort Collection, Huntington Library, FB 1812, January 16, 1869.

14. Lady Strangford, ed., *Original Letters and Papers of the Late Viscount Strangford* (London: Trübner, 1878), 165.

15. Ibid., 211.

16. Lord Strangford, "Chaos," 10.

17. A. Vambery, "To the Memory of Lord Strangford," in Strangford, ed., *Original Letters and Papers*, xvi.

18. Strangford, "Chaos," 8.

19. Ibid., 21.

20. Ibid., 9–10.

21. "Chaos" was intended to be the beginning of a larger work on Eastern Europe that was never finished. It was reprinted posthumously in 1869 as part of *A Selection of the Writings of Viscount Strangford.*

22. Strangford, "Chaos," 39.

23. Ibid., 56.

24. G. R. Berridge, "Nation, Class and Diplomacy," in Markus Mösslang and Torsten Riotte, eds., *The Diplomats' World: A Cultural History of Diplomacy, 1815–1914* (Oxford: Oxford University Press, 2008), 414–16. This loss of local knowledge, according to G. R. Berridge, had negative effects on British information gathering up through World War I.

25. Levantines were local representatives in the employment of the British government; Strangford, ed., *Selection from the Writings of Viscount Strangford*, 1:63–64.

26. Strangford, "Chaos," 67.

27. Reprinted in *Writings of Viscount Strangford*, 1:164.

28. Ibid., ix. She also published a second volume of his writings that same year. In 1878, she published *Original Letters and Papers.*

29. The capitulations were a set of legal and economic privileges granted to European citizens that dated back to the sixteenth century and remained in effect until the 1920s. See Bloxham, *Great Game of Genocide*, 11–12.

30. Austen Henry Layard, *Sir A. Henry Layard, G.C.B., D.C.L: Autobiography and Letters from His Childhood until His Appointment as H.M. Ambassador at Madrid*, ed. William N. Bruce (London: John Murray, 1903), 1:103.

31. Ibid., 145–46.

32. Austen Henry Layard, *Discoveries in the Ruins of Nineveh and Babylon* (London: John Murray, 1853; reprint, Port Chester, NY: Elibron, 2001), part 2, 431.

33. Layard, *Autobiography*, 157–60.

34. Layard, *Nineveh and Its Remains: With an Account of a Visit to Chaldean Christians of Kurdistan* (London: John Murray, 1849), 268. Layard claimed to have helped "discover" these Eastern Churches. To make these connections, according to J. F. Coakley, "Layard minimized the Nestorian heresy, and emphasized the Syrians' antipathy to Rome and kinship with the Protestants." In the end, "What Layard looked for was an improvement in the government of the region." J. F. Coakley, *The Church of the East and the Church of England* (Oxford: Clarendon Press, 1992), 46–47.

35. Ibid., 248–51.

36. Strangford, *Selection of the Writings of Viscount Strangford*, 2:295.

37. Sir Arthur Otoway quoted by Bruce in Layard, *Autobiography*, 112, 267.

38. Layard to Granville, quoted in Gordon Waterfield, *Layard of Nineveh* (New York: Praeger, 1968), 236.

39. Layard to Lady Huntly, April 25, 1853, Layard Papers, British Library Manuscripts, Add. 38944, f. 120.

40. Layard to Lady Huntly, October 23, 1857, Layard Papers, British Library Manuscripts, Add. 38944, f. 164.

41. Layard to Morelli, July 20, 1876, Layard Papers, British Library Manuscripts, Add. 38966, f. 324.

42. Layard to Lady Gregory, November 30, 1876, Layard Papers, British Library Manuscripts, Add. 38966, f. 198.

43. Ibid., f. 195.

44. Layard might have heeded his own advice. In 1878, he found himself in the middle of the Russo-Turkish War, a conflict that critics claimed his political maneuverings behind the scenes with the sultan had helped escalate rather than solve. Layard to Viscount Redcliffe, September 10, 1877, Layard Papers, British Library Manuscripts, Add. 39124, f. 114.

45. Strangford to Layard, September 2, 1877, Layard Papers, British Library Manuscripts, Add. 39015, f. 54.

46. Strangford to Layard, Feb 19, 1880, Layard Papers, British Library Manuscripts, Add. 39031, f. 243.

47. Strangford to Layard, April 5, 1880, Layard Papers, British Library Manuscripts, Add. 39032 f. 240.

48. Strangford to Layard, July 1, 1878, Layard Papers, British Library Manuscripts, Add. 39021, f. 340.

49. Strangford to Layard, September 21, 1878, Layard Papers, British Library Manuscripts, Add. 39022, f. 82.

50. Strangford to Layard, April 30, 1880, Layard Papers, British Library Manuscripts, Add. 39033, f. 95.

51. Personal writings, March 11, 1883, Layard Papers, British Library Manuscripts, Add. 39143, f. 282.

52. Confidential print correspondence on "Protestant Constitution" negotiations, April, May, June 1880, Layard Papers, British Library Manuscripts, Add. 39156.

53. "Our Relations with Turkey," *Contemporary Review* 47 (May 1885), 611.

54. Layard to Granville, June 1, 1880, Layard Papers, British Library Manuscripts, Add. 39156, f. 145.

55. These largely Eastern Orthodox Christians included a number of recent Protestant converts due to the efforts of American and British missionaries operating in the region. On Protestant missionaries in the Ottoman Empire, see Julius Richter, *A History of Protestant Missions in the Near East* (London: Fleming H. Revell, 1910); Stina Katchadourian, ed., *Great Need over the Water: The Letters of Theresa Huntington Ziegler, Missionary to Turkey, 1898–1905* (Ann Arbor, MI: Gomidas, 1999); Frank Andrews Stone, *Academies for Anatolia: A Study of the Rationale, Program and Impact of the Educational Institutions Sponsored by the American Board in Turkey: 1830–1980* (Lanham, MD: University Press of America, 1984); William Strong, *The Story of the American Board: An Account of the First Hundred Years of*

the American Board of Commissioners for Foreign Missions (Boston: Pilgrim Press, 1910); and Barbara Merguerian, "A View from the United States Consulate," in Richard Hovannisian, ed., *Armenian Tsopk/Kharpert* (Costa Mesa, CA: Mazda), 273–325.

56. As Bloxham notes of the millet system, the British helped modernize this structure after 1850 by putting pressure on the Ottoman government to introduce a "Protestant millet" governed along liberal, secular lines. *Great Game of Genocide*, 43–44.

57. Ibid., 37–42.

58. Everett to Maria, October 12, 1884, Everett Collection, GB165-0100, Box 1, File 1, MECA.

59. James Marshall-Cornwall, "Three Soldier-Geographers," *The Geographical Journal* 131, no. 3 (September 1965), 357–65.

60. Lady Ardagh, Susan Countess of Malmesbury, *Life of Sir John Ardagh* (London: John Murray, 1909), 43–81.

61. Everett to Major Trotter, June 25, 1880, in Bilâl N. Şimşir, ed., *British Documents on Ottoman Armenians* (Ankara: Turk Tarih Kurumu Basımevi, 1983), 2:71.

62. Vice Consul Eyres to Everett, in Şimşir, ed., *British Documents*, 493.

63. Ibid., 204.

64. Dufferin to Everett, April 7, 1884, Everett Collection, Box 2, File 4b, MECA.

65. Everett to Granville, April 23, 1883, Everett Collection, Box 2, File 4b, MECA.

66. Everett had asked for between 7,000 and 8,000 pounds. Layard to Everett, February 7, 1880, Everett Collection, Box 2, File 4b, MECA.

67. Bloxham, *Great Game of Genocide*; Richard Hovannisian, ed., *The Armenian Genocide* (New York: St. Martins, 1992); Stina Katchadourian, ed., *Great Need over the Water*.

68. Shannon, *Gladstone and the Bulgarian Agitation 1876* (London: Thomas Nelson, 1963), 59–86.

69. Diary, February 1882, Everett Collection, Box 2, file 2, MECA.

70. Dufferin to Everett, April 7, 1884, Everett Collection, Box 2, File 4b, MECA.

71. Dufferin to Granville, June 27, 1884, in Şimşir, ed., *British Documents*, 496.

72. Layard to Everett, February 7, 1880, Everett Collection, Box 2, File 4b, MECA.

73. Diary, February 8, 1882, Everett Collection, Box 2, File 2c, MECA.

74. Everett to Maria, October 26, 1884.

75. Diary, February, 7, 8, and March 9, 1882, Everett Collection, Box 2, File 2c, MECA.

76. Undated note inserted in Everett's Diary, MECA.

77. Everett Collection, Box 1, File 2a, MECA.

78. Boyajian to Everett, November 17, 1886, Everett Collection, Box 2, File 5/7, MECA.

79. Lady Ardagh, *Life of Sir John Ardagh,* 279–80. Everett was created a KCMG (CMG in 1886) two years later for his services in connection with the treaty delimitating the frontiers in West Africa, in 1898, and died in 1908.

80. Platt, *Cinderella Service,* 133–34, 144–46.

81. Mösslang and Riotte, ed. *The Diplomats' World,* 7–9.

CHAPTER 4

1. Work on missionaries in the Ottoman Empire includes Culi Francis-Dehqani, "CMS Women Missionaries in Persia: Perceptions of Muslim Women and Islam, 1884–1934," and "Being Made Disciples—The Middle East," both in Kevin Ward and Brian Stanley, eds., *The Church Missionary Society and World Christianity, 1799–1999* (Richmond, Surrey: Curzon Press, 2000), 91–119, 120–46; and Ussama Damir Makdisi, *Artillery of Heaven* (Ithaca: Cornell University Press, 2008). Billie Melman has demonstrated that secular British women also traveled extensively and wrote about the "Orient." *Women's Orients: English Women and the Middle East, 1718–1918* (Ann Arbor: University of Michigan Press, 1992).

2. J. F. Coakley, *The Church of the East and the Church of England: A History of the Archbishop of Canterbury's Assyrian Mission* (Oxford: Clarendon, 1992), 11–18.

3. Exact population numbers do not exist. Turkish officials put the number at 1.3 million, while the Armenian patriarch of Constantinople estimated it at 2.1 million. The Foreign Office in 1920 sided with the latter figure, claiming if anything that the number was "too low rather than too high." Nassibian, *Britain and the Armenian Question 1915–1923* (London: Croom Helm, 1984), 3–4.

4. Andrew Porter, *Religion vs. Empire?* (Manchester: Manchester University Press, 2004), 58–63.

5. Over 1,000 charities with incomes totaling more than £6 million were founded, financed, and run by women during the Victorian period. F. K. Prochaska, *Women and Philanthropy in Nineteenth Century England* (Oxford: Oxford University Press, 1980), 22–23. For the American case, see Lori Ginzberg, *Women and the Work of Benevolence* (Yale: Yale University Press, 1992).

6. SPCK secretary to Rassam, February 20, 1838, as quoted in Coakley, *The Church of the East,* 27.

7. The mission suffered continually from a lack of funds and survived due to the dedication of the archbishop himself and fund-raising by largely women-run organizations. The mission only had £1,290 on hand in 1886, for example, until one church member, Mrs. Roe, organized a scheme that raised no less than £1,011 to help endow it. The mission was eventually disbanded in 1938. See chapter 5 for more on the Assyrian mission. Ibid., 145–51.

8. Sandra Holton, *Quaker Women: Personal Life, Memory and Radicalism*

in the Lives of Women Friends, 1780–1930 (London and New York: Routledge, 2007); Thomas Kennedy, *British Quakerism, 1860–1914* (Oxford: Oxford University Press, 2001).

9. Kennedy, *British Quakerism,* 7.

10. John Ormorod Greenwood, *Quaker Encounters,* vol. 1 (London: William Sessions, 1978). On the role of Quakers in business, see David Burns Windsor, *The Quaker Enterprise: Friends in Business* (London: Frederick Muller, 1980).

11. Edward Annett, "Fifty Years among the Armenians: A Brief Record of the Work of Ann Mary Burgess" (London: Stanley Hunt, 1938), 5. Religious Society of Friends in Britain Library (Friends House), London.

12. Quakers had traveled to the region as early as the 1860s. The Quaker activist Joseph Bevan Braithwaite started the mission in 1881 with a group of prominent Friends after visiting Constantinople. Dobrashian and his partner, Dr. H. J. Giragosian, purchased a house for the mission at the behest of the committee in 1884 at the cost of £1,500 in the Armenian quarter of Constantinople in 1884 for "Meeting and Mission purposes." "Medical Mission among the Armenians, Extract of the First Minute of the Committee held at Devonshire House, 1884," Friends House, London.

13. This was an argument made about other Eastern churches, including the Assyrians, who had stayed true to the orthodoxy of their early beliefs. Coakley, *The Church of the East,* 18–35.

14. According to Jo Laycock, the Armenians captured the Victorian imagination in part by offering a symbolic and geographic connection with the cradle of civilization. Jo Laycock, *Imagining Armenia* (Manchester: Manchester University Press, 2009), 43–98.

15. W. E. Gladstone quoted on the masthead of *Friend of Armenia.*

16. Kennedy, *British Quakerism,* 14.

17. Clare Midgley, *Feminism and Empire* (New York: Routledge, 2007), 97; Andrew Porter, *Imperial Horizons of British Protestant Missions, 1800–1914* (Grand Rapids, MI: William Eerdmans, 2003).

18. Donald Bloxham, *The Great Game of Genocide: Imperialism, Nationalism, and the Destruction of the Ottoman Armenians* (Oxford: Oxford University Press, 2005), 51–57. For a contemporary account, see the pamphlet by Emily J. Robinson, "Armenia and the Armenians" (London, 1917).

19. "Medical Mission among the Armenians: Occasional Paper," March 21, 1896, Friends House, London.

20. "Friends' Mission, Constantinople: Letter from A. M. Burgess at the Request of Many Friends and Supporters of the Mission," Friends House, London.

21. Jeffrey Cox, *Imperial Fault Lines* (Stanford, CA: Stanford University Press, 2002), 170–79. Rhonda Semple claims that it was not uncommon for women missionaries to receive inadequate training before going on medical missions; *Missionary Women: Gender, Professionalism, and the Victorian Idea of Christian Mission* (Suffolk: Boydell Press, 2003), 233. See also Maina

Chawla Singh, "Gender, Thrift and Indigenous Adaptations: Money and Missionary Medicine in Colonial India," *Women's History Review* 15, no. 5 (2006), 701–17.

22. Friends of Armenia annual reports, 1897–1902, British Library.

23. The international character of this organization meant that these networks came to include both British and American philanthropic organizations. *Friend of Armenia*, "Constantinople News," January 1920, n.s. 75; "Constantinople News," October 1920, n.s. 78.

24. Ann Mary Burgess (AMB) to Miss [Priscilla] Peckover, Constantinople, January 23, 1921, Friends House, London, Ryan correspondence with Burgess, GB165-0248, Box 5, File 2, MECA.

25. Porter, *Religion vs. Empire?* 314. Kevin Grant argues a similar point about reform efforts in the Congo during the late nineteenth century in *A Civilised Savagery: Britain and the New Slaveries in Africa* (New York: Routledge, 2005).

26. Annett, "Fifty Years," 17.

27. "Medical Mission among the Armenians: Occasional Paper," March 21, 1896, Friends House, London

28. Not everyone took this line on the Eastern Churches. High Anglicans like Gladstone joined the Quakers in believing that they could easily revivify the Eastern Churches, while the Church Missionary Society (CMS) worried that these churches had strayed too far from their Apostolic beginnings. H. C. G. Matthew, *Gladstone, 1809–1898* (Oxford: Oxford University Press, 2001), 264–66; and Porter, *Religion vs. Empire?* 217.

29. "Industrial Work, Constantinople: Letter from Ann M. Burgess," 1904, Friends House, London.

30. "Friends' Mission in Constantinople: Appeal for Completion of New Buildings Fund and for Additional Subscribers," 1906, Friends House, London.

31. The correspondence of the women and men who supported the mission through their purchases has disappeared. However, the Friends Armenian Mission annual reports offer a sense of the extent of this network among Friends in Britain. In 1888, 121 subscribers gave £346 in donations. Similar numbers exist for 1896, with 150 subscribers giving £730 to support the mission. By 1903, the number of contributing members was well over 200, with each giving on average under £1. Subscription lists indicate that these donations came from Friends all over Britain. Friends Armenian Mission annual reports, 1883–1925, Friends House, London. This pattern continued. In 1915, £627 was given by just under 200 donors.

32. AMB to Andrew Ryan, May 21, 1924, Ryan Papers GB165-0248, Box 5, File 2, MECA.

33. At least five English women and a varied number of mostly unnamed Armenian and Greek women and men worked with her at different times in Constantinople. Some were paid employees, while others volunteered for missionary service. One of her English missionary assistants, for exam-

ple, included Margaret Clarke, a member of a prominent philanthropically minded Quaker family.

34. AMB to Peckover, October 12, 1923, Friends House, London

35. Hetty M. Rowe to Algerina Peckover, July 24, 1916, Friends House, London.

36. Friends of Armenia annual report, 1899, 15, British Library.

37. "Ann Mary Burgess," *Gleaner*, May, 1922, 98.

38. AMB to A. Peckover, May 23, 1903, Friends House, London.

39. Brian Harrison, *Peaceable Kingdom: Stability and Change in Modern Britain* (Oxford: Clarendon Press, 1982), 229. See also Prochaska, *Women and Philanthropy*.

40. G.R. Searle, *Morality and the Market in Victorian Britain* (Oxford: Clarendon Press, 1998).

41. Ann Mary Burgess Obituary, Friends House archive, London.

42. Annett, "Fifty Years," 24.

43. Ibid. This item along with other toys generated £750 profit from sales in England alone.

44. Alice Odian Kasparian, *Armenian Needlelace and Embroidery* (McLean, Virginia: EPM Publications, 1983), 19–36.

45. Annett, "Fifty Years," 24. For the actual types of patterns produced in Anatolian villages during this period, see Kasparian, *Armenian Needlelace and Embroidery*, 77–100.

46. "Friends Armenian Mission, Constantinople," 1902, Friends Library, London.

47. This attempt to escape the problems of Western culture provided inspiration for an increasing number of missionaries who joined the foreign mission field, particularly after 1880. Porter, *Religion vs. Empire?* 229.

48. *The Friend of Armenia*, spring 1928, 10.

49. Ibid., September 1919, 9.

50. This distribution network proved such a great success that in 1904 Burgess decided to open a new confectionary business. She relied on these same networks to raise funds for this new scheme: "If one hundred ladies could be found each willing to take a £5 parcel of our Embroideries and make sales among their friend, they could each gain £1 profits and 2/– to cover postage by retailing the articles. . . . The united effort of home Friends would thus make our new undertaking an easy one. They would have the satisfaction of knowing that they had raised £100 toward the new work. "Industrial Work, Constantinople: Letter from Ann M. Burgess," 1904. Friends House, London.

51. Maud A.E. Rowntree, "In the City of the Sultan: The Work of the Friends' Armenian Mission, Constantinople," London, 1917, 22, Friends House, London.

52. In 1899, the balance sheet recorded over £3,278 in receipts for the organization's industrial work centers. Balance sheet, Friends of Armenia annual report, 1899, British Library.

53. Coakley, *The Church of the East*, 244–46.

54. "Aims of the Society," Friends of Armenia annual reports, 1897–1902, British Library.

55. "The Constitution of the Commission of Industries," *Friend of Armenia*, winter 1909.

56. "Orphans of Kharpoot," *Friend of Armenia*, December 1900.

57. Attempts to find suitable employment for women in England during the second half of the nineteenth century resulted in the founding of women-run industrial enterprises by upper-middle-class women that provided remunerative employment for lower-middle-class women. The Society for Promoting the Employment for Women and related institutions like the Women's Printing Society supported work programs that put middle-class women firmly in control of their working-class charges. At the same time, workers were given a financial interest in the businesses where they were employed. Michelle Tusan, "Reforming Work: Gender, Class and the Printing Trade in Victorian Britain," *Journal of Women's History* 16, no. 1 (2004), 102–25.

58. On the Mt. Holyoke school in Bitlis, see Barbara Merguerian, "Mt. Holyoke Seminary in Bitlis: Providing an American Education for Armenian Women," *Armenian Review* 43, no. 1 (spring 1990), 31–65.

59. This letter, originally written in Armenian and translated into English, was forwarded to Peckover by the secretary of the Friends of Armenia, Mary Hickson, and ended up in Burgess's personal papers at the Friends Library in London. Letter from Sara Crecorian, 1908, Friends House, London.

60. "Friends Armenian Mission, Constantinople," 1902, Friends House, London.

61. "Letters from Orphans," *Friend of Armenia*, February 1900.

62. Seth Koven demonstrates the importance of cultivating a sense of loyalty and brotherhood between philanthropists and the children they sponsored in Victorian society. *Slumming* (Princeton, NJ: Princeton University Press, 2004), 228–30.

63. The Friends of Armenia had affiliates throughout Britain. In Wales, for example, they forged connections with the Cardiff Women's Liberal Association. Friends of Armenia general committee report, January 12, 1901. In Scotland, they were associated with the Scottish Armenian Association. *Friend of Armenia*, spring 1904.

64. "Letters from Orphans," *Friend of Armenia*, February 1900.

65. Letter included in Friends of Armenia annual report, 1952. British Library.

66. *Friend of Armenia*, autumn 1903.

67. "The Reward of Labour," *Friend of Armenia*, winter 1905.

68. Clare Midgely, *Feminism and Empire*, 111–12.

69. Annett, "Fifty Years," 22–24.

70. Ibid, 22.

71. "Semi-Jubilee of Miss A. M. Burgess," *The Orient*, January 28, 1914.

72. Bloxham, *Great Game of Genocide*, 1.

73. Hetty M. Rowe to Algerina Peckover, July 24, 1916, Friends House, London.

74. AMB to Mr. Hurnard, March 9, 1916, Friends House, London.

75. Rowe to A. Peckover, July 24, 1916, Friends House, London.

76. Ibid.

77. AMB to A. Peckover, April 20, 1922, Friends House, London.

78. AMB to A. Peckover, January 23, 1921, Friends House, London.

79. AMB to A. Peckover, December 8, 1922, Friends House, London.

80. "Industrial Relief: Conclusions and Proposals," *Friend of Armenia*, March 1917.

CHAPTER 5

1. Peter Balakian cites the number of 250 in *Armenian Golgotha* (New York: Knopf, 2009). On the origins of the Armenian Genocide, see Raymond Kevorkian, *The Armenian Genocide: A Complete History*, (London: I. B Tauris, 2011); Vahakn Dadrian, *The History of the Armenian Genocide*, 4th rev. ed. (New York: Berghahn, 2008); Taner Akçam, *A Shameful Act: The Armenian Genocide and the Question of Turkish Responsibility* (New York: Henry Holt, 2006); Donald Bloxham, *The Great Game of Genocide: Imperialism, Nationalism, and the Destruction of the Ottoman Armenians* (Oxford: Oxford University Press, 2005); Peter Balakian, *The Burning Tigris: The Armenian Genocide and America's Response* (New York: Perennial, 2003); Jay Winter, ed., *America and the Armenian Genocide of 1915* (Cambridge: Cambridge University Press, 2003); and Richard Hovannisian, ed. *The Armenian Genocide: History, Politics, Ethics* (New York: St. Martins Press, 1992). I have adopted the practice of capitalizing "Armenian Genocide" in this chapter and elsewhere.

2. J. Ellis Barker, "Germany and Turkey," *Fortnightly Review* 96 n.s. (December 1914), 1013.

3. World War I's Eastern Front in general has generated less interest than the Western Front. Military histories do not deal with the British response to events on the Eastern Front and make little mention of events outside of major battles and military offensives. See, for example, Norman Stone, *The Eastern Front, 1914–1917* (New York: Scribner, 1975); and Nigel Steel and Peter Hart, *Defeat at Gallipoli* (London: Papermac, 1995).

4. Not enough work has been done to quantify exactly how many Greeks and Assyrians were massacred during the Genocide. Donald Bloxham puts the number of Greek deportations at around 150,000; *Game of Genocide*, 98–99. David Gaunt puts the number of Assyrian victims at over 250,000. "Treatment of the Assyrians," in R. Suny, ed., *A Question of Genocide* (Oxford: Oxford University Press, 2011), 245. Evidence of the wholesale deportation of towns with a majority of Greek and Assyrian residents before and during the war suggests that these populations were victims of the anti-Armenian fervor due to their status as part of the Ottoman Empire's remaining Christian

minority population. See also Ioannis K. Hassiotis, "The Armenian Genocide and the Greeks," in Hovannisian, ed., *The Armenian Genocide,* 129–51; and Thea Halo, *Not Even My Name* (New York: Picador, 2001).

5. W. Williams, "Armenia and the Partition of Asia Minor," *Fortnightly Review* 98 (November 1915), 968.

6. Dadrian, *History of the Armenian Genocide,* 61–68; Arman Kirakossian, *British Diplomacy and the Armenian Question* (Princeton, NJ: Gomidas Institute, 2003), 172–87.

7. Jo Laycock, *Imagining Armenia* (Manchester: Manchester University Press, 2009), 1. In the words of Donald Bloxham, the Genocide became a "useful propaganda tool for the Entente"; *Great Game of Genocide,* 134. See also Akaby Nassibian, *Britain and the Armenian Question 1915–1923* (London: Croom Helm, 1984), 78–119.

8. A. Williams, "Armenian Relief," letter to the *Times,* November 15, 1915. As early as April 1913 members used the opportunity of an international conference held at the House of Commons to argue that the Balkan War settlement should include reforms for Armenians. The committee subsequently met once a week until disbanding in 1924 to discuss effective strategies to influence future policy on Armenia.

9. Obituary, *Times,* January 21, 1924.

10. Armenian Red Cross annual reports, British Library.

11. Appeal for funds, Armenian Red Cross, [n.d.]. MS. Bryce 201, Bryce Papers, Bodleian Library.

12. First annual report, adopted at committee meeting on February 14, 1916, British Library.

13. Most of the money consistently came from subscriptions and donations (£4,739). Lectures brought in £17, drawing-room meetings £2, and bank interest £9. First annual report, 1916, British Library.

14. Events the first year that collected money for the fund included E. T. A. Wigram, "The Cradle of Mankind"; a lecture by Miss Amelia Bernard at St. Matthew's Parish Hall, Brook Green; a drawing-room meeting held at Bolton hosted by the Reynolds; and an address by Mr. N. I. Tiratsoo to School House Kineton on "Armenia Past and Present" and a published companion pamphlet.

15. Armenian Red Cross annual reports, British Library.

16. Nassibian, *Britain and the Armenian Question,* 41.

17. Imperial War Museum (IWM) online collection, Armenia/2.

18. Balakian, *Burning Tigris,* 65–67, 192, 278–79.

19. Nicoletta F. Gullace, *"The Blood of Our Sons": Men, Women, and the Renegotiation of British Citizenship During the Great War* (New York: Palgrave, Macmillan 2002), 17–34.

20. K. D. Watenpaugh, "The League of Nations' Rescue of Armenian Genocide Survivors and the Making of Modern Humanitarianism, 1920–1927," *American Historical Review* 115, no. 5 (December 2010), 1315–39.

21. Robinson to Douglas, June 3, 1923, Douglas Papers 61, Lambeth Palace Library, London.

22. Armenian Red Cross, 4th annual report, adopted January 23, 1919. British Library.

23. Manoug Somakian, *Empires in Conflict: Armenia and the Great Powers, 1895–1920* (London: I. B. Tauris, 1995), 77–82.

24. Armenian Red Cross, 4th annual report, adopted January 23, 1919, British Library.

25. Somakian, *Empires in Conflict*, 82. For an analysis of the so-called provocation thesis, see Ronald Grigor Suny, "Writing Genocide," in Suny, ed., *A Question of Genocide: Armenians and Turks at the End of the Ottoman Empire* (Oxford: Oxford University Press, 2011), 24–28.

26. Steel and Hart, *Defeat at Gallipoli*, 21–27.

27. Ibid., 364. The Foreign Office refused an earlier offer of help from Armenian volunteers living in France during the Dardanelles campaign under the leadership of Boghus Nubar. Born in Constantinople in 1851, the French-educated Nubar spent much of his life in Egypt. His work as head of the Armenian national delegation put him into regular contact with European leaders during the war, making him according to his biographer "politically the most centripetal Armenian figure during the years 1913 through 1918." Vatche Ghazarian, ed. and trans., *Boghos Nubar's Papers and the Armenian Question, 1915–1918* (Waltham, MA: Mayreni, 1996), xviii.

28. Undated Armenian Red Cross pamphlet, Davidson Papers 371, Lambeth Palace Library, London.

29. IWM Armenia/2.

30. *Ararat* 2, no. 25 (July 1915).

31. "Armenian Relief," *Times*, November 15, 1915.

32. Near East Relief was the most active relief organization in the region, raising money and providing humanitarian relief throughout the 1920s. See James Levi Barton, *The Story of Near East Relief* (New York: Macmillan, 1930); Stanley Kerr, *The Lions of Marash: Personal Experiences with American Near East Relief, 1919–1922* (Albany: State University of New York Press, 1973).

33. Lord Mayor's Fund (LMF) pamphlet. Bryce Papers, MS. Bryce 210, Bodleian Library.

34. *Ararat* 2, no. 25 (July 1915).

35. Ibid.; Mark Sykes, T. P. O'Connor, and Lady Ramsey quoted in LMF appeal for refugees, March 25, 1919.

36. In an LMF flyer of March 1919 the figure cited was 800,000.

37. LMF appeal, March 25, 1919, Bryce Papers, MS. Bryce 210, Bodleian Library.

38. Ibid.

39. Armenian-run organizations in Britain included the Armenian Ladies' Guild of London. It was organized on November 2, 1914, and made clothes to send to volunteers and refugees through Robinson's contacts in Russia. Asking for help from all British dominions, the organization raised about £1,192 in 1915. The Armenian Refugees' Relief Fund was run by prominent Arme-

nians living in London and collected money from "Armenian colonies in the Far East" that was then given to the Catholicos (the head of the Armenian church). It had raised £7,249 by fall 1915. Information from *Ararat*, July–September 1915.

40. Nassibian, *Britain and the Armenian Question*, 253.

41. J. A. R. Marriott, *Fortnightly Review* 99 (June 1916), 943.

42. Viscount James Bryce, *The Treatment of Armenians in the Ottoman Empire: 1915–16* (New York and London: G. Putnam's Sons, 1916; facs., Whitefish, MT: Kessinger Publishing), xvi.

43. H. A. L. Fisher, *James Bryce* (New York: Macmillan, 1927), 1:157–60.

44. "Armenians" to Bryce, April 1878, Bryce Papers, MS. Bryce 191, Bodleian Library.

45. Vartabed Astvazatourian wrote from the Armenian rectory on behalf of the Armenian Community of Manchester to congratulate him on his election to Parliament in April 1880. Bryce Papers, MS. Bryce 191, Bodleian Library.

46. Obituary, *Times*, January 31, 1922.

47. Bryce was made viscount in 1914 shortly after returning from his post as ambassador to the United States.

48. Gullace, "*The Blood of Our Sons*," 17–34; Fisher, *James Bryce*, 2:132–36. John Horne and Alan Kramer argue that the report represented in the German case "systematic terror as military doctrine," *German Atrocities, 1914: A History of Denial* (New Haven: Yale University Press, 2001), 237.

49. Williams to Primrose, May 2, 1915, FO 371/2488.

50. Sir G. Buchanan to Sir Edward Grey, May 11, 1915, Petrograd, FO 371/2488.

51. Joint declaration to Sublime Porte, May 24, 1915, quoted in Gary Bass, *Stay the Hand of Vengeance* (Princeton, NJ: Princeton University Press, 2000), 117.

52. Donald Bloxham has argued that although Germany did play a significant role in the massacres, "the German role should still be seen in a comparative, interactive context with those of the other Great Powers," *Great Game of Genocide*, 115. See also Margaret Anderson, "'Down in Turkey Far Away': Human Rights, the Armenian Massacres, and Orientalism in Germany," *Journal of Modern History* 79, no. 1 (March 2007), 80–111.

53. J. M. Read, *Atrocity Propaganda, 1914–1919* (New Haven: Yale University Press, 1941), 216–22.

54. Boldface in original; Toynbee quoting from the *New York Tribune*, October 1915. Arnold Toynbee, *Armenian Atrocities: The Murder of a Nation* (London: Hodder and Stoughton, 1915), 117. Blaming Germany for the massacres became a familiar trope that continued beyond the war. Suny, "Writing Genocide," 18–20; Isabel Hull, *Absolute Destruction: Military Culture and the Practices of War in Imperial Germany* (Ithaca: Cornell University Press, 2005), ch. 11.

55. Bryce quoted in Toynbee, *Armenian Atrocities*, 7.

56. R. Ahmad, "A Moslem View of Abdul Hamid and the Powers," *Nineteenth Century*, July 1895, 156.

57. The disloyalty argument was later outlined and refuted by American Ambassador Henry Morgenthau in his memoirs published in 1918; Suny, "Writing Genocide," 19–20.

58. Toynbee to Bryce, July 22, 1916, Bryce Papers, MS. Bryce 203, Bodleian Library.

59. Toynbee, *Armenian Atrocities*, 58.

60. Ibid.

61. Bryce, *Treatment of Armenians*, xvii.

62. Nassibian, *Britain and the Armenian Question*, 78–84.

63. Toynbee Papers, Bodleian library, Box on Armenia, "Memorial," September 26, 1924. Quoted in ibid., 81.

64. Charles Masterman to Bryce, June 14, 1916, Bryce Papers, MS. Bryce 202, Bodleian Library.

65. Masterman to Bryce, June 20, 1916, FO 96/207.

66. Masterman to Bryce, June 14, 1916, Bryce Papers, MS. Bryce 202, Bodleian Library.

67. "Lord Bryce's Report on Turkish Atrocities in Armenia," *Current History* (New York) 5, no. 2 (November 1916), 321.

68. CFGM (Masterman) to Sir John Simon, June 20, 1916, FO 96/207.

69. Toynbee to Bryce, June 20, 1916, FO 96/207.

70. Ibid.

71. Toynbee to Bryce, March 11, 1920, Bryce Papers, MS. Bryce 206, Bodleian Library. Though he does not name the book, it most likely was Johannes Lepsius's *Deutschland und Armenien, 1914–1918* (Potsdam: Der Tempelverlag, 1919).

72. Pamphlet in Bryce Papers, MS. Bryce 209, Bodleian Library.

73. A. S. Safrastian to Bryce, March 14, 1917, Bryce Papers, MS. Bryce 204, Bodleian Library.

74. For a comparative treatment of the Armenian and Assyrian case, see David Gaunt, "The Ottoman Treatment of the Assyrians," in Suny, ed., *A Question of Genocide*, 244–59.

75. J. F. Coakley, *The Church of the East and the Church of England: A History of the Archbishop of Canterbury's Assyrian Mission* (Oxford: Clarendon, 1992), 336–40.

76. Lord Archbishop of York to Archbishop of Canterbury, October 1, 1915, Davidson papers 371, Lambeth Palace Library, London.

77. Archbishop of Canterbury to Archbishop of York, November 24, 1915, Lambeth Palace Library, London.

78. Ibid.

79. Fisher, *James Bryce*, 2:144.

80. Toynbee correspondence with V. Chirol, Chatham House archives.

81. Arnold Toynbee, *Acquaintances* (Oxford: Oxford University Press, 1967), 149.

82. Lewis Einstein, "The Armenian Massacres," *Contemporary Review* 111 (April 1917), 494.

83. "Turks Talk of Reform: Punishment for Armenian Massacres," *Times*, November 30, 1918.

84. "More Armenian Massacres," *Times*, January 4, 1919.

85. Vahakn Dadrian has undertaken a comprehensive analysis of these trials most recently with Taner Akçam in *Judgment at Istanbul: The Armenian Genocide Trials* (New York: Berghahn, 2011). See also Dadrian, "The Turkish Military Tribunals' Prosecution of the Authors of the Armenian Genocide: Four Major Court-Martial Series," *Holocaust and Genocide Studies* 11, no. 1 (spring 1997), 28–59.

86. Bass, *Stay the Hand of Vengeance*, 114–17.

87. The phrase "crimes against humanity and civilization" appeared for the first time in a joint Allied declaration issued in May 1915. Admiral Somerset Calthorpe labeled the acts being tried during the trials as "crimes against humanity." See below.

88. Bass, *Stay the Hand of Vengeance*, 106–7; Akçam, *Shameful Act*, 368–72.

89. Louis Mallet to Sir R. Graham, "Necessity of punishing Turks responsible for Armenian Massacres and other outrages," January 17, 1919, FO 371/4172.

90. "Situation Report," H. V. Whittall, Lieut., document received May 17, 1919, FO 608/79.

91. Admiral Calthorpe, Constantinople, January 7, 1919, FO 371/4173.

92. "Treatment of British Prisoners of war and Armenians," British High Commissioner to Balfour[?], January 7, 1919,FO 371/4172.

93. Calthorpe, Constantinople, January 24, 1919, FO 371/4172.

94. Calthorpe, report from Constantinople, January 28, 1919, FO 371/4172.

95. Bass, *Stay the Hand of Vengeance*, 128.

96. Vahakn Dadrian, "A Textual Analysis of the Key Indictment of the Turkish Military Tribunal Investigating the Armenian Genocide," *Armenian Review* 44, no. 1/173 (spring 1991), 3.

97. Calthorpe, report from Constantinople, January 28, 1919.

98. Bass, *Stay the Hand of Vengeance*, 127.

99. Ibid., 136–39.

100. FO 371/6504.

101. "Turks' British Captives: Exchange for War Criminals," *Times*, October 5, 1921; "Turkish War Criminals: Double Negotiations," *Times*, October 17, 1921.

102. Muriel Bromley Davenport, "Turkish War Criminals," letter to the editor, *Times*, October 19, 1921.

103. "Turkish War Criminals," editorial, *Times*, October 6, 1921.

104. These experiences are recounted in documents found in FO 371/6505.

105. Lt. Col. A. Rawlinson, *Adventures in the Near East 1918–1922* (New York: Dodd, Mead, 1924), 342.

106. Akçam describes the shift from the National Movement's condemnation of the massacres to a more "equivocal stance" during this period, *Shameful Act*, 349–51.

107. Frederick James Smith's review published in *Motion Picture Classic* in August 1919, quoted in Anthony Slide, *Ravished Armenia and the Story of Aurora Mardiganian* (Lanham, MD: Scarecrow Press, 1997), 15.

108. Reviews of the film are contained in the series of files, HO 45/10955/312971/89-105.

109. January 8, 1920, HO 45/10955/312971/89.

110. The case came to trial in 1921 and was decided against the council. "Exhibition of 'The Auction of Souls,'" *Times*, July 13, 1921.

111. "Metropolitan Police: Criminal Investigation Department, New Scotland Yard," January 15, 1920, HO 45/10955/312971/89.

112. Ibid.

113. Shortt to Harris (Prosecutions department), n.d., HO 45/10955/312971/89.

114. Home Office memorandum, received January 22, 1920, HO 45/10955/312971/98.

115. Home Office memorandum from Foreign Office officials who viewed the film, n.d., HO 45/10955/312971/89.

116. Letter from head of the Woking Mosque, November 5, 1919. HO 45/10955/312971/90.

117. Islamic Information Bureau representative to secretary of state for Home Affairs, November 5, 1919, HO 45/10955/312971/99.

118. Mr. A. Mirza to Home Office, received February 6, 1920, HO 45/10955/312971/105.

119. Letter forwarded from Curzon, January 5, 1920, HO 45/10955/312971/92.

120. See the following *Times* articles: "Police Objections Referred to Mr. Shortt," January 20, 1920; "Film Approved after Alterations," January 21, 1920; "First Public Exhibition," January 27, 1920.

121. "Response to Secretary of State's Objections," January 24, 1920, HO 45/10955/312971/98.

122. Ibid., censored titles and subtitles of *Auction of Souls*, received by Home Office, January 22, 1920.

123. Foreign Office official memorandum, HO 45/10955/312971/89, [n.d.].

124. Reviews of the film included: *Times*, October 30, 1919; *Daily Telegraph*, October 30, 1919; *Daily Mail*, October 30, 1919; *Daily Sketch*, October 30, 1919; *Daily Graphic*, October 30, 1919; *Evening News*, October 25, 1919; *Daily Express*, October 30, 1919; *Westminster Gazette*, October 30, 1919; *Evening Standard*, October 30, 1919; *People*, November 2, 1919; *The Star*, October 29; *Pall Mall Gazette*, October 30, 1919; *Cinema*, October 16, 1919; *Liverpool Courier*, October 30, 1919; *Liverpool Daily Post and Mercury*, October 29, 1919; *Norwich Eastern Daily Press*, October 31, 1919; *Belfast Cinema*, October 23, 1919.

125. Lady Baird to Home Office, January 22, 1920, HO 45/10955/312971/101.

126. Excerpt from *Evening Standard*, October 30, 1919, HO 45/10955/312971/95.

127. Ibid., letter from Arthur Webster, November 12, 1919.

128. Iris Constance Fitzgerald Marriot to Home Office, January 24, 1920, HO 45/10955/312971/102.

129. L. Johnson, YMCA Hostel, London Bridge, November 13, 1919, HO 45/10955/312971/95.

130. J.D. Rees to secretary of state for Home Office, February 19, 1920, HO 45/10955/312971/104.

131. Excerpt from the *Times*, HO 45/10955/312971/98.

132. Advertisement, *Times*, January 20, 1920.

133. Excerpt from the *Universe*, n.d., HO 45/10955/312971/95.

134. November 5, 1919, HO 45/10955/312971/89.

135. "The Movies," *English Review*, May 1920, 472.

136. Sidney Low, "Propaganda Films and Mixed Morals on the 'Movies,'" *Fortnightly Review* 107 (May 1920), 717–28.

137. The Armenian Film Foundation issued a twenty-minute segment of the film in 2009 on DVD, the only part seeming to remain of the nine reels originally produced. My thanks to Walter Karabian and the Armenian Film Foundation for providing me with a copy of the film segment.

138. David Lloyd George, *War Memoirs*, vol. 1 (London: Odhams Press, 1938), 224–26; Nassibian, *Britain and the Armenian Question*, 125–26.

139. R.W. Seton-Watson, *Disraeli, Gladstone, and the Eastern Question* (1935; reprint, New York: Norton, 1972), 1.

140. Jay Winter, "Under the Cover of War: The Armenian Genocide in the Context of Total War," in Winter, ed., *America and the Armenian Genocide* (Cambridge: Cambridge University Press, 2003), 38–42.

CHAPTER 6

1. "Memoir," T.W. Bunter Papers, Imperial War Museum (IWM), London, 87/22/1 (1444).

2. "Anonymous Account of the Burning of Smyrna," September 13, 1922, entry, IWM, Misc 97 (1473). Transcript diary kept by an unknown midshipman on the HMS *Serapis*, who was present at Smyrna during September 1922.

3. Charles James Howes, "Smyrna 1922," C.J. Howes Papers, IWM, 86/14/1 (2286).

4. See Giles Milton, *Paradise Lost: Smyrna 1922* (New York: Basic Books, 2008); Marjorie Housepian, *The Smyrna Affair* (New York: Harcourt Brace Jovanovich, 1971); George Horton *The Blight of Asia* (Indianapolis: Bobbs Merrill Co., 1953); Edward Hale Bierstadt, *The Great Betrayal: A Survey of the Near East Problem* (New York: McBride, 1924).

5. Claudena Skran, *Refugees in Interwar Europe* (Oxford: Clarendon Press, 1995), 1–3.

6. "Anonymous Account," September 6 entry, IWM, Misc 97 (1473).

7. Bruce Clark, *Twice a Stranger* (Cambridge, MA: Harvard University Press, 2006), 9–10.

8. Lord Curzon to Sir H. Rumbold, September 2, 1922, FO 141/580.

9. Lord Curzon to Sir H. Rumbold, September 3, 1922, FO 141/580.

10. Henry Lamb to Curzon, September 4, 1922, FO 141/580.

11. "Evacuation of British Colony at Smyrna: Memorandum," S. L. Vereker Papers, IWM, 7497 75/87/1.

12. Milton, *Paradise Lost,* 48–53; Housepian, *Smyrna Affair,* 112–13. Numerous eyewitnesses record the arrival of the Turkish irregulars in Smyrna and the brutal treatment of Greek and Armenian residents. See Howes, "Smyrna 1922," 2; Dora Sakayan, trans., *An Armenian Doctor in Turkey: Garabed Hatcherian, My Smyrna Ordeal 1922* (Montreal: Arod Books, 1997); Hovakim Uregian and Krikor Baghdjian,"Two Unpublished Eyewitness Accounts of the Holocaust in Smyrna," *Armenian Review* 35 (1982), 362–89; Lysimachose Oeconomos, *The Martyrdom of Smyrna and Eastern Christendom* (London: George Allen, 1922); Whittall Papers on Smyrna, MS 259/7, University of Exeter.

13. "Anonymous Account," September 9 entry, IWM, Misc 97 (1473).

14. Howes, "Smyrna 1922," C. J. Howes Papers, IWM, 86/14/1 (2286), 4.

15. Housepian, *Smyrna Affair,* 220–23; Krikor Baghdjian, "Court Evidence: American Tobacco Company vs. Guardian Assurance," in Uregian and Baghdjian, "Two Unpublished Accounts," 384–89.

16. "Anonymous Account," September 13 entry.

17. Interview with C. S. B. Swinley, IWM, July 12, 1977, IWM interview 996.

18. "Anonymous Account," September 13 entry, IWM, Misc 97 (1473).

19. Ibid., September 14, 1922 entry.

20. Interview with C. H. Drage, March 22, 1982, IWM, 6131-05 (Reel 4).

21. "Anonymous Account," September 14 entry, IWM, Misc 97 (1473).

22. "Last Days of Smyrna," *Times,* September 19, 1922.

23. "Evacuation of Smyrna," University of Exeter Library Special Collections, MS 259/7.

24. Ibid.

25. "The Ruins of Smyrna," *Times,* September 22, 1922.

26. The American ships joined the rescue effort first with orders to land and protect aid workers who had been working on shore since the fire started. Housepian, *Smyrna Affair,* 98; Esther Pohl Lovejoy, *Certain Samaritans* (New York: Macmillan, 1927), 140–52.

27. "Anonymous Account," September 14 entry, IWM, Misc 97 (1473).

28. Ibid., September 16 entry.

29. Drage interview, March 22, 1982, IWM, 6131-05 (Reel 4).

30. Howes, "Smyrna 1922," C. J. Howes Papers, IWM, 86/14/1 (2286), 6.

31. "S.N.O Smyrna: Diary of Events," September 20, 1922, Document 230,

"Rear Admiral Tyrwhitt to Brock," in Paul Halpern, *The Mediterranean Fleet, 1919–1929* (Burlington, VT: Ashgate, 2011), 389–90.

32. Press cutting, n.d., Swinley Papers, IWM, 4280.

33. Acting Vice-Consul Urquhart to Rumbold, October 10, 1922, FO 141/580.

34. C.S.B. Swinley, "Diary, 1922," Swinley Papers, IWM, 4280.

35. Ibid.

36. Acting Vice-Consul Urquhart to Sir H. Rumbold, September 29, 1922, FO 141/580.

37. Ibid.

38. Urquhart to Rumbold, October 13, 1922, FO 141/580.

39. Ibid.

40. Rumbold to Curzon, November 11, 1922, FO 141/580.

41. Housepian, *Smyrna Affair,* 218.

42. Stephen Evans, *The Slow Rapprochement: Britain and Turkey in the Age of Kemal Ataturk, 1919–38* (Beverly, North Humberside: Eothen Press, 1982), 69.

43. Howes, "Smyrna 1922," C.J. Howes Papers, IWM, 86/14/1 (2286), 7.

44. "Anonymous Account," conclusion, IWM, Misc 97 (1473).

45. Telegram, Paris, Mr. Balfour to High Commissioner for Egypt, May 11, 1919, FO 141/580.

46. Letter from Sydney La Fontaine, March 15, 1919, FO 141/580.

47. Clark, *Twice a Stranger,* xv.

48. William Rappard, *International Relations as Viewed from Geneva* (New Haven: Yale University Press, 1925), 40. On minority treaties as they emerged immediately after the war, see Carole Fink, *Defending the Rights of Others* (Cambridge: Cambridge University Press, 2004), 133–69.

49. Fink, *Defending the Rights of Others,* 267–68; Blanche E.C. Dugdale and Wyndham A. Bewes, "The Working of the Minority Treaties," *Journal of the British Institute of International Affairs* 5, no. 2 (March 1926), 79–95, http://www.jstor.org/stable/3014590, accessed July 13, 2009.

50. Rappard, *International Relations,* 58–9.

51. On the formation of the Eastern Committee, March 1918, Curzon Papers, British Library, MSS Eur F112/273. Criticism was voiced early on by Cecil that this committee could not handle the enormous charge with which it had been given. In a letter to Balfour on July 20, 1918, Cecil suggested that a more formalized command structure for the Eastern settlement be created under the auspices of the Foreign Office. Robert Cecil Papers, Add. MSS 51071A f. 48, British Library.

52. "Eastern Committee," December 9, 1918, Curzon Papers, MSS Eur F112/273, British Library.

53. Ibid., December 2, 1918.

54. Montagu to Curzon, April 4, 1921, Curzon Papers, MSS Eur F112/221B, British Library.

55. T. P. O'Connor to Curzon, December 24, 1921, Curzon Papers, MSS Eur F112/221B, British Library.

56. A letter from a Friends of Armenia representative described conditions from November 18 and 22, 1921, indicating that officials did have reports on the ground. Correspondence found in British Armenian Committee (BAC) minutes, MSS Brit. Emp. s. 22, British Library of Commonwealth and African Studies, University of Oxford (Rhodes House).

57. For example, see meetings of December 20, 1920, January 3, 1921, and February 14, 1921, BAC minutes, MSS Brit. Emp. s. 22, Rhodes House.

58. British Armenian Committee (BAC) minutes, March 23, 1920, MSS Brit. Emp. s. 22, Bodleian Library of Commonwealth and African Studies, University of Oxford (Rhodes House).

59. BAC minutes, September 7, 1920, Rhodes House.

60. August 6, 1937, BAC Armenia file, MSS Brit. Emp. s. 22, Rhodes House.

61. Violet R. Markham, "Greece and the Refugees from Asia Minor," *Fortnightly Review* 117 (February 1925), 177–78.

62. Letter to Douglas from the BAC, June 20, 1923, Douglas Papers, vol. 61, Lambeth Palace Library, London.

63. Mark H. Ward, "The Deportations in Asia Minor, 1921–22" (London, 1922). Ward claimed that the only assistance deportees received was from American volunteers working in the interior. Deportation to the interior was essentially a death sentence. Of the estimated 30,000 mainly Greek refugees deported between May 1921 and January 1922 only 6,000 made it to their destination. Ward described the circumstances that these remaining refugees faced: "The deportees all knew that they were being sent there to die. The Turkish officials knew it. There was no possibility that many could find shelter or food among those high mountains" (5).

64. "Review of Six Prisons and Two Revolutions," *Saturday Review* 11 (October 3, 1925), 375.

65. E. N. Bennett, "Our Anatolian Policy and the Suppressed Report," *English Review* 30 (April 1920), 361.

66. Published statement of the Near and Middle East Association held in the Harry St. John Philby Collection, GB165-0229, MECA.

67. Toynbee quoted in Housepian, *Smyrna Affair,* 225.

68. "The Denouement in the Near East," *Contemporary Review* 122 (October 1922), 409–14.

69. Toynbee's increasingly strident anti-Greek position did not win him many friends at home. This was a particular problem after he took up the chair of Modern Greek Studies in the mid-1920s. See "Memorandum on the Journalistic and Political Activity of Professor Toynbee," which criticized Toynbee for focusing too much time on politics over his academic affairs: "At the time of the burning of Smyrna Mr. Toynbee went so far as to accuse the Greeks of responsibility, although he could not quote one word of evidence for the charge and admitted that it was only a 'presumption of guilt.'"

(2) SSEES archives, Seton-Watson Collection SEW 17/29/1, University College London.

70. Curzon to Williams, December 6, 1921, FO 286/879.

71. A. Hulme-Beaman, "Lausanne and Its Lessons," *Nineteenth Century* 93 (March 1923), 321.

72. *The Sphere*, November 18, 1922, quoting Mr. Scotland Liddell on the "fate of 400,000 Constantinople Christians." The Lausanne Conference opened on November 20, 1922.

73. Sir Andrew Ryan, *The Last of the Dragomans* (London: Geoffrey Bles, 1951), 27.

74. Ibid., 39–46.

75. Ibid., 121.

76. Ibid., 123.

77. Ibid., 139

78. Robert Graves, *Storm Centres of the Near East: Personal Memories 1879–1929* (1933, reprint, London: Hutchinson, 1975), 325.

79. Letter from E. Paul to Andrew Ryan, Aleppo, June 18, 1919. Ryan Papers GB165-0248, Box 4, File 1, MECA.

80. Graves, *Storm Centres*, 324.

81. Ibid., 236.

82. Ibid., 130.

83. Ibid., 327.

84. Ibid., 329.

85. Ibid., 330–32.

86. Ryan, *Last of the Dragomans*, 150–51.

87. Graves, *Storm Centres*, 147. The work of the AGS officially wound up at the end of January 1922.

88. Ibid., 352.

89. G. D. Clayton argues that Britain's main focus in the settlement after the war was the Arab lands of the Ottoman Empire; see his *Britain and the Eastern Question* (London: University of London Press, 1971), 235–39.

90. Hulme-Beaman, "Lausanne," 324.

91. Harold Nicolson, *Curzon: The Last Phase* (London: Constable, 1934), 315.

92. Clark, *Twice a Stranger*, xii. As the passage of Nansen's plan became a foregone conclusion, Ryan and others began to worry about the details. A plan to abolish the Greek Patriarchate at Constantinople concerned Ryan due to "the emotion which would be caused in Anglican circles at home if Great Britain made herself a party to the expulsion of the Patriarchate." He cited potential objections by the Archbishop of Canterbury.

93. Treaty of Sevres, Articles 140–51, supplement to the *American Journal of International Law*, vol. 15, *Official Documents* (New York: Oxford University Press, 1921), 208–13; and Treaty of Lausanne, Articles 37–45, *Lausanne Conference on Near Eastern Affairs, 1922–23: Records of Proceedings and Draft Terms of Peace* (London: Stationary Office, 1923), 698–702.

94. As described in Ryan, *Last of the Dragomans,* 198.

95. Ibid., 218.

96. W. D. W. Matthews to Andrew Ryan, October 1, 1923, Ryan Papers GB165-0248, Box 5, File 3, MECA.

97. A large number of these refugees arrived from Smyrna and its surrounding areas before the signing of the treaty. Skran, *Refugees in Interwar Europe,* 44–46; Elisabeth Kontogiori, *Population Exchange in Greek Macedonia* (Oxford: Oxford University Press 2006), 6.

98. Bruce Clark, *Twice a Stranger,* 11–12; According to Skran, "Refugee movements in inter-war Europe dwarfed all previous ones"; *Refugees in Interwar Europe,* 14.

99. "Armenia" as a territory had a precarious existence after declaring independence as a republic in April 1918. It was eventually taken over by Communist Russia and became part of the Soviet Union in December 1922. Widespread starvation and inadequate resources made it a difficult place to support settlement despite efforts by the League to make it a permanent home for the Armenians. See Richard Hovannisian, *The Republic of Armenia,* vol. 4: *Between Crescent and Sickle* (Berkeley and Los Angeles: University of California Press, 1996); Housepian, *Smyrna Affair,* 117.

100. A small Christian minority population was allowed to remain in Constantinople after Lausanne. The story of victims of the massacres who remained behind in other regions is just beginning to be told by a new generation of Turkish authors. See Fethyne Çetin, *My Grandmother: A Memoir* (New York: Verso, 2008).

101. The Archbishop of Canterbury supported the founding of the church and himself preached at St. Sarkis in October 1925. A small community of Armenians also existed in Liverpool and Manchester. See Joan George, *Merchants in Exile: The Armenians in Manchester, 1835–1935* (Princeton: Gomidas, 2002).

102. John Hope Simpson, *The Refugee Problem: Report of a Survey* (London: Oxford University Press, 1939), 337. The Chatham House study was a survey which resulted from a tour of the region in fall 1937 that was funded by the Rockefeller Foundation.

103. Akaby Nassibian has demonstrated the unevenness of government pledges of support for refugees in the postwar period even within areas where they held a mandate; *Britain and the Armenian Question 1915–1923* (London: Croom Helm, 1984), 255–60.

104. Curzon to Williams, December 6, 1921, FO 286/879.

105. Lancelot Oliphant to Australian and Canadian Consulates, January 8, 1923, FO 286/879.

106. Correspondence with New Zealand Consulate, January 9, 1923, and April 10, 1923, FO 286/879.

107. Correspondence with Canadian Consulate, December 20, 1922, FO 286/879.

108. Typescript to Douglas from Buxton on LMF stationary, June 30, 1924, Douglas Papers, vol. 61, Lambeth Palace Library, London.

109. Ibid., Jan 1926. They estimated rescue costs of £8 per girl.

110. *Saturday Review,* June 16, 1928, 779.

111. *English Review Advertiser,* December 1928, 626.

112. Augusta to Harris, December 28, 1929, BAC Armenia file, Rhodes House. This shift in attitude can be seen in the statement announcing proposed contributions to Armenian resettlement in 1924. According to the secretary of Save the Children, "The cause of voluntary aid received considerable moral support from the proposal made to the PM of Great Britain (Ramsey MacDonald) by the leaders of the Opposition parties in the House of Commons (Asquith and Baldwin) in Sept 1924 that the British Government should make a grant of 1 million from the Exchequer 'for the final liquidation of the Armenian problem'" because of their support for the Allies during the war. Edward Fuller, "Voluntary Aid and the Refugees," Refugee Survey: Special Deports (draft), vol. 11, [n.d.], Chatham House. The proposed aid never materialized.

113. Nassibian, *Britain and the Armenian Question,* 248.

114. The Refugee camp in Bakuba was discussed as part of the Iraq settlement immediately after the war. T 161/50.

115. Northcote to mother, December 3, 1918, Northcote Papers, Add MSS 57559, British Library.

116. Northcote reported speaking Armenian "quite well" by July 5, 1919, in a letter home. Northcote Papers, Add MSS 57559, British Library. Refugee statistics come from Simpson, *The Refugee Problem,* 49.

117. Letter dated July 18, 1919, Northcote Papers, Add MSS 57559, British Library.

118. Letter dated October 3, 1920, Northcote Papers, Add MSS 57559, British Library.

119. "Iraq settlement," as discussed in T 161/50. David Gaunt chronicles the widespread massacre of Assyrian civilians during World War I in *Massacres, Resistance, Protectors: Muslim-Christian Relations in Eastern Anatolia during World War I* (Piscataway, NJ: Gorgias Press, 2006).

120. "The Assyrian Problem," speech by Rev. W. A. Wigram (British chaplain to the Athens legation) at the 72nd anniversary of the Anglican and Eastern Church Association, November 18, 1936, Renton Papers GB165-0239, Box 4, File 11, MECA.

121. LMF memorandum to Under Secretary of State Colonial Office, October 25, 1922, FO 286/879; Randall Cantuar to Sir John Shuckenburgh (Colonial Office), December 20, 1922, FO 286/879.

122. Foreign Office memo no. 697, December 1, 1922, FO 286/835.

123. J. E. Shuckburgh, January 9, 1923, FO 286/879.

124. Robert Hewsen, *Armenia: A Historical Atlas* (Chicago: University of Chicago Press, 2001), 242. On the history of modern Armenia, see Richard Hovanissian, *The Armenian People from Ancient to Modern Times,* vol. 2

(New York: Palgave Macmillan, 2004); and Razmik Panossian, *The Armenians* (New York: Columbia University Press, 2006), 246–56.

125. Letter dated July 13, 1921, Northcote Papers, Add MSS 57559, British Library,

126. Letters dated September 23 and 24, 1921, Northcote Papers, Add MSS 57559, British Library.

127. Nassibian, *Britain and the Armenian Question*, 248–49.

128. Northcote was still employed by the LMF in March 1926 but expressed his wish to "come home." Funding given by Save the Children discussed in a letter dated February 3, 1922, Northcote Papers, Add MSS 57559, British Library.

129. Dr. Nansen, High Commissioner of the League for Refugees, "Report on Refugees in Near East," January 26, 1923, FO 286/879.

130. Britain's most important pledge of aid was a loan guarantee to Greece to help with the refugee crisis: Clark, *Twice a Stranger*, 151–57. The *League of Nations Official Journal* recorded that by January 1923 Britain also had pledged £50,000 in aid to "refugees from Asia Minor." "Refugees from Asia Minor," January 1923, 1140–1141.

131. Major General Sir Patrick Hehir, "Enclosure No. 1 respecting Greek Refugees," Nansen Report, January 26, 1923, FO 286/879.

132. "Greek Refugees," January 26, 1923, FO 286/879.

133. Vice Consul (Arguit)[?] to Bentinck, December 23, 1922, FO 286/404.

134. Bentinck to Cyprus Consulate, February 8, 1923, FO 286/879.

135. FO 286/879.

136. Simpson, *The Refugee Problem*, 344.

137. Evacuation orders, Smyrna September 5, 1922, S.L. Vereker Papers, IWM 75/87/1.

138. Letter to the British legation, Athens, December 4, 1922, FO 286/806.

139. Caps in original. Ibid., December 9, 1922.

140. Caps in original. Ibid.

141. The reply to Athens's inquiry is not recorded, and it is not clear whether or not the Smyrna refugees did get their allowances cut. Undated letter to Bentinck, FO 286/806.

142. Nicholas Sanson first applied for help on September 30, 1922. George Sanson wrote the Foreign Office on behalf of his cousin, Nicholas, and Martin on November 4, 1922, asking to admit them to London or have them sent back to Malta rather than stranding them in Calais. They were denied entry on November 17, 1922, on grounds cited by H.J. Read that "it would not seem that either of the persons in question has any connection with Malta or any other British colony," FO 286/879.

143. Bentinck to FO, January 11, 1923, FO 286/806.

144. Acting British Consul at Smyrna Urquhart to Bentinck, February 20, 1923, FO 141/580.

145. Ibid., January 12, 1923.

146. Bentinck to Urquhart, April 21, 1923, FO 141/580.

147. Hubert Montgomery on behalf of Curzon, November 9, 1922, FO 286/806.

148. December 4 and 13, 1922, FO 286/806.

149. Simpson, *The Refugee Problem*, 344.

150. Donald Bloxham has suggested that ineffectual British diplomacy at Lausanne and the ultimate acceptance of the Kemalist revolution in 1923 amounted to a "tacit support for Turkey's policies": *Great Game of Genocide: Imperialism, Nationalism, and the Destruction of the Ottoman Armenians* (Oxford: Oxford University Press, 2005), 170. For Jo Laycock, the refugee problem coupled with the Russian annexing of Armenia in 1922 further strained ties after the war as "sympathy gave way to wariness": *Imagining Armenia* (Manchester: Manchester University Press, 2009), 173, 219.

EPILOGUE

1. Laurence Grafftey-Smith, *Bright Levant* (London: John Murray, 1970), 1.

2. "The Near East," *Gleaner*, January 1913.

3. "Editorial Notes," *Gleaner*, September 1918.

4. Captain Alfred Thayer Mahan used the term in 1902 to refer to lands from Suez to Singapore. Rodric Davison, "Where Is the Middle East?" *Foreign Affairs* 38 (1960), 667. The term itself, however, had earlier origins. It was used in an American missionary periodical, *Zion's Herald*, in 1876 to describe a similar area. though without its imposing capital letters. T. E. Gordon used the term to describe "Persia and Afghanistan" in March 1900 in the *Nineteenth Century:* "the most sensitive part of our external policy in the Middle East is the preservation of the independence and integrity of Persia and Afghanistan" ("The Problem of the Middle East," 413).

5. W. R. Kermack, *W. and A. K. Johnston's Atlas of World History: Ancient, Mediaeval and Modern* (Edinburgh, 1931).

6. Cecil Beaton, *Near East* (London: B. T. Batsford, 1943), vii.

Bibliography

ARCHIVES

Armenian Film Foundation
Ravished Armenia (Auction of Souls)

Bodleian Library, University of Oxford
James, Viscount Bryce Papers
Toynbee Box

Bodleian Library of Commonwealth and African Studies,
University of Oxford (Rhodes House)
British Armenian Committee Papers

British Library
Balfour Papers
George Douglas Campbell Papers
Robert Cecil Papers
G. N. Curzon Papers
Gladstone Papers
Austen Henry Layard Papers
Map Collection

Chatham House, London
Refugee Survey Papers
Toynbee Correspondence

Sherman Grinberg Film Library, courtesy of the Armenian Film
Foundation
Film footage of Smyrna burning

Huntington Library, San Marino, California

Francis Beaufort (Sir) Papers

Imperial War Museum (IWM), London

Private Papers: Captain E. P. Argyle; Captain B. E. Batt; T. W. Bunter; Lieutenant M. M. Carus-Wilson; J. Coffey; C. J. Howes; Mr. Philips Price; Major J. G. Sitwell; Captain C. S. B. Swinley; Commander S. L. Vereker
Miscellaneous Documents, Misc 97 (1473)
Oral interviews: Commander C. H. Drage; J. W. L. Napier; Captain C. S. B. Swinley
"Report of Mr. Grescovich, Commander of the Smyrna Insurance Fire Brigade on the Great Fire in Smyrna"
Online documents, Armenia/2

Lambeth Palace Library, London

Davidson Papers
Douglas Papers

Middle East Centre Archive (MECA), St. Antony's College, Oxford University

Sir William Everett Collection
Cecil Hallward Collection
Harry St. John Philby Collection
Morgan Philips Price Collection
Maj.-Gen. James Malcolm Leslie Renton Collection
Sir Andrew Ryan Collection
Sir Mark Sykes Collection
Whittall and Co. Collection

National Archives of the UK

Colonial Office Records: CO 323
Foreign Office Records: FO 78, 96, 141, 195, 286, 383, 369, 371, 395, 608, 925
Treasury Records: T 161, 171

Religious Society of Friends in Britain Library, London

Burgess Collection
Marshall Fox Papers
Friends of Armenia Papers

Royal Geographical Society, London

Library Manuscript Collection
Map Collection
Special Collections: Sir Mark Sykes; Sir Percy Cox

SSEES Archives, University College London
Seton-Watson (Professor Robert William) Collection

University of Exeter, England
Whittall Papers, Special Collections

PERIODICALS

Ararat
Blackwood's Magazine
Christian Literature and Review
Contemporary Review
Cornhill Magazine
Dublin Review
Edinburgh Review
English Review
Fortnightly Review
The Forum
Fraser's Magazine
The Friend
The Friend of Armenia
Geographical Journal
Gleaner (Church Missionary Society)
Illustrated London News
League of Nations Official Journal
London Quarterly
Macmillan's Magazine
National Geographical Magazine
National Quarterly Review
National Review
Nineteenth Century
Northern Echo
The Orient
Our Sisters
Quarterly Review
The Quiver
Review of Reviews
Saturday Review
Shafts
Times (London)
Times Literary Supplement (London)
Woman's Herald
Woman's Signal
Women's Penny Paper

UNPUBLISHED THESES

McReynolds, Madeline. "The Quaker Family of Wisbech: A Study of Quaker Business and Benevolence." University of California, Riverside, 1984.

Swails, John. "Austen Henry Layard and the Near East, 1839–1880." University of Georgia, 1983.

PUBLISHED PRIMARY AND SECONDARY SOURCES

Afalo, Frederick George. *An Idler in the Near East.* London: Milne, 1910.

Akçam, Taner. *A Shameful Act: The Armenian Genocide and the Question of Turkish Responsibility.* New York: Henry Holt, 2006.

Altholz, Josef. *The Religious Press in Britain, 1760–1900.* London: Greenwood Press, 1989.

Anderson, Dorothy. *The Balkan Volunteers.* London: Hutchinson, 1968.

Anderson, Ewan. *The Middle East: Geography and Geopolitics.* London: Routledge, 2000.

Anderson, Margaret. "Down in Turkey, Far Away: Human Rights, the Armenian Massacres, and Orientalism in Wilhelmine Germany." *Journal of Modern History* 79, no. 1 (March 2007), 80–111.

Anderson, M. S. *The Eastern Question, 1774–1923.* London: Macmillan, 1966.

Appleyard, Ernest Silvanus. *Eastern Churches.* London: Darling, 1850.

Ardagh, Lady, Susan Countess of Malmesbury. *Life of Sir John Ardagh.* London: John Murray, 1909.

Argyll, George Douglas Campbell. *The Eastern Question: From the Treaty of Paris 1856 to the Treaty of Berlin 1878 and the Second Afghan War.* 2 vols. London: Strahan, 1879.

Ash, Timothy. "Mitteleuropa?" *Daedalus: Journal of the American Academy of Arts and Science* 119, no. 1 (winter 1990), 1–21.

Asmar, Maria Theresa. *Prophecy and Lamentation: A Voice from the East.* London: Hatchard, 1845.

Auchterlonie, Paul. "From the Eastern Question to the Death of General Gordon: Representations of the Middle East in the Victorian Periodical Press, 1876–1885." *British Journal of Middle Eastern Studies* 28, no. 1 (May 2001), 5–24.

Auerbach, Jeffrey, and Peter H. Hoffenberg, eds. *Britain, the Empire, and the World at the Great Exhibition of 1851.* Aldershot: Ashgate, 2008.

B., M. A. *Diary of Travels through Palestine.* London: Women's Printing Society, 1898.

Bailey, John, ed. *Diary of Lady Frederick Cavendish, vol II.* New York: Frederick Stokes, 1927.

Balakian, Peter. *The Burning Tigris: The Armenian Genocide and America's Response.* New York: Perennial, 2003.

——, trans., with Aris Sevag. *Armenian Golgotha.* New York: Knopf, 2009.

Ballantyne, Tony. *Orientalism and Race.* New York: Palgrave, 2002.

Barber, Peter, and Christopher Board, *Tales from the Map Room: Fact and Fiction about Maps and Their Makers*. London: BBC Books, 1993.

Baring, Maurice. *Letters from the Near East, 1909 and 1912*. London: Smith, Elder, 1913.

Barkey, Karen. *Empire of Difference: The Ottomans in Comparative Perspective*. Cambridge: Cambridge University Press, 2008.

Barton, James Levi. *The Story of Near East Relief*. New York: Macmillan, 1930.

Bar-Yosef, Eitan. *The Holy Land in English Culture, 1799–1917*. Oxford: Clarendon, 2005.

Bass, Gary. *Freedom's Battle*. New York: Vintage, 2008.

———. *Stay the Hand of Vengeance*. Princeton, NJ: Princeton University Press, 2000.

Baumgart, Winifred. *The Crimean War 1853–1856*. London and New York: Oxford University Press, 1999.

Beaton, Cecil. *Near East*. London: B. T. Batsford, 1943.

Bell, Gertrude, and William Ramsey. *The Thousand and One Churches*. London: Hodder, 1909.

Bevis, Richard. *Bibliotheca Cisorientalia: An Annotated Checklist of Early English Travel Books on the Near and Middle East*. Boston: G. K. Hall, 1973.

Bierstadt, Edward Hale. *The Great Betrayal: A Survey of the Near East Problem*. New York: McBride, 1924.

Blount, Sir Henry. *A Voyage into the Levant*. London: Crooke, 1636.

Bloxham, Donald. "The Armenian Genocide of 1915–1916: Cumulative Radicalisation and the Development of a Destruction Policy." *Past and Present* 181, no. 1 (2003), 141–91.

———. *The Great Game of Genocide: Imperialism, Nationalism, and the Destruction of the Ottoman Armenians*. Oxford: Oxford University Press, 2005.

Blunt, Fanny Janet. *The People of Turkey: Twenty Years Residency among the Bulgarians, Greeks, Albanians, Turks and Armenians*. By a consul's daughter and wife, ed. Stanley Lane Poole, vol. 1 and 2. London: Murray, 1878.

Booth, Charles, ed. *Labour and Life of the People*. Vols. 1–3. 2nd ed. London: Williams and Norgate, 1889.

Bradshaw, George. *Bradshaw's Hand-Book to the Turkish Empire*. 2 vols. London: Adams, 1870.

Brake, Laurel, and Marysa Demoor, eds. *Dictionary of Nineteenth-Century Journalism*. London: Academia Press/British Library, 2009.

Brotton, Jerry. *Trading Territories: Mapping the Early Modern World*. Ithaca, NY: Cornell University Press, 1998.

Bryce, James. "Edward Augustus Freeman." *English Historical Review* 7, no. 27 (July 1892), 497–509.

———. *Transcaucasia and Ararat*. 1877. Reprint, New York: Arno Press, 1970.

———. *Treatment of Armenians in the Ottoman Empire: 1915–1916*. New York and London: G. Putnam's Sons, 1916. Facsimile, Whitefish, MT: Kessinger Publishing.

Buisseret, David, ed. *Monarchs, Ministers and Maps: The Emergence of Cartography as a Tool of Government in Early Modern Europe.* Chicago: University of Chicago Press, 1992.

Buxton, Noel. *Travels and Politics in Armenia.* London: Smith and Elder, 1914.

Cameron, Verney. *Our Future Highway: The Euphrates Valley.* 2 vols. London: Macmillan, 1880.

Campbell, Sir George. *A Handy Book on the Eastern Question.* London: Murray, 1876.

Carlucci, April, and Peter Barber. *Lie of the Land: The Secret Life of Maps.* London: British Library, 2001.

Çetin, Fethyne. *My Grandmother: A Memoir.* Trans. Maureen Freely. New York: Verso, 2008.

Chapman, Maybelle Kennedy. *Great Britain and the Baghdad Railway, 1888–1914.* Northampton, MA: Smith College, 1948.

Childs, W. J. *Across Asia Minor on Foot.* Edinburgh: Dodd, Mead and Co., 1917.

Chirol, Valentine. *The Middle Eastern Question, or Some Political Problems of Indian Defense.* London: John Murray, 1903.

Church Missionary Society. *One Hundred Years: Being the Short History of the Church Missionary Society.* 3rd ed. London: Church Missionary Society, 1899.

Clark, Bruce. *Twice a Stranger.* Cambridge, MA: Harvard University Press, 2006.

Clayton, G. D. *Britain and the Eastern Question.* London: University of London Press, 1971.

Clogg, Richard. *A Short History of Modern Greece.* Cambridge: Cambridge University Press, 1986.

Coakley, J. F. *The Church of the East and the Church of England: A History of the Archbishop of Canterbury's Assyrian Mission.* Oxford: Clarendon, 1992.

Conzen, Michael P., ed. *Chicago Mapmakers: Essays on the Rise of the City's Map Trade.* Chicago: Chicago History Society, 1984.

Coryat, Thomas. *Coryat's Crudities.* 1615. Reprint, London: W. Cater, 1776.

Cox, Jeffrey. *Imperial Faultlines.* Stanford, CA: Stanford University Press, 2002.

Creagh, James. *Armenians, Koords and Turks.* 2 vols. London: Tinsley, 1880.

Crone, G. R. *Maps and Their Makers: An Introduction to the History of Cartography.* 4th ed. London: Hutchinson, 1968.

Curzon, George N. *Persia and the Persian Question.* 2 vols. London: Longman, 1892.

———. *Problems of the Far East.* 3rd ed. London: Longmans, 1894.

———. *Russia in Central Asia in 1889.* London: Longmans, 1889.

———. *Tales of Travel.* London: Hodder and Stoughton, 1923.

Curzon, Robert. *Armenia: A Year at Erzeroom.* London: Murray, 1854.

Cutts, Rev. Edward Lewes. *Christians under the Crescent in Asia.* London: SPCK, 1887.

Dadrian, Vahakn. *The History of the Armenian Genocide*. 4th rev. ed. New York: Berghahn, 2008.

——."A Textual Analysis of the Key Indictment of the Turkish Military Tribunal Investigating the Armenian Genocide." *Armenian Review* 44, no. 1/173 (spring 1991), 1–36.

——. "The Turkish Military Tribunals' Prosecution of the Authors of the Armenian Genocide: Four Major Court-Martial Series." *Holocaust and Genocide Studies* 11, no. 1 (spring 1997), 28–59.

Dadrian, Vahakn, and Taner Akçam. *Judgment at Istanbul: The Armenian Genocide Trials*. New York: Berghahn, 2011.

Davis, Tom. *Shifting Sands*. Oxford: Oxford University Press, 2004.

Davison, Roderic H. "Turkish Attitudes concerning Christian-Muslim Equality in the Nineteenth Century." *American Historical Review* 59, no. 4 (July 1954), 844–64.

——. "Where Is the Middle East?" *Foreign Affairs* 38 (1960), 665–75.

De Azcarate, P. *The League of Nations and National Minorities: An Experiment*. Trans. from the Spanish by Eileen Brooke. Washington: Carnegie Endowment for International Peace, 1945.

Denton, W. *The Christians of Turkey: Their Conditions under Mussulman Rule*. London: Dalday, Isbister and Co., 1876.

Dickie, John. *The British Consul*. New York: Columbia University Press, 2007.

Dugdale, Blanche E.C., and Wyndham A. Bewes. "The Working of the Minority Treaties." *Journal of the British Institute of International Affairs* 5, no. 2 (March 1926), 79–95.

Earle, Edward Mead. *Turkey, the Great Powers, and the Baghdad Railway: A Study in Imperialism*. New York: Macmillan, 1923.

Eastern Question Association. *Papers on the Eastern Question*. London: Cassell Petter and Galfin, 1877.

Emin, Joseph. *The Life and Adventures of Joseph Emin: An Armenian*. London, 1792.

Eton, William. *A Survey of the Turkish Empire*. London: Cadell and Davies, 1798.

Evans, Arthur J. *Through Bosnia and the Herzegovina on Foot during the Insurrections, August and September 1875*. 2nd ed. London: Longmans, Green, and Co., 1877.

Evans, Stephen. *The Slow Rapprochement: Britain and Turkey in the Age of Kemal Ataturk, 1919–38*. Beverley, North Humberside: Eothen Press, 1982.

Feldman, David. *Englishmen and Jews*. New Haven: Yale University Press, 1994.

Fink, Carole. *Defending the Rights of Others*. Cambridge: Cambridge University Press, 2004.

Finkel, Caroline. *Osman's Dream*. New York: Basic Books, 2005.

Fisher, H.A.L. *James Bryce*. 2 vols. New York: Macmillan, 1927.

Fraser, David. *The Short Cut to India: The Record of a Journey along the Route of the Baghdad Railway*. Edinburgh: Blackwood, 1909.

Friederici, Karl. *Bibliotheca Orientalis: Vollständige Liste der vom Jahre 1876 bis 1883 erschienenen Bücher, Broschüren, Zeitschriften, usw. über die Sprachen, Religionen, Antiquitäten, Literaturen und Geschichte des Ostens.* Leipzig: Otto Schulze, 1876–83.

Freeman, E. A. *The Historical Geography of Europe.* 3rd edition, 2 vols. London: Longmans, 1912.

———. *The Ottoman Power in Europe: Its Nature, Its Growth and Decline.* London: Macmillan, 1877.

Fromkin, David. *A Peace to End All Peace: The End of the Ottoman Empire and the Creation of the Modern Middle East.* London: Phoenix, 2000.

Gaillard, Gaston. *The Turks and Europe.* London: Thomas Murby and Co., 1921.

Gatrell, Peter. *A Whole Empire Walking: Refugees in Russia during World War I.* Bloomington: Indiana University Press, 1999.

Gaunt, David. *Massacres, Resistance, Protectors: Muslim-Christian Relations in Eastern Anatolia during World War I.* Piscataway, NJ: Gorgias Press, 2006.

George, Joan. *Merchants in Exile: The Armenians in Manchester, 1835–1935.* Princeton: Gomidas, 2002.

Ghazarian, Vatche, ed. and trans. *Boghos Nubar's Papers and the Armenian Question, 1915–1918.* Waltham, MA: Mayreni, 1996.

Gibbons, Herbert Adams. *Reconstruction of Poland and the Near East: Problems of Peace.* New York: The Century Co., 1917.

Gibson, Matthew. *Dracula and the Eastern Question.* New York: Palgrave Macmillan, 2006.

Gilkes, Gilbert, and Henry Hodgkin. *Report of the Deputation to Friends Mission in Syria.* London: Friends' Foreign Mission Assoc., 1911.

Ginzberg, Lori. *Women and the Work of Benevolence.* Yale: Yale University Press, 1992.

Goldsworthy, Vesna. *Inventing Ruritania: The Imperialism of the Imagination.* New Haven: Yale University Press, 1998.

Grafftey-Smith, Laurence. *Bright Levant.* London: John Murray, 1970.

Grant, Kevin. *A Civilised Savagery: Britain and the New Slaveries in Africa.* New York: Routledge, 2005.

Graves, Sir Robert. *Storm Centres of the Near East: Personal Memories 1879–1929.* 1933. Reprint, London: Hutchinson, 1975.

Greenwood, John Ormorod. *Quaker Encounters.* Vol. 1. London: William Sessions, 1978.

Gullace, Nicoletta F. *"The Blood of Our Sons": Men, Women, and the Renegotiation of British Citizenship During the Great War.* New York: Palgrave Macmillan, 2002.

Hall, Duncan. *Mandates, Dependencies and Trusteeship.* London: Stevens and Sons, 1948.

Halo, Thea. *Not Even My Name.* New York: Picador, 2001.

Halpern, Paul, ed. *The Mediterranean Fleet, 1919–1929*. Burlington, VT: Ashgate, 2011.

Hambloch, Ernest, *British Consul: Memoirs of Thirty Years Service in Europe and Brazil*. London: George G. Harrap, 1938.

Hammerton, J.A., ed. *Harmsworth's Atlas of the World and Pictorial Gazetteer with an Atlas of the Great War*. London: Amalgamated Press, 1919.

Hancock W.K., and Jean Van Der Poel, eds. *Selection from the Smutts Papers*. Vol. 4. Cambridge: Cambridge University Press, 1966.

Harley, J.B. *The New Nature of Maps: Essays in the History of Cartography*. Ed. Paul Laxton. Baltimore: The Johns Hopkins University Press, 2001.

Harmsworth Atlas and Gazetteer. London: Carmelite House, 1909.

Harris, David. *Britain and the Bulgarian Horrors of 1876*. Chicago: University of Chicago Press, 1939.

Harris, James Rendel. *Letters from the Scenes of the Recent Massacres in Armenia*. London: Nisbet, 1897.

Harris, Stephen M. *British Military Intelligence in the Crimean War, 1854–1856*. London and Portland, OR: Frank Cass, 1999.

Harrison, Brian. *Peaceable Kingdom: Stability and Change in Modern Britain*. Oxford: Clarendon Press, 1982.

Heller, Joseph. *British Policy towards the Ottoman Empire, 1908–1914*. London: Frank Cass, 1983.

Hertslet, Sir Edward. *Recollections of the Old Foreign Office*. London: John Murray, 1901.

Hewsen, Robert. *Armenia: A Historical Atlas*. Chicago: University of Chicago Press, 2001.

Hirschon, Renee. *Heirs of the Greek Catastrophe*. 1989. Reprint, New York: Berghahn Books, 2009.

Hogarth, D.G. *The Nearer East*. London: W. Heinemann, 1902.

Holton, Sandra. *Quaker Women: Personal Life, Memory and Radicalism in the Lives of Women Friends, 1780–1930*. London and New York: Routledge, 2007.

Horne, John, and Alan Kramer. *German Atrocities, 1914: A History of Denial*. New Haven: Yale University Press, 2001.

Horton, George. *The Blight of Asia*. Indianapolis: Bobbs Merrill Co., 1953.

Housepian, Marjorie. *The Smyrna Affair*. New York: Harcourt Brace Jovanovich, 1971.

Hovannisian, Richard. *The Armenian People from Ancient to Modern Times*. New York: Palgrave Macmillan, 2004.

———. *The Republic of Armenia*. 4 vols. Berkeley and Los Angeles: University of California Press, 1971–96.

———, ed. *The Armenian Genocide: History, Politics, Ethics*. New York: St. Martins Press, 1992.

———. *Armenian Tsopk/Kharpert*. Costa Mesa, CA: Mazda, 2002.

———. *Confronting the Armenian Genocide: Looking Backward, Moving Forward*. New Brunswick: Transaction, 2003.

———. *Remembrance and Denial: The Case of the Armenian Genocide.* Detroit: Wayne State University Press, 1999.

Hovhannisyan, Nicolay. *Arab Historiography on the Armenian Genocide.* Yerevan, 2005.

Howel, Thomas. *A Journal of a Passage from India, by a Route Partly Unfrequented, through Armenia and Anatolia or Asia Minor.* London: C. Foster, 1789.

Huber, Mary Taylor, and Nancy Lutkehaus, eds. *Gendered Missions: Women and Men in Missionary Discourse and Practice.* Ann Arbor: University of Michigan Press, 1999.

Hull, Isabel. *Absolute Destruction: Military Culture and the Practices of War in Imperial Germany.* Ithaca, NY: Cornell University Press, 2005.

Hulme-Beaman, Ardern George. *Twenty Years in the Near East.* London: Methuen, 1898.

Hupchick, Dennis, and Harold Cox. *The Palgrave Concise Historical Atlas of Eastern Europe.* New York: Palgrave, 2001.

Ingram, Edward, ed. *Anglo-Ottoman Encounters in the Age of Revolution: Collected Essays of Allan Cunningham.* Vol. 1. London: Frank Cass, 1993.

Ingrams, Doreen. *The Palestine Papers, 1917–1922.* London: John Murray, 1972.

Iseminger, Gordon L. "The Old Turkish Hands: The British Levantine Consuls, 1856–76." *Middle East Journal* 22, no. 3 (summer 1968), 297–316.

Jacob, Christian. *The Sovereign Map: Theoretical Approaches in Cartography throughout History.* Trans. Tom Conley. Chicago: University of Chicago Press, 2006.

Jasanoff, Maya. *Edge of Empire.* New York: Knopf, 2005.

Jewitt, A. Crispin. *Maps for Empire: The First 2000 Numbered War Office Maps, 1881–1905.* London: British Library, 1992.

Johnson, H. H. *Reminiscences in the Near East, 1891–1913.* London: Drane, 1914.

Johnston, Anna. "British Missionary Publishing, Missionary Celebrity and Empire." *Nineteenth Century Prose* 32, no. 2 (fall 2005), 22–25.

———. *Missionary Writing and Empire, 1800–1860.* Cambridge: Cambridge University Press, 2003.

Johnston, W., and A. K. Johnston. *One Hundred Years of Map Making: The Story of A. K. Johnston.* Edinburgh: W. and A. K. Johnston, 1925.

Jolliffe, Thomas Robert. *Narrative of an Excursion from Corfu to Smyrna.* London: Black and Young, 1827.

Jones, Dora. *Great Cities of the Near East, the Story of a Winter Cruise: The Byzantine Capital.* London: Extr. Travels, 1897.

Jowett, Rev. William. *Christian Researches in the Mediterranean.* London: Watts, 1822.

Joyce, Patrick. *Democratic Subjects: The Self and the Social in Nineteenth Century England.* Cambridge: Cambridge University Press, 1994.

Judt, Tony. *Postwar: A History of Europe since 1945.* New York: Penguin, 2006.

———. *Reappraisals.* New York: Penguin, 2008.

Kasparian, Alice Odian. *Armenian Needlelace and Embroidery.* McLean, VA: EPM Publications, 1983.

Katchadourian, Stina, ed. *Great Need over the Water: The Letters of Theresa Huntington Ziegler, Missionary to Turkey, 1898–1905.* Ann Arbor, MI: Gomidas, 1999.

Kayat, Asaad. *A Voice from Lebanon.* London: Madden, 1847.

Kennedy, Thomas. *British Quakerism, 1860–1914.* Oxford, Oxford University Press, 2001.

Kermack, W. R. *W. and A. K. Johnston's Atlas of World History: Ancient, Mediaeval and Modern.* Edinburgh, 1931.

Kerr, Stanley. *The Lion of Marash: Personal Experiences with Near East Relief.* Albany: State University of New York Press, 1973.

Kevorkian, Raymond. *The Armenian Genocide: A Complete History.* London: I. B Tauris, 2011.

King, Peter. *Curzon's Persia.* London: Sidwick and Jackson, 1986.

Kirakossian, Arman. *British Diplomacy and the Armenian Question from the 1830s to 1914.* Princeton, NJ: Gomidas Institute, 2003.

———, ed. *The Armenian Massacres, 1894–1896: British Media Testimony.* Dearborn: University of Michigan, 2008.

Klatt, Johannes, and Ernst Kuhn, eds. *Literatur-Blatt für Orientalische Philologie.* Vols. 1–4. Leipzig: Otto Schulze, 1883–85.

Kontje, Todd. *German Orientalisms.* Ann Arbor: University of Michigan Press, 2004.

Kontogiori, Elisabeth. *Population Exchange in Greek Macedonia.* Oxford: Oxford University Press, 2006.

Koven, Seth. *Slumming.* Princeton, NJ: Princeton University Press, 2004.

Kuklick, Bruce. *Puritans in Babylon.* Princeton, NJ: Princeton University Press, 1996.

Laqueur, Thomas. "Bodies, Details, and the Humanitarian Narrative." In *The New Cultural History,* ed. Lynn Hunt. Berkeley and Los Angeles: University of California Press, 1989.

Latham, R. G. *The Ethnology of Europe.* London: John Van Voorst, 1852.

———. *The Varieties of Human Species.* London: Houlston and Stoneman, 1856.

Lausanne Conference on Near Eastern Affairs, 1922–23: Records of Proceedings and Draft Terms of Peace. London: Stationers Office, 1923.

Layard, Austen Henry. *Discoveries in the Ruins of Nineveh and Babylon, Part I and II.* London: John Murray, 1853. Reprint, Port Chester, NY: Elibron, 2001.

———. *Nineveh and Its Remains: With an Account of a Visit to Chaldean Christians of Kurdistan.* London: John Murray, 1849.

———. *Sir A. Henry Layard, G.C.B., D.C.L: Autobiography and Letters from His Childhood until His Appointment as H.M. Ambassador at Madrid.* 2 vols. Ed. William N. Bruce. London: John Murray, 1903.

Laycock, Jo. *Imagining Armenia.* Manchester: Manchester University Press, 2009.

Lefebvre, Henri. *The Production of Space.* Trans. D. Nicholson-Smith. Oxford: Blackwell, 1991.

LeQueux, William. *An Observer in the Near East.* New York: Doubleday, Page and Co., 1907.

Lloyd George, David. *War Memoirs.* Vol. 1 London: Odhams, 1938.

Lovejoy, Ester Pohl. *Certain Samaritans.* New York: Macmillan, 1927.

Lumsden, Lieut. Thomas. *A Journey from Merut to India to London through Arabia, Persia, Armenia, Georgia, Russia, Austria, Switzerland, and France.* London: Black, 1822.

MacCallum, Elizabeth. *The Near East: A Survey of Political Trends in 1925.* New York: Foreign Policy Association, 1926.

Maccoll, Malcolm. *England's Responsibility towards Armenia.* New York: Longmans, 1895.

——. *The Sultan and the Powers.* London: Longmans, 1896.

Macfarlane, Charles. *The Armenians: A Tale of Constantinople.* 3 vols. London: Saunders and Otley, 1830.

Mackenzie, G. Muir, and A. P. Irby. *The Slavonic Provinces of Turkey in Europe.* 1866. Facsimile, New York: Arno Press, 1971.

MacLean, Gerald. *The Rise of Oriental Travel.* Palgrave Macmillan, 2004.

MacMillan, Margaret. *Peacemakers.* London: John Murray, 2001.

Makdisi, Ussama Damir. *Artillery of Heaven.* Ithaca, NY: Cornell University Press, 2008.

Mandel, Maud. *In the Aftermath of Genocide: Armenians and Jews in Twentieth-Century France.* Durham: Duke University Press, 2003.

Mander, Peter, ed. *Liberty and Authority in Victorian England.* Oxford: Oxford University Press, 2006.

Marchand, Suzanne. *German Orientalism.* Cambridge: Cambridge University Press, 2009.

Markovits, Stefanie. "Rushing Into Print: 'Participatory Journalism' During the Crimean War." *Victorian Studies* 50, no. 4 (summer 2008), 559–86.

Marriott, J. A. R. *The Eastern Question: A Study in European Diplomacy.* 4th ed. Oxford: Clarendon Press, 1940.

Marsden, Philip. *The Crossing Place.* New York: Kodansha, 1995.

Marsh, Peter. "Lord Salisbury and the Ottoman Massacres." *Journal of British Studies* 11, no. 2 (1972), 63–83.

Marshall, P. J. *The Making and Unmaking of Empires.* Oxford: Oxford University Press, 2005.

Martyn, Henry. *Journals and Letters of the Rev. Henry Martyn.* London: Seeley, 1837.

Marx, Karl. *The Eastern Question.* London: Swan Sonnenschein, 1897.

Matthew, H. C. G. *Gladstone, 1809–1898.* Oxford: Oxford University Press, 2001.

——. "Gladstone, Vaticanism, and the Question of the East." In *Studies in Church History*, vol. 15, ed. D. Baker (1978), 417–42.

——, ed. *The Gladstone Diaries*. Vol. 13. Oxford: Clarendon Press, 1994.

Maunsell, F. R. "The Geography of Eastern Turkey in Asia." Lecture given for the Aldershot Military Society Lectures, January 16, 1894.

——. *Military Report on Eastern Turkey in Asia*. 2 vols. London: Harrison and Sons, 1893.

Mayer, Arno. *Politics and the Diplomacy of Peacemaking, 1918–1919*. New York: Knopf, 1967.

Mazower, Mark. *The Balkans*. London: Phoenix, 2001.

——. *No Enchanted Palace: The End of Empire and the Ideological Origins of the United Nations*. Princeton, NJ: Princeton University Press, 2009.

——. *Salonica: City of Ghosts*. New York: Vintage, 2004.

——. "Violence and the State in the Twentieth Century." *American Historical Review* 107, no. 4 (2002), 1158–78.

McMeeken, Sean. *The Berlin to Baghdad Express: The Ottoman Empire and Germany's Bid for World Power*. Cambridge, MA: Harvard University Press, 2010.

Medlicott, W. N. *The Congress of Berlin and After: A Diplomatic History of the Near Eastern Settlement, 1878–1880*. 2nd ed. London: Frank Cass, 1963.

Meinertzhagen, Richard. *Middle East Diary: 1917–1956*. New York: Thomas Yoseloff, 1959.

Melman, Billie. *Women's Orients: English Women and the Middle East, 1718–1918*. Ann Arbor: University of Michigan Press, 1992.

Mentzel, Peter. *Transportation Technology and Imperialism in the Ottoman Empire, 1800–1923*. Washington, DC: American Historical Association, 2006.

Merguerian, Barbara."Mt. Holyoke Seminary in Bitlis: Providing an American Education for Armenian Women." *Armenian Review* 43, no. 1 (spring 1990), 31–65.

Meyer, Karl, and Shareen Blair Brysac. *Kingmakers: The Invention of the Modern Middle East*. New York: Norton, 2008.

Midgley, Clare. *Feminism and Empire*. New York: Routledge, 2007.

Miller, William. *Travels and Politics in the Near East*. London: Unwin, 1898.

Millman, Richard. *Britain and the Eastern Question, 1875–1878*. Oxford: Clarendon Press, 1979.

Milton, Giles. *Paradise Lost: Smyrna 1922*. New York: Basic Books, 2008.

Moorehead, Alan. *Gallipoli*. New York: Harper and Brothers, 1956.

Mösslang, Markus, and Torsten Riotte, eds. *The Diplomats' World: A Cultural History of Diplomacy, 1815–1914*. Oxford: Oxford University Press, 2008.

Moyn, Samuel. *The Last Utopia*. Harvard: Harvard University Press, 2010.

Murray, Eustace Clare Grenville. *Turkey: Being Sketches from Life*. London: Routledge, 1877.

Nalbandian, Louise. *The Armenian Revolutionary Movement*. Berkeley: University of California Press, 1963.

Nassibian, Akaby. *Britain and the Armenian Question 1915–1923*. London: Croom Helm, 1984.

Nebenzahl, Kenneth. *Mapping the Silk Road and Beyond*. London: Phaidon, 2004.

Newbigin, Marion. *Geographical Aspects of the Balkan Problems in Their Relation to the Great European War (with a Coloured Map of South-Eastern Europe and Sketch Maps)*. 2nd ed. London: Constable, 1915.

———. *The Mediterranean Lands*. 4th printing. London: Christophers, 1928.

———. *Modern Geography*. London: Williams and Norgate, 1911.

Nicolson, Harold. *Curzon: The Last Phase*. London: Constable, 1934.

———. *Peacemaking 1919*. 2nd ed. London: Constable, 1945.

Nightingale, Florence. *Letters from Egypt*. London: Spottiswoode, 1854.

Noyes, James O. *Roumania: The Borderland of the Christian and the Turk*. New York: Rudd and Carleton, 1858.

Oeconomos, Lysimachos. *The Martyrdom of Smyrna and Eastern Christendom*. London: George Allen, 1922.

Padron, Ricardo. *The Spacious Word: Cartography, Literature, and Empire in Early Modern Spain*. Chicago: University of Chicago Press, 2004.

Palgrave, William Gifford. *Essays on Eastern Questions*. London: Macmillan, 1872.

"Pamphlets on Armenia." Vol. 4 from the Rodman Wanamaker Collection, Princeton University.

Panossian, Razmik. *The Armenians*. New York: Columbia University Press, 2006.

Parry, William. *Remarks on the Present Aspect of the Turkish Question*. London: Masters, 1853.

Patrick, Mary Mills. *Bosporus Adventure: Constantinople Womens College, 1871–1924*. Stanford, CA: Stanford University Press, 1934.

Payaslian, Simon. *The History of Armenia*. New York: Palgrave, 2007.

Pedersen, Susan. "The Meaning of the Mandates System: An Argument." *Geschichte und Gesellschaft* 32 (2006), 560–82.

Penson, Lillian M. "The Principles and Methods of Lord Salisbury's Foreign Policy." *Cambridge Historical Journal* 5, no. 1 (1935), 87–106.

Permanent Bureau of the Turkish Congress Lausanne. "Inquiries in Anatolia" (pamphlet), 1919.

Platt, D. C. M. *The Cinderella Service: British Consuls since 1825*. Hamden, CT: Archon Books, 1971.

Pope, R. Martin. *Here and There in the Historic Near East*. London: Epworth Press, 1923.

Porter, Andrew. *Imperial Horizons of British Protestant Missions, 1800–1914*. Grand Rapids, MI: William Eerdmans, 2003.

———.*Religion vs. Empire?* Manchester: Manchester University Press, 2004.

Porter, Sir James. *Turkey: Its History and Progress*. London: Hurst and Blackett, 1854.

Power, Samantha. *The Problem from Hell: America and the Age of Genocide.* New York: Harper, 2007.

Pratt, Mary Louise. *Imperial Eyes: Travel Writing and Transculturation.* London: Routledge, 1992.

Price, William. *Journal of the British Embassy to Persia.* London, 1825.

Prime, Samuel Irenaeus. *The Bible in the Levant, or The Life and Letters of the Rev. C.N. Righter, Agent of the American Bible Society in the Levant.* New York: Sheldon, 1859.

Prochaska, F.K. *Women and Philanthropy in Nineteenth Century England.* Oxford: Oxford University Press, 1980.

Quataert, Donald. *The Ottoman Empire, 1700–1922.* 2nd ed. Cambridge: Cambridge University Press, 2005.

Rappard, William. *International Relations as Viewed from Geneva.* New Haven: Yale University Press, 1925.

Rawlinson, Lt. Col. A. *Adventures in the Near East 1918–1922.* New York: Dodd, Mead, 1924.

Read, J.M. *Atrocity Propaganda, 1914–1919.* New Haven: Yale University Press, 1941.

Redgate, A.E. *The Armenians.* Oxford: Blackwell, 2000.

Reynolds-Ball, E.A. *Practical Hints for Travellers in the Near East.* London: E. Marlborough, 1903.

Richter, Julius. *A History of Protestant Missions in the Near East.* New York: Fleming H. Revell, 1910.

Riley, John Athelstan. *The Archbishop of Canterbury's Mission to the Assyrian Church.* London: SPCK, 1891.

Robinson, Arthur. *Early Thematic Mapping in the History of Cartography.* Chicago: University of Chicago Press, 1982.

Robinson-Dunn, Diane. *The Harem, Slavery and British Imperial Culture.* Manchester: Manchester University Press, 2006.

Roe, James Moulton. *The British and Foreign Bible Society, 1905–1954.* London: British and Foreign Bible Society, 1965.

Roy, Douglas. "Britain and the Armenian Question." *Historical Journal* 19, no. 1 (1976), 113–33.

Royle, Trevor. *Crimea: The Great Crimean War, 1854–1856.* New York: Palgrave, 2004.

Ryan, Sir Andrew. *Last of the Dragomans.* London: Geoffrey Bles, 1951.

Rycaut, Sir Paul. *The Present State of the Greek and Armenian Churches.* London: John Starkey, 1679.

Saab, Ann Pottinger. *Reluctant Icon: Gladstone, Bulgaria and the Working Classes, 1856–1878.* Cambridge, MA: Harvard University Press, 1991.

Said, Edward. *Orientalism.* New York: Vintage, 1979.

Sakayan, Dora, trans. *An Armenian Doctor in Turkey: Garabed Hatcherian, My Smyrna Ordeal 1922.* Montreal: Arod Books, 1997.

Salaman, Redcliffe N. *Palestine Reclaimed: Letters from a Jewish Officer in Palestine.* London: Routledge, 1920.

Salt, Jeremy. *Imperialism, Evangelism and the Ottoman Armenians, 1878–1896*. London: Frank Cass, 1993.

——. *The Making of the Modern Middle East*. Berkeley and Los Angeles: University of California Press, 2009.

Sandwich, Humphrey. *A Narrative of the Siege of Kars*. London: Murray, 1856.

Sarafian, Ara, and Eric Avebury. *British Parliamentary Debates on the Armenian Genocide 1915–1918*. London: Gomidas Institute, 2003.

Sarafian, Ara, ed. *The Treatment of Armenians in the Ottoman Empire, 1915–1916: Documents Presented to Viscount Grey by Viscount Bryce*. Princeton, NJ: Gomidas Institute, 2000.

Satia, Priya. *Spies in Arabia: The Great War and the Cultural Foundations of Britain's Covert Empire in the Middle East*. Oxford: Oxford University Press, 2008.

Schevill, F. *The Balkan Peninsula and the Near East*. G. Bell: London, 1922.

Scott, James. *Seeing Like a State: How Certain Schemes to Improve the Human Condition Have Failed*. New Haven: Yale University Press, 1999.

Semple, Rhonda. *Missionary Women: Gender, Professionalism, and the Victorian Idea of Christian Mission*. Suffolk: Boydell Press, 2003.

Searle, G. R. *Morality and the Market in Victorian Britain*. Oxford: Clarendon Press, 1998.

Seton-Watson, R. W. *Disraeli, Gladstone, and the Eastern Question*. 1935. Reprint, New York: Norton, 1972.

Shannon, Richard. *Gladstone and the Bulgarian Agitation 1876*. London: Thomas Nelson, 1963.

Sherley, Sir Anthony. *Travels into Persia in 1599*. London: Butter and Bagfet, 1613.

Simpson, John Hope. *The Refugee Problem: Report of a Survey*. London: Oxford University Press, 1939.

Şimşir, Bilâl N. *British documents on Ottoman Armenians*. 4 vols. Ankara: Türk Tarih Kurumu Basımevi, 1983.

Singh, Maina Chawla. "Gender, Thrift and Indigenous Adaptations: Money and Missionary Medicine in Colonial India." *Women's History Review* 15, no. 5 (2006), 701–17.

Skelton, R. A. *Maps: A Historical Survey of their Study and Collecting*. Chicago: University of Chicago Press, 1975.

Skran, Claudena. *Refugees in Interwar Europe*. Oxford: Clarendon Press, 1995.

Slide, Anthony. *Ravished Armenia and the Story of Aurora Mardiganian*. Lanham, MD: Scarecrow Press, 1997.

Sluglett, Peter. *Britain in Iraq: Contriving King and Country*. New York: Columbia University Press, 2007.

Smith, Eli. *Researches on Armenia*. Boston: Crocker and Brewster, 1833.

Smuts, J. C. *The League of Nations: Practical Suggestions*. London: Hodder and Soughton, 1918.

Somakian, Manoug. *Empires in Conflict: Armenia and the Great Powers, 1895–1920*. London: I. B. Tauris, 1995.

Spencer, Edmund. *Travels in European Turkey.* London: Colburn, 1851.

Stansky, Peter. *Gladstone: A Progress in Politics.* Boston: Little Brown, 1979.

Stead, W. T., ed. *The MP for Russia: Reminiscences and Correspondence of Madame Olga Novikoff.* 2 vols. New York: Putnam, 1909.

Steel, Nigel, and Peter Hart. *Defeat at Gallipoli.* London: Papermac, 1995.

Stephens, W. R. W. *The Life and Letters of Edward A. Freeman.* 2 vols. London: Macmillan, 1895.

Stock, Eugene. *The History of the Church Missionary Society.* 3 vols. London: Church Missionary Society, 1899.

Stockdale, Nancy. *Colonial Encounters among English and Palestinian Women.* Gainesville: University Press of Florida, 2007.

Stocking, George. *Victorian Anthropology.* New York: Free Press, 1991.

Stone, Frank Andrews. *Academies for Anatolia: A Study of the Rationale, Program and Impact of the Educational Institutions Sponsored by the American Board in Turkey: 1830–1980.* Lanham, MD: University Press of America, 1984.

Stone, Norman. *The Eastern Front, 1914–1917.* New York: Penguin, 2004.

Strangford, Lady, ed. *The Eastern Shores of the Adriatic.* London: Richard Bently, 1864.

———. *Egyptian Sepulchers and Syrian Shrines.* London: Macmillan, 1874.

———. *Original Letters and Papers of the Late Viscount Strangford.* London: Trübner, 1878.

———. *A Selection from the Writings of Viscount Strangford.* 2 vols. London: Richard Bently, 1869.

Stratford de Redcliffe, Viscount Stratford Canning. *The Eastern Question.* London: John Murray, 1881.

———. *Why Am I a Christian?* 4th ed. London: Henry S. King, 1873.

Strong, William. *The Story of the American Board: An Account of the First Hundred Years of the American Board of Commissioners for Foreign Missions.* Boston: Pilgrim Press, 1910.

Stuga, Glenda. *The Nation, Psychology, and International Politics, 1870–1919.* London: Palgrave, 2006.

Suny, Ronald Grigor, et al., eds. *Looking toward Ararat: Armenia in Modern History.* Bloomington: Indiana University Press, 1993.

———. *A Question of Genocide: Armenians and Turks at the End of the Ottoman Empire.* Oxford: Oxford University Press, 2011.

Sykes, [Sir] Mark. "The Future of the Near East." London: Pelican Press, 1918.

———. *Through Five Turkish Provinces.* London: Bickers, 1900.

Temperley, Harold William. "The Bulgarian and Other Atrocities, 1875–78." *Proceedings of the British Academy* (1931), 105–46.

Thompson, Geo. Carslake. *Public Opinion and Lord Beaconsfield, 1875–1880.* 2 vols. London: Macmillan, 1886.

Thorne, Susan. *Congregational Missions and the Making of an Imperial Culture in Nineteenth-Century England.* Stanford, CA: Stanford University Press, 1999.

Todorova, Maria. *Imagining the Balkans.* New York: Oxford University Press, 1997.

Townshend, Arthur FitzHenry. *A Military Consul in Turkey.* London: Seeley, 1910.

Toynbee, Arnold. *Acquaintances.* Oxford: Oxford University Press, 1967.

———. *Armenian Atrocities: The Murder of a Nation.* London: Hodder and Stoughton, 1915.

———. *International Affairs, 1920–1923.* Oxford: Oxford University Press, 1925.

———. *The Murderous Tyranny of the Turks.* Preface by Viscount Bryce. New York: Doran, 1917.

Tusan, Michelle. "Reforming Work: Gender, Class and the Printing Trade in Victorian Britain." *Journal of Women's History* 16, no. 1 (2004), 102–25.

Uregian, Hovakim, and Krikor Baghdjian. "Two Unpublished Eyewitness Accounts of the Holocaust in Smyrna." *Armenian Review* 35 no. 4 (1982), 362–89.

Villa, Susie Hoogasian, and Mary Kilbourne Matoossian. *Armenian Village Life before 1914.* Detroit: Wayne State Press, 1982.

Walker, Christopher. *Visions of Ararat.* London: I. B. Tauris, 2005.

Walkowitz, Judith. *City of Dreadful Delight.* Chicago: University of Chicago Press, 1992.

Ward, Kevin, and Brian Stanley, eds. *The Church Missionary Society and World Christianity, 1799–1999.* Richmond, Surrey: Curzon Press, 2000.

Washburn, George. *Fifty Years in Constantinople and Recollections of Robert College.* Boston: Houghton Mifflin, 1909.

Watenpaugh, K. D. "The League of Nations' Rescue of Armenian Genocide Survivors and the Making of Modern Humanitarianism, 1920–1927." *American Historical Review* 115, no. 5 (December 2010), 1315–39.

Waterfield, Gordon. *Layard of Nineveh.* New York: Praeger, 1968.

Watson, Sir Charles Moore. *Fifty Years of Work in the Holy Land: A Record and Summary, 1865–1915.* London: Palestine Exploration Fund, 1915.

Watson, William. *The Purple East: A Series of Sonnets on England's Desertion of Armenia.* London: John Lane, 1896.

West, Maria. *Romance of Missions: or, Inside Views of Life and Labor in the Land of Ararat.* New York: Randolph, 1875.

West, Rebecca. *Black Lamb, Grey Falcon.* New York: Penguin Classics, 2007.

Werfel, Franz. *Forty Days of Musa Dagh.* New York: Viking, 1934.

Wheeler, Susan. *Missions in Eden.* New York: Revell, 1899.

Wherry, E. M., ed. *Islam and Missions.* New York: Revell, 1911.

Whigham, H. J. *The Persian Problem: An Examination of the Rival Positions of Russia and Great Britain in Persia with Some Account of the Persian Gulf and the Baghdad.* New York: Charles Scribner's Sons, 1903.

Whyte, Frederic. *Life of W. T. Stead.* 2 vols. 1925. New York: Garland, 1971.

Windsor, David Burns. *The Quaker Enterprise: Friends in Business.* London: Frederick Muller, 1980.

Winter, Jay, ed. *America and the Armenian Genocide of 1915*. Cambridge: Cambridge University Press, 2003.

Wohl, Anthony S. "'Dizzi-Ben-Dizzi': Disraeli as Alien." *Journal of British Studies* 34, no. 3 (July 1995), 375–411.

Wokoeck, Ursula. *German Orientalism: The Study of the Middle East and Islam from 1800–1945*. London: Routledge, 2009.

Wolff, Larry. *Inventing Eastern Europe: The Map of Civilization on the Mind of the Enlightenment*. Stanford, CA: Stanford University Press, 1994.

Wratislaw, A. C. *A Consul in the East*. Edinburgh: William Blackwood and Sons, 1924.

Yeghiayan, Vartkes. *British Foreign Office Dossiers on Turkish War Criminals*. La Verne, CA: AAIC, 1991.

Young, Robert. *The Idea of English Ethnicity*. Oxford: Blackwell, 2008.

Zeidner, Robert. "Britain and the Launching of the Armenian Question." *International Journal of Middle East Studies* 7, no. 4 (October 1976), 465–83.

Zwemer, Samuel Marinus. *The Mohammedan World of Today*. New York: Revell, 1906.

———. *The Nearer and Farther East*. New York: Macmillan, 1908.

Index

Ingram Content Group UK Ltd.
Milton Keynes UK
UKHW011821010623
422734UK00001B/161